WINNER TAKES ALL

WINNER TAKES ALL

STEVE WYNN, KIRK KERKORIAN, GARY LOVEMAN, AND THE RACE TO OWN LAS VEGAS

Christina Binkley

HYPERION

NEW YORK

Library of Congress Cataloging-in-Publication Data is available upon request.

ISBN: 978-1-4013-0236-8

Hyperion books are available for special promotions and premiums.
For details contact Michael Rentas, Assistant Director, Inventory Operations, Hyperion,
77 West 66th Street, 12th floor, New York, New York 10023, or call 212-456-0133.

Book design by Fearn Cutler de Vicq

FIRST EDITION
10 9 8 7 6 5 4 3 2 1

To James, Harper, and Saskia.

CONTENTS

FRIENDLY

I'm a Buddhist and I think Buddhist things.

—STEVE WYNN

as Vegas. It is April 2006.

Steve Wynn is eating a yogurt-covered energy bar in an office with walls lined in chocolate velvet. He is spiffy in a snug yellow sweater; on the back is a rampant black panther with crimson eyes.

This place is a circus of Wynn-ness. There are three dogs in the room—two precision-trained German shepherds on the floor and a cocker spaniel named Loopy Lou who dances on Wynn's lap for kisses and baby talk.

Wynn's wife, Elaine, is in an office next door. His nephew and brother-in-law are somewhere around. A valet, eyes downcast, delivers two bottles of water and two napkins to Wynn's desk.

Two women outside the door control access to the sanctum. One is Cindy Mitchum with her big hair and unflappable cool, a Wynn veteran since 1979. The other is new—a cutie pie with bursting décolletage.

Two men await an audience with Wynn out there. One has the red robes and shorn head of a Buddhist monk. He is Tensing, a kind-looking emissary from the Dalai Lama. The other is Patrick Woodroffe, the Rolling Stones' lighting designer.

The valet is back. More water. Another napkin.

Sitting across from the desk is Wynn's former dolphin trainer, who has stopped by to give his regards. And there's me. I am headed for the door. But before I go, Wynn has an urgent question.

"Is there going to be anything in this book that I won't like?" he demands. And then loudly, face reddening, "WAS IT A FRIENDLY OR AN UNFRIENDLY DEAL?"

The dolphin guy looks confused by the non sequitur, but this subject has obsessed Wynn for six years. Pride and legacy. The syntax is vital: When *I sold* Mirage Resorts to Kirk Kerkorian, Wynn says. Not: when Kerkorian *took* my company, the one I spent twenty-seven years building with my own meaty fists.

Wynn is yelling now and he is big and loud. He is just over six feet tall. His body is broad but self-consciously svelte. At sixty-four, he has recently allowed a tickle of gray hair to appear at his sideburns—the rest of his expensively maintained head is jet-black, like when he was a cocky young stud. His capped teeth gleam white, white, white.

His big head swivels, searching. Wynn is going blind with a sort of tunnel vision, and I had slipped out of his view upon returning to my seat.

"It was a FRIENDLY deal!" he says, answering his own question.

The day after Wynn's nemesis Kirk Kerkorian bought Mirage Resorts in the spring of 2000, the London *Independent* headline stabbed Wynn in the gut: THE KING IS DEAD. Six years later, Wynn's fury and frustration at being written off are still palpable.

To Wynn's way of thinking, Kerkorian's coup wasn't a hostile takeover, it was a lucky break. Nothing was out of his control. Got it?

"Kirk called me up when it closed. I told him it was the happiest day of my life," Wynn says, strident. "I made more money in five minutes than I made in twenty-seven years."

In a few weeks, Wynn will receive two honorary PhDs—one from his alma mater, the University of Pennsylvania. He will be named by *Time* magazine as one of the 100 most influential people in the world, alongside Pope Benedict XVI and Bono. Elaine Wynn is recently returned from fashion week in Paris, where she spent time with their friends Oscar de la Renta and Karl Lagerfeld.

Theirs is a high life.

But the issue on Steve Wynn's front burner is free will.

Why can't he get it through my thick skull? Suggesting in this book that it was a hostile takeover would be "illegal." Do I understand what he's getting at? What's more, we will be finished, he and I. No more interviews. Steve will be mad. He will Cut. Me. Off.

The phone rings. Cindy announces a call from National Security Secretary Michael Chertoff. Wynn says he'll call him back—"It's personal"—and he turns to me to say wickedly, "I'll bet you wanna know what that's about."

He blusters on, still red-faced, "It was a friendly deal. The only thing that Kirk Kerkorian did was give me my price!"

Wynn doesn't blame Kirk for leaving the impression that he vanquished Wynn. Nope, Kirk is a nice guy. They played tennis together, eons ago.

One can't help thinking it's an artful thing to make a man sell you his life, convinced of your generosity. Of course, Wynn has come back from the dead.

"Kirk is a gentle, kind man. He is my friend," says the once-again king of Vegas. And if it wasn't for him, I wouldn't be as rich as I am."

There is, after all, some Zen in this thought—that goodness can be hidden in adversity. A man can enjoy building his kingdom twice.

The audience is over. Outside, there is Tensing, the monk waiting patiently and perhaps a bit tentatively, smiling in his red robes.

WINNER
TAKES
ALL

chapter one

BULLDOZED

In this town, nobody likes each other. It's all veneer covering the seething hate.

—Jan Jones, former Las Vegas mayor

he dust has cleared. Kirk Kerkorian controls the western half of the Las Vegas Strip. Gary Loveman and the vast Harrah's and Caesars empire commands the central zone. Steve Wynn is the overlord of an island to the north.

So Las Vegas is set for a showdown. The town is in the full swing of its most robust renaissance. A good $60 billion worth of new casino resorts is under way there—more than the United States' planned spending on Homeland Security in 2007.

A recent Google search for "Las Vegas" revealed 179 million hits. This compared with 132 million hits for "Rome," a city some 2,700 years older than Las Vegas but with a similar history of gluttony. What this tells us is that Las Vegas, as a cultural reference and as a city, has taken on greater worldwide significance than the place may deserve. Also, it's heavily advertised.

Yet there it is. Las Vegas is visited annually by forty million people and it is growing like mad. Like *mad*.

Las Vegas has been reborn many times, always emerging bigger and more boisterous, wriggling and howling to make its presence known. Pioneers Bugsy Siegel and Gus Greenbaum built the Flamingo in 1946: a two-hundred-room resort that cost $6 million. That is less than one-third the $20 million that Caesars Palace recently spent on *each* of six snazzy new high-roller suites.

These huge casinos are the result of an extraordinary partnership of ego, nerve and greed on the part of a handful of men. But they couldn't fill them without you, the public—people who can't get enough of Las Vegas, and those who hate it but go anyway.

Each year, at least a million more people visit Las Vegas than the year before. The city has twice as many hotel rooms as New York City, and on many weekends all 135,000 of them are sold out.

The town's popularity conquers many inconveniences. Las Vegas Boulevard is tackier than the old Times Square—children can collect prostitution fliers from the sidewalk in front of Caesars Palace. In Las Vegas, visitors stand in queues: at airports, hotels, buffets, valet parking, taxi stands, and theater box offices. The only places where there are no lines are at the slot machines.

Yet in a time when vacations have been so curtailed that they amount to long weekends, people visit Las Vegas for a whopping average of 4.5 days. They arrive prepared to spend cash and, while there, they dutifully participate in an ecstasy of consumerism.

Roughly as many people visit Las Vegas as New York City each year, but Sin City's visitors spent 62 percent more in 2005 than their counterparts touring the Big Apple. This explains why Guy Savoy has opened a restaurant in Las Vegas; by most estimates, it is the most expensive restaurant in the world. Luxury retailers have noticed too. By 2009, if all goes as planned, Chanel will have more clothing boutiques in Las Vegas than in New York. And if you desire a pair of Manolo Blahnik shoes, you will find no larger a collection anywhere than at the Blahnik boutique in Las Vegas.

One might easily assume that people go to Las Vegas to gamble. But of the $36.7 billion that sinners spent in Las Vegas in 2005, only $9.7 billion was wagered away, according to the Las Vegas Convention and Visitors Authority. If not to gamble, why go? When it's all averaged out, most folks see a show, spend $248 on food and drinks, $136 on shopping, and $60 on local transportation. Those who did gamble sat at slot machines or tables for an average 3.6 hours per day.

Which is, when you think about it, a long stretch spent on your butt.

People go to Las Vegas for things that are plastic but couldn't happen anyplace else. Kobe beef for breakfast, lunch, and dinner. A Nordic sake sommelier. A massage at Canyon Ranch before a six-hour blackjack spree. Even the entertainment is mind-bending: if you haven't seen Cirque du Soleil in Las Vegas, then you haven't seen what Cirque can do on a stage that will disappear underwater or flip sideways and toss its actors into space.

There are many other stunning and stimulating parts of Nevada, but few visitors bother to venture even a few miles to see Hoover Dam, Lake Mead or the vast, lovely lunar landscape that stretches past Death Valley to the west and the Grand Canyon to the east. On average, sightseeing absorbed a mere $8.21 of visitors' trip budgets. That won't buy entry to the Liberace Museum—not even with the senior discount.

The convention authority understandably did not account for how much people spent on sex, sex shows, drugs, or other illegal activities. Given the billboards, advertising fliers, and prostitutes visible around Las Vegas, it's a safe bet that this, too, plays as significant a role in the Las Vegas economy as gambling.

So. If that many people are having so much fun visiting Las Vegas casinos, just imagine what it's like to own one. No industrial titan is likely to equal the lifestyle of an average Las Vegas casino boss. A trip to the Far East for a casino mogul is likely to include socializing with the wealthiest industrialists in China as well as eager dignitaries in Thailand, Hong Kong, and Singapore. For a dinner at his home several years ago, Steve Wynn simultaneously hosted his friends former U.S. President George H. W. Bush and the actor Bruce Willis. Clint Eastwood got married on the Wynns' Las Vegas terrace; Wynn has vacationed with former British Prime Minister Tony Blair and has hosted the Dalai Lama at his home.

Kirk Kerkorian has owned his own movie studio and spends part of nearly every year on the French Riviera. Glenn Schaeffer, the former president of Mandalay Resort Group, snared a recurring role on the television show *Las Vegas*. He played a casino owner alongside actor James Caan, whom Schaeffer took to calling "Jimmy."

As investments go, casinos sure beat pork bellies.

Las Vegas is headed toward being a "major city," visited each year by more than four million international travelers, including business and political leaders who come to use Las Vegas for their own devices.

Yet, for all its phenomenal growth, Las Vegas behaves like a small town. The Strip pulses with the testosterone of casino bosses who are locked in treacherous rivalries but attend one another's birthdays and charity galas and send their kids to the same two private schools.

Las Vegas may be plastic and modern, but it retains a libidinous frontier air—a pioneering, can-do zeal to improve. This is a city that will send in road-building crews on the graveyard shift in order to avoid disrupting the flow of traffic into a new casino. It's a mindset that comes from the knowledge that Las Vegas initially had nothing, really nothing, going for it except its willingness to be bulldozed.

And imploded. And bulldozed again into resurrection.

chapter two

"RIFLE RIGHT"

There was a time I was aiming at $100,000. Then I thought I'd have it made if I got a million dollars. Now it isn't the money.

—KIRK KERKORIAN

Kirk Kerkorian, clad in gray pants and a blue dinner jacket, strolled into the ballroom of the Mirage hotel in late November 2005. He was flanked by a couple of old friends. His little entourage made its way to a table front and center, where a line of white-coated waiters stood at attention—the only line of waiters in the ballroom.

This year, the Nevada Cancer Institute's Rock for the Cure gala had an angelic theme. Hors d'oeuvres were served by leggy "rock angels" wearing white hot pants, white platform go-go boots, and four-foot-long feathered wings. A topless angel with silver sparkles painted on her nipples swung lazily from a trapeze bar on the ceiling. She looked bored. The actor George Hamilton strolled by with his famous ochre complexion.

Onstage, television personality Larry King chitchatted from a dais. King's trademark suspenders were slung over his bony shoulders.

"He's gonna hate me for doing this," King confided to the microphone, "but he's one of the world's great entrepreneurs and he's here tonight! Kirk Kerkorian, folks! Give 'im a hand. Take a bow, Kirk."

The room rose en masse, people in gowns and tuxedoes throwing their hands together in applause. Kerkorian nodded politely, a movie studio owner who waits in line to see films anonymously in theaters, a casino mogul who views boxing bouts in his own casinos from the nosebleed section.

Rock for the Cure is one of the big charity balls in Las Vegas, where the town's elite bid each year on such desirables as a golden retriever puppy, Muhammad Ali boxing mitts, and dinners cooked by Wolfgang Puck. The other elite charity events of the year in Las Vegas are an Alzheimer's gala headed by Larry Ruvo, who runs the region's dominant wine and liquor distributorship, Southern Wine and Spirits; and Andre Agassi's annual Grand Slam for local children's causes.

"There's no more Howard Hughes," King continued, his gravelly basso rising like a carnival barker. "We have Kirk Kerkorian!"

The Mirage's ballroom was full of designer gowns glued to artificially augmented bodies—a blend of Hollywood va-va-voom and Kansas City spangles. At some point during the evening, a Bentley Continental Flying Spur was auctioned off for $220,000, and an outing with Tiger Woods went for $350,000.

A date with flirtatious Fox weathergirl Jillian Barberie was sold twice—each time for $100,000—with coaxing from Larry King. "Larry's my pimp," Barberie joked from the stage.

Later, the comedienne Rita Rudner performed. Rudner lives in Las Vegas. She began her routine by voicing one of Las Vegans' fondest hopes: that they might become a legitimate city. Not just white-glove, but world-class.

The Nevada Cancer Institute, one month old, was promising Las Vegans the panache of real medical research. It was founded by one of the town's new power couples, Heather and Jim Murren. Jim Murren was president and chief financial officer of Kerkorian's casino company, MGM Mirage. Heather Murren had abandoned a seven-figure income as a Wall Street analyst to found the institute.

In her speech that evening, Heather Murren noted that patients had already flown in for treatment from as far as Arkansas. A murmur of awe rippled through the ballroom. "We're getting so sophisticated," Rudner said dryly. "I tell people in New York not to get too uppity."

Then she gazed across a glittering sea of rock angels and trophy wives. "Here, breasts—they're more than a body part," Rudner dead-panned, "they're entertainment."

The singer Stevie Nicks was preparing to take the stage as Kerkorian was leaving, still flanked by his pals, a few minutes before ten p.m. Larry King was back at the microphone.

"On Saturday, I am seventy-goddamned-two years old and Kirk Kerkorian is my hero," King told the crowd. "He'll live forever. And if he doesn't, he'll buy heaven and sell shares."

♣ ♦ ♥ ♠

Kerkorian's office is in the leafy commercial district of Beverly Hills, on Rodeo Drive, just around the corner and across the street from the Barneys New York store. It is separated from the paparazzi tourist movie-star hubbub part of Rodeo by the automotive whoosh of Wilshire Boulevard. Down one more block, the neighborhood turns to homes with small, neatly kept backyards.

The office building, a modern low-rise with a dozen or so tenants, is unmarked by Kerkorian's name or the names of any of the companies that he controls. One must simply know.

Kerkorian stands 5'11" or thereabouts and has an etched face, a pugilist's nose, and stubborn, wavy white hair. Even in his ninth decade, he is tennis svelte. He goes just about everywhere with a posse of loyal cronies who are willing and able to jet off with him at a moment's notice. Yet aside from being a billionaire, a sometime Hollywood studio mogul, and a casino tycoon, Kerkorian is quirky and old-fashioned—a relic. Most of his contemporaries are six feet underground. At midlife, he was Howard Hughes's nemesis and Cary Grant's buddy. In his youth, he boxed and flew airplanes.

He keeps life as simple as any mogul can. He doesn't use credit cards or wear a watch most days, according to friends. Embarrassed about his lack of formal education, he doesn't make speeches or accept awards. He has donated millions of dollars to charitable causes—many of them in Armenia, and even including the Armenian government—but he won't allow any of the roads, buildings, or other projects to be named for him and he has not so much as visited any of them, according to a longtime friend. Kerkorian is as likely to lunch with his bookkeeper as with another business titan—perhaps more likely. He drives himself around in regular-guy vehicles. Recently it was a pair of white Jeep Cherokees—one in L.A., another in Las Vegas.

To meet Kerkorian is to receive a polite handshake, a nod, a restrained smile. He is unreadable. People say it's an adrenaline rush to do business with Kerkorian, but this comes as much from people's imaginations—"He is a legend!"—than from anything in his unextraordinary behavior.

Kerkorian runs two primary companies. One is called the Tracinda Corporation. The other is the Lincy Foundation. Both are an amalgam of the names of Tracy and Linda—his two grown daughters from his second marriage to a former Las Vegas showgirl named Jean Maree Hardy. Linda is adopted, according to several accounts. Kerkorian is legally the father of a third daughter, Kira Rose Kerkorian, though the girl turned out to be another rich man's progeny.

Tracinda owns his holdings in the other companies that Kerkorian controls. Its offices on Rodeo are quiet and genteel, according to several people who have worked there. The receptionists, accountants, and lawyers begin to arrive around nine a.m. to begin a day that is steeped in tradition, as some have worked there for three decades. They leave at the stroke of noon to lunch together, typically at one of three restaurants. The choices include a Mexican eatery, a French bistro, or a soup-and-sandwich shop. Kerkorian often eats a sandwich at his desk or lunches at a restaurant around the corner at the Beverly Wilshire Hotel, his colleagues say.

No one seems to be particularly clear on how Kerkorian spends his hours in his office, other than to say that he isn't pushing papers or sweating details. He speaks on the telephone. He thinks.

Everyone heads home around five p.m.

Widespread beliefs that Kerkorian leads a frugal life are just false.

Kerkorian maintains large homes in Los Angeles and Las Vegas. He travels in his own Boeing 737, which according to legal records is furnished with a living room, kitchen, two bedrooms, and seats for twenty-one passengers. In addition to walking around with a wad of thousands of dollars in his pocket, he has also had a long and fickle relationship with a yacht—a 192-foot, German steel-hulled boat with two 1,750 horsepower Caterpillar engines, a teak sun deck, a gymnasium—plenty of comfort but no "frou-frou" details—with room for ten guests and a dozen crew members.

It's the twenty-second largest yacht in the world, according to *Power & Motoryacht* magazine's 2005 rankings. The yacht is one of those assets, like the MGM movie studio and his early airline, that Kerkorian keeps buying and selling.

Kerkorian chartered the yacht in her earlier life, liked her, bought her, named her the *October Rose* (his sister's name is Rose), sold her, and after she underwent a series of new owners (including Larry Ellison) and new names (*Libertad, Sakura*), bought her back again. And named her *October Rose* again. Then sold her again.

"It's a guy's boat," says Douglas Sharp, of Sharp Design in San Diego. Kerkorian hired Sharp to refurbish the yacht, but didn't seem much interested in the details. "We just met him once," says Sharp, who had traveled to Las Vegas with a set of plans for the yacht's refurbishment.

"One of the meetings was really bizarre. We sat in the outer office and sent the designs into an inner office," Sharp says. Kerkorian sent an emissary with his comments, but didn't bother to step outside his office or invite Sharp in. "We never saw him."

When Kerkorian kept the yacht in San Diego, Sharp says, "She was always on the move. His crew would get a call and have to take her out. It was for his friends to use—and for him to use. It was never chartered."

Later, Kerkorian kept her on the French Riviera. By April 2006, yachting circles were chattering that Kerkorian had moved on again. The yacht was spotted in France and Italy with yet another name, *Magna Grecia,* signifying another new owner.

Kerkorian belongs to the Beverly Hills Tennis Club, which is located on Maple Drive in the shady, flat part of Beverly Hills. The club roster is posted on a wall near the pool. There is Neil Simon, the play-wright, and the actor Kirk Douglas. There is Henry Gluck, the for-mer chairman of Caesars World. And there are several of Kerkorian's close crowd: Terry Christensen, his longtime lawyer, and Alex Ye-menidjian, his onetime protégé.

The Beverly Hills Tennis Club is venerable now, but it was founded by rejects. Groucho Marx and several other Jewish tennis lovers founded it after they weren't welcomed into the restricted Los Angeles Tennis Club in blue-blooded Hancock Park. That was back when Beverly Hills was nouveau riche. Cheery pictures of Charlie Chaplin, Carole Lombard, and Errol Flynn in tennis togs still adorn the walls.

On any given afternoon, the average age of the players at the club is in the neighborhood of seventy years and at the casual restaurant over-looking the pool it is possible to lunch with former Secretary of State Warren Christopher on one side and a movie studio chief on the other.

In a room to one side known as the "card room," there is what amounts to the club's wall of honor, hung with youthful photographs of members who served in the armed forces. There is a baby-faced Jo-seph Wapner, who would later become television's "Judge Wapner."

Kerkorian was a civilian flight instructor and "too smart" to serve in the armed forces, says one member whose photo is also on the wall. But there he is anyway, standing against a small plane and wearing a leather jacket, palming a cigarette. His eyes look smoky with shyness—or impatience.

During heavyweight bouts at his casinos, Kerkorian can be found plunging into the crowd far from the VIP seats where Steve Wynn and Donald Trump vie for spots in the limelight. He likes action, not pampering. When gunfire broke out in the MGM Grand Casino after the Mike Tyson–Evander Holyfield match, Kerkorian was in the crowd, elbow-to-elbow with Dan Wade, the MGM Grand's president.

He can be curiously helpless, in the manner of one who has other people handle details. One day not long after 9/11, when Holly-wood feared its movie studios were terrorist targets, Kirk Kerkorian drove himself onto the lot of the Metro-Goldwyn-Mayer studio, which he controlled. The guard at the gate had no idea who this gentleman in the Jeep was, recalls Alex Yemenidjian, who was then the studio's chairman.

The guard asked Kerkorian to pop open his trunk for a security check. Kerkorian said courteously that he didn't know how, but the guard was welcome to open it if he could find the button.

♣ ♦ ♥ ♠

Kerkorian's control of casinos, movie studios, and other businesses is de facto but not de jure. MGM Mirage, for instance, is run by an executive committee and the board of directors. Kerkorian attends the meetings, and the company's executives are careful to brief him beforehand. "No surprises," says Yemenidjian. Technically, Kerkorian is just another board member and big shareholder. J. Terrence "Terry" Lanni is the company's meticulous chairman and chief executive.

The way Lanni got his job says a lot about the way Kerkorian leads his life and his businesses.

Terry Lanni spent nearly two decades at Caesars before Kirk Kerkorian and Steve Wynn came calling at about the same time. Kerkorian needed help fixing the MGM Grand, which was being picketed by the powerful local Culinary Union and was suffering the ills of poor design and management. He asked Lanni to meet him at a hotel near his office in Beverly Hills.

"He asked me about what I thought of the MGM Grand," Lanni recalls of his interview. "I said it wasn't very well run, it was too big, and there must not have been an architect. He asked me about the union. I said it would be very hard for me to work at a place in Las Vegas without the union."

"I don't get involved in any of those things," Kerkorian replied. "I leave it all up to the management."

Often a phone will ring in Las Vegas in an office of the casinos that Kerkorian controls. It might be the chief financial officer's office or the general counsel's or the chief executive's. More often than not, the caller won't be "Mr. K," but another of his trusted executives who is seeking a piece of information: Why is the stock price down 1.5 percent? Who is exercising their stock options and why?

Kerkorian moves people back and forth between Tracinda and his other enterprises, even sometimes convincing his attorneys and accountants to come work for him. Alex Yemenidjian rose from tax accountant to movie studio head this way. When MGM Mirage needed a general counsel, Kerkorian plucked Gary Jacobs out of private legal practice and put him in the job.

Many of these people at Tracinda don't have traditional job titles that would clarify what they do for a living. There are cloudy, generic titles, such as "executive."

For many years, Kerkorian has played aggressive games of tennis with a group of close friends at his home each weekend that he is in Los Angeles. Being included in these sessions is a coveted privilege. When Yemenidjian stopped working for Kerkorian, he made a point of saying he was still invited to play tennis.

"Kirk is a god," Yemenidjian says.

♣ ♦ ♥ ♠

One of the rare photos of Kirk Kerkorian in public circulation shows him in the Las Vegas sun with the steel girders of the rising structure of the International Casino and Hotel behind him. It is 1969. He looks lean and masculine. He's holding a small sheaf of papers in one hand and he is smiling broadly.

He looked younger, but Kerkorian was already fifty-two years old, with two young daughters and a company named after the first— the Tracy Investment Company. He was in the midst of taking over the Metro-Goldwyn-Mayer movie studios in Los Angeles, for the first time. Much like the *October Rose* yacht, he would later sell, buy, and sell it again.

Caesars Palace had opened three years earlier. Its playful, full-body Grecian theme began at the streaming fountains in front and continued through to the "goddess" cocktail waitresses with their fake blond tresses. Caesars was built with Teamsters money, but it was the brainchild of an imaginative fellow named Jay Sarno whose bacchanalian life mirrored that of his resort.

Sarno in 1968 opened another groundbreaker—Circus Circus—

where a baby elephant wandered around for entertainment. Sarno was a creator, not a mogul, and he was forced to sell off both his ill-managed casinos. After a sixty-three-year lifetime of fun and debauchery, he would die of a heart attack in 1984, a virtual pauper. His lifeless body was found in a luxury suite at Caesars Palace, where, according to an executive there, he had been enjoying the female fruits of a night's gambling.

But Sarno lives on. His cherubic visage is the model for the cartoonish "Caesar" seen around Caesars Palace and on some of the hotel's stationery—being fed grapes, appropriately enough, by a female serf. Years later, Steve Wynn would become a great admirer of Sarno and closely study his ideas.

Caesars Palace generated so much excitement that it wasn't long before Ol' Blue Eyes moved over from the Sands, heralding the end of the Rat Pack and Las Vegas's fondest era.

Snazzy new casinos had been rising on the Strip since 1941, when the El Rancho Vegas first combined gambling, restaurants, entertainment, and hotel rooms. Some, like the Sands and the Desert Inn, remain landmarks years after being imploded. One incredible year, 1955, saw the grand openings of six new hotels, including the Stardust, the Riviera, the Dunes, and the Hacienda.

As Mob money and Teamsters pension funds dried up under legal pressures, Howard Hughes conveniently bought the aging Mob associates out before going mad in his Desert Inn suite.

What with the town's reputation and all, investing in Las Vegas in the 1970s and 1980s took a strong stomach. From 1969 until 1989, Kirk Kerkorian was just about the only person able and willing to build a major new casino on the Strip.

When that photo was taken, the 1,568-room International Hotel was going to be the biggest hotel in the world. Its land and construction cost $65 million—a huge sum at the time.

Kerkorian was convinced that the International's location east of the Las Vegas Strip, on Paradise Road, would effectively create a second Strip. Howard Hughes feared this, and he set about trying unsuccessfully to get Kerkorian's financing killed.

Hughes and Kerkorian shared interests in aerospace, Hollywood, and Las Vegas. But Hughes was well educated, born an heir to a fortune.

Kerkorian is a self-made eighth-grade dropout. He was born near Fresno, California, on June 6, 1917, the youngest of the four children of Armenian-born Ahron and Lily Kerkorian. The arrival of Kerkor (his given name) was a surprise, and initially an unwelcome one. According to a profile in the *Los Angeles Times,* his mother tried to abort the baby with hot baths.

Kerkorian's father drove a Lincoln and owned farmland around Fresno in an area called Weedpatch. It's the same place John Steinbeck settled in to research *The Grapes of Wrath,* only Steinbeck came along years after the Kerkorians had left. When the recession of the early 1920s hit, Ahron Kerkorian tried to save his assets by putting them into his young children's names, but the banks came after them anyway, even suing four-year-old Kirk as recounted in Dial Torgesson's 1974 book, *Kerkorian, An American Success Story.* The family's holdings were auctioned off, and they moved to a precarious life in Los Angeles.

In L.A. Kerkor grew up to be something of a juvenile delinquent, albeit a hard-working one. He was expelled from Foshay Junior High for punching a teacher's son in the throat and was sent to Jacob Riis reform school, but he sold newspapers and hustled odd jobs as a sometime bouncer and golf caddy. He dropped out of school in the eighth grade—a choice that would hound him later when his ill-educated speech and manners would make him reticent in public.

In order to hit a person, you have to be just a little bit sadistic. After Kerkorian left school, he followed his older brother Nishon's path into boxing, and as "Rifle Right Kerkorian," won a welterweight championship. He quit after winning twenty-nine of his thirty-three amateur fights, advised that he was too slight and not aggressive enough to survive as a pro.

While installing furnaces as an hourly wage worker in Los Angeles, Kerkorian took a flight in a Piper Cub with a friend and caught the flying bug. He would later lie about his education to get into a flight academy and would end up a civilian flight instructor for the

U.S. Army. During World War II, he delivered Canadian bombers to the Royal Air Force's bases in Europe for $1,000 a trip, according to several accounts—a stunt that was akin to a suicide run. Later he traveled around the world buying and selling surplus planes, flying these jalopies himself to deliver them.

Kerkorian first arrived in Las Vegas as a pilot in 1945, flying gamblers in on a single-engine Cessna. The Strip at the time consisted of an old gambling joint called the 91 Club (formerly the Pair-O-Dice), the El Rancho Vegas (1941), and the Last Frontier (1942). The Flamingo was under construction. Kerkorian's passengers included gangster Bugsy Siegel.

Kerkorian worked hard at the airline for twenty years. He sold it and bought it back in a move that would become a habit with his other assets. It may be the best job he ever did of managing a business, for the airline flourished. He took Trans International Airlines public in 1965 with the help of a fellow Armenian stockbroker in Fresno named George Mason. Mason convinced the Armenian community to buy the stock. Three years later, Kerkorian sold the airline again, in the same era that a young Steve Wynn chose to move to Las Vegas from the East Coast.

Kerkorian bet big sums at the sailors' game craps—placing a wager and walking away a winner or a loser. It came to light that Kerkorian had once written a check in 1961 to pay off $21,300 in sports bets to Charles "Charlie the Blade" Tourine. Tourine was believed to be a member of the Cosa Nostra Family of Vito Genovese. Casino regulators in 1970 failed to prove that Kerkorian knew who Charlie the Blade was when he wrote that check.

Kerkorian gambled on Las Vegas with a land-speculation deal when he bought eighty-two acres of flood-prone land across the street from the Flamingo. He did some savvy land trades to expand it, rented it to the folks who were building Caesars Palace, and eventually sold the parcel to Caesars in 1968.

Over the years he bought and sold the Flamingo, the Desert Inn, and the Sands. He very nearly lost his shirt a few times, but righted himself by selling something. Kerkorian confessed to one early interviewer that he had learned as a child not to be "married" to anything because everything was easily lost.

Hollywood caught his interest shortly after Kerkorian sold the airline the second time to Transamerica, a conglomerate that also owned the film company United Artists. After sniffing around for an undervalued studio, in 1969 he launched a hostile takeover of the ill-managed Metro-Goldwyn-Mayer, thinking he could turn it around.

He couldn't. Over the next thirty-five years, Kerkorian would buy and sell the MGM studio three times, run through a slate of failed studio executives, fail at running it himself, and make a string of forgettables like *Buddy Buddy* while passing on *Jaws* and *The Sting*, which both became big hits for Universal.

Kerkorian sold the studio to Ted Turner in 1986, then bought part of it back when Turner got strapped for cash. Then he did one of those things that makes people scratch their heads. Kerkorian deliberately passed up an opportunity to wrest control of Turner Broadcasting, which owned the CNN network. Rather than buying back parts of the studio, Kerkorian was advised that he could have forced the struggling Turner to pay him with so much common stock that he would have gained voting control of Turner Broadcasting. He told people he liked Turner and didn't want to take control of his company.

Not long after building the International in Las Vegas, Kerkorian became overextended and sold it to Hilton Hotels, whereupon it came to be called the Las Vegas Hilton. Then he built another "biggest hotel" across the street from the Dunes in 1973. He connected his Hollywood and Vegas interests and called it the MGM Grand. This was a stretch, for "grand" it just wasn't.

The last major casino to be built on the Strip for seventeen years, the Grand had 2,100 shoddily built rooms. A tragic grease fire spread out of control at the Grand in 1980, killing eighty-seven people. Among the contributing factors, according to authorities, was slap-dash construction. Kerkorian settled the lawsuits quickly, paying the victims before his insurers paid him.

He seemed thereafter to find the place unbearable, and while he rebuilt it, Kerkorian tried to sell the hotel to Henry Gluck, then chairman of Caesars. Gluck says he would have bought the place, but Kerkorian refused to part with the MGM Grand name. "I might do something else someday," Kerkorian said, according to Gluck.

So the Grand became Bally's when Bally's Manufacturing bought it. Kerkorian's legacy there, like at the Las Vegas Hilton, is remembered only by the history buffs. The casino gave its new owner the same headaches it's given every owner it has ever had. It's only a matter of time until Bally's is imploded.

Kerkorian took up tennis during those intervening years in Las Vegas. He liked to play at the Desert Inn, which was as much a country club as a casino. One of Kerkorian's young doubles partners there was a brash, well-connected Jewish kid with jet-black hair named Steve Wynn.

chapter three

SAY "HAIR-UHS"

Casino gamblers are more likely than nongamblers to have bought a car new. . . . Nongamblers are far more likely to drive a car that is five or more years old.

—2006 HARRAH'S SURVEY

ill Harrah had no intention of getting involved in the whole Las Vegas imbroglio. In fact, he'd be dead and gone for a quarter century before his casino company would make its bones in Sin City.

At eighteen, Harrah got his start in Venice, California, in 1929 working for his father at something that in those days was called a bingo parlor. The place was built on a pier that led off the beach. Venice was a holiday town at the time, with actual canals built to replicate the original Venice in Italy. At the Circle Game bingo parlor, players perched on fold-up stools surrounding a table, a hopper, and a flashing board. They paid a dealer fifty cents for a set of cards, then rolled a ball into the hopper, trying to make the flashboard register a number and suit matching the player's cards. This was not exactly legal.

Young Bill eventually bought the place from his dad for $500. He fixed it up, buying new chairs and adding curtains. Business was good, but he lacked sway with the district attorney: He got shut down every year around Christmas when the Santa Anita Racetrack opened for betting.

It took Harrah longer than some to see the benefit when Nevada legalized gambling again in 1931. Six years later, in 1937, Harrah bought a bingo parlor in Reno, Nevada, and moved there. He struggled for four years, going in and out of several bingo businesses with various partners.

In a stroke of luck for him, though, the Japanese bombed Pearl Harbor in 1941. The ensuing persecution of Japanese Americans forced many to sell their businesses cheaply. A week after Pearl Harbor, Bill Harrah offered to buy one of the town's most successful bingo parlors, the Reno Club, from a gentleman named Freddie Aoyama and his silent Japanese partners. Harrah renamed it Harrah's Reno Club.

He opened his first casino four years later and called it Harrah's Club. From his perch in Reno, and later when he expanded to Lake Tahoe, Bill Harrah brought all sorts of innovations to the casino business. His consultants set up models for keeping track of the doings in "count rooms"—the highly guarded rooms in casinos where cash is counted. He created daily accounting reports called the "daily report" and the "daybook" to inform himself and his management of the operations of each casino over the previous twenty-four hours. In those days, that was real science.

To raise money for expansion, Bill Harrah listed his company on the over-the-counter exchange in 1971, raising $4 million and selling off 13 percent of the holdings. A few years later, Harrah's became the first casino company to trade on the New York Stock Exchange. But Harrah didn't spend his new wealth building a place in Las Vegas. Quite the opposite, he pledged never to do business there, where he believed he would have had to deal with the Mob.

Harrah's northern Nevada location made it difficult to entice entertainers, though, so Harrah started treating performers like high rollers. He loaned Sammy Davis Jr. the use of a Rolls Royce, gave a custom Jeep with a Ferrari engine to Bobby Darin, and housed performers in a pair of Lake Tahoe mansions or special sprawling hotel suites. Those were glory days for Las Vegas entertainment, and Harrah's rode its coattails, drawing regular appearances from stars like Bill Cosby, Frank Sinatra, Don Rickles, and Bob Hope.

Naturally, Bill Harrah had a lot of fun at his places. He was a drinker (until he quit) and a womanizer—married seven times, to six women. He was also obsessive about keeping his places top-notch. Sinatra used to say Bill Harrah ran the nicest hotel around, and

Sammy Davis Jr. agreed. According to an account in *Jackpot!,* a book by Robert L. Shook, Harrah wouldn't allow notes to be taped to any surface in his properties. Pictures had to be hung from two nails to be sure they hung straight; leather upholstery was preferred and vinyl was banned as tacky. Flowers and plants had to be real. When he opened his Lake Tahoe hotel in 1973, each room had his-and-her bathrooms with a television and a phone in each one. Bill Harrah wore Brioni suits when you still had to fly to Rome to get them.

One wonders how Harrah would have felt about the smoky, vinyl-cushioned, honky-tonk casinos that would, by the 1990s, populate the country and bear his name. But he died in 1978, so he never knew about that.

It turned out that Bill Harrah wasn't much for estate planning. To pay off his debts and estate taxes upon his death, his company had to be sold. It was acquired by Holiday Inns Incorporated, which operated only 1,600 hotels at the time. Holiday Inns was a morally upright company based in Memphis, Tennessee. Two of its board members resigned over moral objections to the Harrah's purchase. This did not stop the remaining hotel bigwigs at Holiday Inns from expanding the casinos into Atlantic City with the help of a young attorney named Phil Satre, who had coincidentally once done legal work for Bill Harrah.

For the next fifteen years, Harrah's was tossed around the markets like so much flotsam: purchased by Bass PLC along with Holiday Inns, spun off into the Promus Companies, which would eventually spin off the hotels in 1995, leaving Harrah's—finally—on its own as a casino company once again.

The Holiday Inn years had an unintended impact on Harrah's. The move to Memphis removed its leaders from clubby, competitive Nevada. This helped Harrah's separate from the pack—something Phil Satre later said was the key to the company's success.

When riverboat gambling began to spread in the early 1990s, the Harrah's fellows didn't come across as flashy Vegas operators. They weren't fancy-pants, and they didn't scoff at small casinos that catered to people who couldn't afford to fly to Las Vegas. Their Wal-Mart reputation was just fine with them.

chapter four

It was always Steve's fantasy to have a place on the Strip.
—Elaine Wynn

By now, people know Las Vegas as a frivolous place, rife with fakery and unabashed silliness. So it's worth envisioning Sin City in 1989, when the New Las Vegas story really begins.

George Herbert Walker Bush was inaugurated president of the United States that January. The Berlin Wall came down and *Rain Man* won the Oscar for best picture. Las Vegas was known for gambling and sex. It had no medieval castle, no pyramid, no imitation Venice, Paris, or New York—not even a pirate ship.

Mormons controlled the county's politics, creating a peculiar balance of power between the morally relaxed and the decently uptight. Mormons were the first white guys to settle in the Las Vegas Valley—so named because springs burbled from the ground there, creating grassy meadows: *las vegas* in Spanish. Nevada became a United States territory in 1861. Las Vegas, down south in the desert, wasn't a metropolis at the time. The Nevadans preferred to be up north in places like in Virginia City, where twenty-six-year-old Samuel Clemens once took a job at the *Territorial Enterprise* and began writing under the pseudonym Mark Twain.

Despite our Protestant leanings, gambling has been an American pastime since at least 1612, when the first lottery in America raised £29,000 for the Virginia Company. Lotteries—a form of gambling with generally far worse odds than a slot machine—also helped pay for some of the first buildings at Harvard, Princeton, and Dartmouth. Revolutionary soldiers gambled at Valley Forge, much to George Washington's consternation. Later, the streets and backrooms of New York, Philadelphia, Chicago, and other big cities served as training grounds for future casino operators who would flee to Nevada to get the law off their backs.

Gambling was legal in Nevada for most of the nineteenth century until a moral majority got it banned. It was a mining and railroad–inspired land rush that created the town of Las Vegas, which was incorporated in 1911. Twenty years later, with the Great Depression pressuring the state's coffers, gambling was again legalized in Nevada.

Of course, there were plenty of gambling joints in Las Vegas even when they were illegal. One pioneering place was called the Pair-O-Dice, whose operators were reputedly connected to Al Capone. It was located south of the town on Highway 91, a road that rolled and rumbled another three hundred arid miles to Southern California.

That was the Strip in utero.

♣ ♦ ♥ ♠

By 1989, the Strip was more famous than the town. On prom nights, casino floors bubbled with pimply kids in tuxedos and evening gowns. In summers, it was a sport for local youngsters to infiltrate the resorts' swimming pools, starting with the Tropicana and sneaking northward up the Strip in a pool-by-pool race.

As for tourists, unless one was headed to Las Vegas to gamble, one was unlikely to be headed to Las Vegas at all in 1989. Fine dining amounted to a single decision: steak or Italian. The entertainment was literally a bad joke. With the Rat Pack long gone and Elvis buried, washed-up or short-lived stars tried to rekindle their careers there. Barbara Mandrell and Jimmie Walker—remember them?—were playing in Las Vegas when the Mirage was opening.

Having lost the Mob, the Teamsters, and Howard Hughes, Las Vegas had been starving for investment capital for two decades. The general view on Wall Street was that the casino industry wasn't *nice*. Investors would rather buy tobacco stocks.

After all, the dicey past wasn't so long gone. Aged Mafia barons were still dining on the osso buco at Piero's Italian restaurant, their canes hanging from their chairs. Meyer Lansky's friend Moe Dalitz, who sold the Desert Inn to Howard Hughes, died that September, beloved for his contributions to schools and parks and for buzzing around town in a canary yellow Volkswagen Bug. In 1989, it had been only three years since the pulpy body of Tony "The Ant" Spilotro, one of the city's most notorious residents, was discovered several feet deep in an Indiana cornfield.

Later, this would all look like Hollywood fun. Spilotro's attorney, Oscar Goodman, quit keeping mobsters out of jail and got himself elected Mayor Goodman. Among the gin-guzzling mayor's truly original proposals: cutting a thumb off the hands of graffiti artists who defaced public property. He also proposed televising the punishment. (The Goodmans were civic contributors. Goodman's wife, Carolyn, founded the city's most prestigious private school, the Meadows, whose campus has buildings named for casino kingpins. It's where all the gambling bigwigs send their littlewigs.)

In the 1980s, it took imagination to compare Las Vegas to Disneyland. Steve Wynn had that imagination and he loved Disney. In fact, his fascination with the highly detailed theme parks would come up again and again over the years.

Wynn moved to Las Vegas at the age of twenty-five with his wife, Elaine, and a ten-month-old daughter in tow. He sought out some of his dad's old connections and managed to get invited to the opening of Caesars Palace in 1966, where he says he was upgraded to suite 1066—the suite he says was occupied the night before by Teamsters honcho Jimmy Hoffa.

Wynn's first attempt to enter the casino business was inauspicious, to say the least. He made, at best, an ill-informed investment in the mobbed-up Frontier casino. Law enforcement soon prosecuted the management for its underworld ties. Wynn wasn't implicated, but he was forced by financial circumstance to leave the casino industry to work as a liquor distributor for a few years.

This would become one of those incidents that people would later use to suggest that Wynn has had an unusual number of brushes with organized crime. Numerous law enforcement investigations for gambling licenses have failed to conclude that Wynn ever worked for or with organized crime, and Wynn has vigorously denied any such involvement. It can be safely said, though, that many people living in Las Vegas in those years bumped into folks who were connected to the Mob.

It was an imaginative local banker named Parry Thomas who became a mentor to the fatherless Steve Wynn. Thomas used his considerable influence to help this kid with moxie buy a piece of land from Howard Hughes. Wynn then sold the land to Kirk Kerkorian in 1969 and used the profits to buy stock in a real casino—a rundown place called the Golden Nugget in seedy downtown Las Vegas. The Nugget's primary advantage was that it was a publicly traded company. That enabled the shareholder Wynn, four years later, to oust the management on a tip that employees were stealing from the mismanaged casino. He installed himself as the Nugget's president and chairman. It was a hostile takeover, but from the inside.

"The key to my progress was that I had the stock and voted myself in," Wynn says.

The Golden Nugget quickly became a mom-and-pop thing, and that's pretty much the way Wynn has run his businesses ever since. Elaine arrived each day with a cup of coffee in her hand. Wynn hired his twenty-one-year-old brother, Kenny, who had been working at a men's store. He also hired people he figured were smart, like Bobby Baldwin.

Wynn discovered Bobby Baldwin while being thrashed by him at poker. Three decades before poker became a televised sport, in 1978 the Oklahoma native won the famous gold bracelet of Binion's World Championship of Poker. He later wrote a folksy book of poker advice called *Tales out of Tulsa*, by Bobby "The Owl" Baldwin.

In a typical Wynn move—spying someone talented and creating a job for him—Wynn hired the professional poker player as a poker-room consultant in 1982. For the next twenty years, Baldwin would keep track of Wynn's details, freeing the boss to be creative. Wynn "never really enjoyed operations, because it involves a lot of interaction with a lot of people at a lot of different levels," Baldwin says. "Steve frustrates easily with that stuff. He's short on patience. I'm long on patience."

Wynn renovated the Golden Nugget, expanded it, and hired casino hosts who knew how to bring in high rollers. He even tried to create a Disney-esque animatronic dinner theater using robotic actors. The plans never came to fruition, but according to a former Disney employee who worked on the project, he created mock-ups of Asian and Mexican shows, created to appeal to regions where high rollers were coming from.

When he expanded into Atlantic City in 1980, Wynn launched a corny television advertising campaign that featured Frank Sinatra treating Wynn like a towel boy. He was on his way to stardom.

♣ ♦ ♥ ♠

In 1989, the cementlike calichi soil at 3400 South Las Vegas Boulevard heaved up the Mirage Hotel and Casino Resort. It isn't an exaggeration to say that Las Vegas was never the same.

The Mirage initially cost $630 million—more money than anyone had ever spent building a casino resort. Michael Milken made it all possible. In addition to helping finance the place with junk bonds, Milken told Wynn how to dress (in a suit) when he met Wall Street investors.

The Mirage was the first place where Wynn was able to meld his own wacky passions with a resort. Vacations in Hawaii gave him the idea of putting a fifty-four-foot-high volcano in front of the hotel. The volcano was really a water fountain with natural gas burners. Sound was piped into speakers that were planted in trees and along the sidewalk and the lagoon on Las Vegas Boulevard. The volcano was rimmed with waterfalls that sent 100,000 gallons of water per minute cascading down the rocks into the lagoon. The lagoon's 2.3 million gallons of water were lit with 1,000-watt lights. Invisible under the water was a special-effects plumbing system with jets that spewed gas that was set afire by pilot lights, creating bubbles and flames that erupted like molten lava for the seven-minute show. All this was controlled from underground rooms that smelled of chlorine and were accessible only through the maze of car-valet tunnels.

Wynn discovered, during the test phase, that the gas was stinky. He added a piña colada scent, then installed filters to remove the gassy odor.

The volcano's job was to lure people from Caesars Palace next door or the Sands across the street. "People today just stand there and stare because they're used to sinking ships and all sorts of special effects," says Jaime Cruz, a mechanical engineer who helped build the volcano at the Mirage. "But on opening night, I remember hundreds of people standing on the street, watching the volcano, going, 'Oooh, aaah.'"

At the Mirage's front desk, four-foot sharks sliced the water of a 20,000-gallon aquarium. An indoor tropical rain forest grew in the tall atrium, where orchids clung to trees and bridges in a humid microclimate. This would become a Wynn signature—a sylvan garden under glass. "I was trying to appeal to women," Wynn says, proving himself the first Las Vegas casino operator to recognize that women were customers worth catering to in a big way.

The Mirage had a convention center and ballroom, swimming pools, retail shops, and 3,100 hotel rooms—including Las Vegas's most lavish high-roller suites. Wynn rolled the dice, building a $20 million show around white tigers and a little-known pair of *bruder*-like German illusionists who called themselves Siegfried and Roy.

Wynn gets the credit, but there was a lot of Bobby Baldwin in the Mirage's details. Baldwin insisted on having sixteen service elevators in the Mirage so that room service didn't share elevators with guests, speeding delivery. "Bobby was all about the nuts and bolts," said Alan Feldman, the Mirage's former spokesman. "How you get the lettuce from the warehouse making sure it doesn't wilt."

"It was my job to decide how many restaurants and how big," Baldwin says, "and it was his job to make it beautiful."

The Mirage was so big and costly that many people on the Strip and on Wall Street predicted disaster. Analysts calculated the Mirage would require revenues of $1 million a day to break even. Unheard of.

"It would be hard for Steve to get his $1 million a day even if we all were sitting on our duffs," Henry Gluck, the chairman and chief executive of rival Caesars World, told *BusinessWeek*.

Wynn offered braggadocio in response. The Mirage would be "a wonderment the world will flock to see," he insisted. "We're gonna skate."

Gluck, a German-Jewish refugee from Nazi Germany who bussed tables in a hotel before he ran one, wasn't sitting on his lanky duff. Nor was the rest of Las Vegas. Instead, out came the bulldozers.

Gluck began to remodel Caesars Palace, adding high-roller suites and a conveyor belt designed to ferry 9,000 people a day from the Mirage's doorstep. The conveyor belt operated only in one direction. People had to walk back out.

Gluck also lit on an innovation that forever changed Las Vegas: shopping. The idea came from his wife, who spent more than her share of time in Las Vegas wishing she was at home in Beverly Hills. She told her husband that women would be happy to have a little more Rodeo Drive on the Las Vegas Strip. This revelation led in 1992 to the Forum Shops at Caesars Palace, a partnership with mall developer Sheldon Gordon. Rivals and even some friends warned Gluck that the shops would be his Roman tomb. But the Forum Shops would one day produce the highest revenue per square foot of any shopping center in the nation.

November 22, 1989, thousands of people crowded Las Vegas Boulevard next door to Caesars Palace and across from the Sands, the latter of which had hired Sha Na Na to compete with the new opening. The crowds were looking toward three golden towers, whose panels consisted of two sheets of glass that encased 24-carat gold mylar film. More expensive than colored glass, this maintained its golden color no matter the conditions of the sun. Steve Wynn had noticed that the Golden Nugget's colored-glass tower often looked greenish depending on the sun's angle. He did not want greenish glass on his Mirage.

In addition to the Mirage's volcano and lagoon, there were palm trees—1,100 of them—as well as pines, ferns, flowers, and grass. Lawns and pools abutted private entrances into high-roller bungalows, one of which housed the singer Michael Jackson, with whom Wynn was planning a "Jackson Attraction" that would feature the performer's memorabilia.

At the opening moment, Wynn stood by a palm tree, queasy with fear and flanked by Michael Milken. This is how indebted Wynn felt to Milken for helping him finance his dream: Wynn said a few years later, "I would do anything for Michael, without limit. I would do just about anything to extend his life a week."

People predicted that 100,000 people would visit the Mirage that day. As it happened, the number was more like 200,000. They skipped *Doogie Howser, M.D.* and *Night Court* on television that evening for the opportunity to see this newfangled Mirage. They overran the casino floor upon the opening of the doors and they snatched up so many coins for slot machines that the casino was caught short of cash.

Two days later, Wynn got an inkling of the monster he had created. He surveyed $800,000 worth of trampled grass and muddied flowerbeds around his lagoon. He also got one of the scares of his life.

"There were some kids and they were drinking and they were all excited and wanted to be macho, so one of them walks across the grass and climbs in the water. He's standing there up to his waist," Wynn says. The volcano was scheduled to erupt any moment in gas bubbles and flames. "He's about to get third-degree burns in his crotch."

Wynn says there are three kinds of possible mistakes in opening a new resort. Category 1 mistakes are fixable—broken equipment and the like. Category 2 mistakes are more costly and "more painful"—requiring redesign. Of Category 3 mistakes, he says, "This is the one you have nightmares about," when you're trying something no one has done before. "You open the hotel and you're completely blindsided. The volcano was one of those."

"It was a nightmare," Wynn said. "It was a Category 3 mistake. I should have seen it. Sometimes you just misfire."

As it happened, someone saved the day. "One of my plainclothes guys jumped in and grabs this guy by the neck and pulled the dipshit out," Wynn says.

The volcano represents the moment that Las Vegas slipped into its goofy modern era. Gamblers became outnumbered by wilding tourists in golf shirts, more interested in eating and shopping than wagering.

As Wynn stood in front of the Mirage and took it all in forty-eight hours after the opening, it hit him that he had made another mistake. He turned to his PR guy, Alan Feldman, and said, "I can't believe I didn't build something overlooking the volcano."

In the following year, the number of visitors to Las Vegas increased 16 percent, to 21 million. The Mirage surpassed the Hoover Dam as southern Nevada's number-one tourist attraction. This led to a decade-long building boom during which thirteen crazy new megacasinos shot up on the Strip at a cost of $8.8 billion. Las Vegas became so overwrought that people came to associate the city with silly theme parks and fakery.

Shortly after the opening, Wynn had the Mirage's lawn replaced with a wider sidewalk and a wrought-iron fence. And then, said Wynn, "because people won't be daunted, we put [in] a beam-and-eye system where if someone steps through all that, it shuts the whole volcano down."

The old Las Vegas was already beginning to die. Sammy Davis Jr. was suffering with throat cancer and a new Las Vegas was being born. Wynn announced he was teaming up with Michael Jackson to build a replica of Diamond Head Mountain in Hawaii behind the Mirage that would feature two swimming pools, a water slide, and luxury high-roller villas. This mountain was not to be. But Steve Wynn recycles his ideas. The mountain would return.

Completely outside of Steve Wynn's radar that year, 1989, a twenty-nine-year-old MIT-trained economist named Gary William Loveman finished his doctoral dissertation, *Changes in the Organization of Production and the Skill Composition of Unemployment.* Loveman had conducted field research on why unemployment rates differ around the world and used mathematics to solve the complex problems.

The sandy-haired Loveman had grown up in a blue-collar family in Indiana. He earned an undergraduate degree from Wesleyan University in Connecticut, which did not prepare him for the rigorous mathematics required by MIT's doctoral program. "Sitting in class was like listening to Swahili," he says. Despite his rough start on the north shore of the Charles River, he had managed to catch up with such sheer grit that he secured himself an Alfred Sloan Doctoral Dissertation Fellowship and a shot at economic stardom.

This made him a hot commodity in 1989's market for young economists. Loveman was offered jobs by Duke University, the University of Chicago, Cornell, and Harvard—the latter offering him no fewer than two jobs (at Harvard Business School and the Kennedy School of Government). Princeton interviewed him, but didn't offer him a job. MIT was in the process of producing an offer when Loveman accepted one of the jobs at Harvard.

So as Steve Wynn was swaggering through the final construction stage of the Mirage, Loveman was joining the faculty of the Harvard Business School and entering his first semester of teaching.

Loveman was well received at Harvard, where several of the department's more senior professors predicted he would become one of the country's foremost labor economists.

That would have been a bad bet. Loveman, after a few years at Harvard, would move on to much bigger things.

chapter five

THE GREAT RACE

Las Vegas exists because of that almost violent hand-to-hand combat place that is the Strip.

—STEVE WYNN

f you feel a need to blame someone for the Las Vegas skyline of the 1990s, consider pinning a blue ribbon on the fellows at Circus Circus Enterprises. As the plans for the Mirage were being drawn up, Glenn Schaeffer sent a memo to his boss at Circus Circus, Bill Bennett. Shaeffer proposed building a casino at the southernmost end of the Las Vegas Strip.

The result was the medieval-themed Excalibur. Hokey beyond belief. Bigger than the Mirage by 900 rooms and costing half as much—$290 million—it opened seven months after the Mirage.

Bennett and Schaeffer were skilled at running what's known in Vegas as a "grind joint," so termed because it grinds the cash out of its customers the hard way—nickel by nickel. Their primary property was the clown-headed monstrosity, Circus Circus, which had been developed by Jay Sarno.

Excalibur was inspired by Neuschwanstein Castle in the Bavarian alps—a crazy concoction of Romanesque, Gothic, and fairy-tale architecture built by Bavaria's King Ludwig II, who really should have lived in twentieth-century Las Vegas. King Ludwig was a sort of nineteenth-century Liberace, known as much for moonlight picnics with his stable boys as his rococo taste.

Ludwig's insatiable urge to develop grandiose castles has uncanny parallels to Wynn. Ludwig went deeply into debt building three out-landish palaces: Neuschwanstein, Linderhof, and Herrenchiemsee. One biography says that Ludwig "took a special interest in the build-ing of all his palaces, sometimes to the extreme irritation of his archi-tects and craftsmen." Having alarmed his cabinet with his spending, Ludwig was declared insane by a kangaroo court and drowned mys-teriously in 1886. He left behind plans for two even grander palaces, which were to have been themed: Chinese and Byzantine.

A century later, Excalibur was a papier-mâché version of Neuschwanstein. More Disney than Bavarian, its crenellated walls and white turrets spindled over the Strip like an overgrown child's toy. It became an instant, if comical, success.

Wynn established his territory by pissing on theirs. The fellows at Circus Circus were very good "with the Kmart set," Wynn said snidely.

But one evening in mid-1991, Wynn and his poker-playing right-hand man, Bobby Baldwin, showed up at Excalibur and asked to be shown around. They were casing the joint.

♣ ♦ ♥ ♠

Inveterate gamblers are driven by the adrenaline and endorphins that their bodies release as they lay it on the line. Once accustomed to $100-a-hand blackjack, $5 hands no longer offer a thrill. When it comes to developing casinos, the same can be said for Kirk Kerkorian, who outdid himself and Wynn with his next project, for which he would recycle the name MGM Grand. It was to cost $1 billion—an Emerald City of Oz–green extravaganza on the corner of the Strip and Tropicana Avenue.

Kerkorian wasn't as shy in the early 1990s as he would become. Rather than avoiding the limelight, he was joined by Burt Reynolds and Loni Anderson for the October 1991 groundbreaking of the world's largest hotel. He was also flanked by hired actors dressed as Dorothy and her companions from *The Wizard of Oz*.

By 1991, every Las Vegas casino needed to be slathered with a theme—heavy on the schmaltz, hold the irony. Hollywood was to be the MGM Grand's theme. Conveniently, Kerkorian controlled Metro-Goldwyn-Mayer and its vast library of films, including *The Wizard of Oz*. The casino would help publicize the studio's stars like Burt Reynolds and Loni Anderson, whose animated video, *All Dogs Go to Heaven*, was being distributed by Metro-Goldwyn-Mayer/United Artists. A perfect film for the resort's primary market: families with kids.

Three weeks after Kerkorian stuck his shovel in the ground, Steve Wynn donned a pirate's cap and coat to announce plans for his own new resort. It would be called Treasure Island. Located on a parking lot on a corner of the Mirage site, the $430-million resort would have 2,900 hotel rooms that would sell for roughly $75 a night—a smorgasbord for the Kmart set that Wynn had so recently criticized.

Advisors suggested that Wynn call it Treasure Island by Steve Wynn. Wynn refused, recalls Alan Feldman, his longtime communications director. "He said he would never, ever put his name on a hotel," Feldman says. "He said, 'That's what Trump does.'"

Two weeks after Treasure Island was announced, Circus Circus unveiled plans for a massive, Egyptian-themed resort, temporarily called Project X. You may know it now as the giant black-glass pyramid casino called the Luxor.

The great casino race was on.

♣ ♦ ♥ ♠

Instead of a volcano, Treasure Island offered passersby a British frigate, the HMS *Britannia* (it had been called the *Sir Francis Drake* until African-American groups pointed out that the British explorer had also been a slave-trader) that sailed around Skull Point to confront pirates in a manmade lagoon called Buccaneer Bay. The ensuing battle involved more than thirty actors and stunt performers who fired muskets and cannons. At the end of every show, the *Britannia* sank under the chilly water in a pit that Wynn had dug deep into the soil of the Strip.

The pirates won. Wink, wink.

With Treasure Island, Wynn made his big break from traditional Las Vegas entertainment and the Tom Jones, Wayne Newton style of show. A French-Canadian circus troupe called Cirque du Soleil had been having conversations with other Las Vegas operators, but they seemed too avant-garde. Wynn was fearless. He installed their *Mystère* show at Treasure Island. The December 1993 premiere was the troupe's launch to worldwide stardom. Las Vegas entertainment would never be the same. As of 2006, an estimated seventeen million people had seen one of the five resident Cirque du Soleil shows in Las Vegas.

To promote his new venture, Wynn produced a television movie in which he flashed his brilliant smile and played the role of the owner of a fantastic, kid-friendly resort called Treasure Island. The movie, primarily a one-hour infomercial called "Treasure Island: The Adventure Begins," aired that January on NBC. Its star was thirteen years old. Any remaining questions about Wynn's demographic could be settled by his choice of time slot: right at the eight-p.m. family viewing hour.

To celebrate Treasure Island's opening, Wynn pressed a small red button at ten p.m. on October 27, 1993. This led to a chain of explosions that reduced the twenty-three-story tower of the famous old Dunes casino to a thirty-foot pile of rubble in twenty-seven seconds.

The Dunes, built during the heady rush of 1955, was a Rat Pack gem fallen on hard times. The spectacular show of fireworks, black powder, and aviation fuel that destroyed it was watched by 200,000 people, many of whom cried. Not Wynn. "For me, it was the beginning of a new project, not the end of the Dunes," he said.

The location of Wynn's next project came as a nasty surprise to Caesars Palace's Henry Gluck, who had been negotiating to buy the Dunes. Wynn had nimbly slipped in and picked it up for $75 million in November 1992, leaving Caesars forever sandwiched between two Wynn casinos. "I never for a moment thought he'd buy it," recalls Gluck.

Wynn was joined at the Dunes implosion by forty-six-year-old Michael Milken, who had been released in March after serving twenty-two months of a ten-year sentence for his conviction on six felony stock trading violations.

"I met Steve in 1978 and felt that Steve embodied Walt Disney," Milken told reporters, explaining why he had backed Wynn those years ago. "I think we are seeing some of that embodiment tonight."

Over the next decade or so, Controlled Demolition of Baltimore would handle more than a dozen implosions in Las Vegas. Attendees at the parties would collect the party favors—dust masks, plastic ponchos, identification badges.

♣ ♦ ♥ ♠

The year 1993 produced an all-out race to open new mega casinos. Luxor crossed the finish line first on October 15, followed closely by Treasure Island twelve days later. Kerkorian's MGM Grand limped across the line on December 18, panting to catch up to the four-year-old Mirage.

"Our typical rooms, at four hundred forty-six square feet, will be about twenty-five percent larger than the typical rooms at the Mirage," Bob Maxey, president of MGM Grand Incorporated, told reporters. He said the MGM's showroom would be larger than the Mirage's. The valet service would be more efficient than the Mirage's. The elevators would be closer to the front desk than the Mirage's, eliminating a long walk that disgruntled Mirage guests.

"This is not a bigger and more expensive Mirage," Maxey said. "This is something new."

Among the resort's features were more than 5,000 hotel rooms, a dozen restaurants, three swimming pools, five tennis courts, and a thirty-three-acre theme park. There was to be a day-care center for the children of guests—one of the hotel industry's first kids' clubs.

Kerkorian really had Wynn beat in one area: He had a 15,000-seat arena built to rival Madison Square Garden—the kind of place where Rifle Right had dreamed of fighting in his youth.

Boxing is one of those events—like rodeos and trucking conventions—that draws real gamblers to Las Vegas. Boxing makes Las Vegas sizzle. All the rival casinos buy tickets for their customers and throw parties. Hollywood celebrities and Donald Trump cadge great seats.

The Mirage and Caesars Palace held matches in temporary arenas in their parking lots. Kerkorian aimed to knock their lights out. The MGM Grand Garden "means no more fights in parking lots in Las Vegas," said Maxey.

Kerkorian was so excited, he wanted to share the arena with his friend George Mason, whose support had launched his airline so many years earlier. During the construction, he led Mason to the arena doors, where they were confronted by a guard, Mason said about the incident several years later.

The guard failed to recognize Kerkorian, who was rarely around, and he informed the visitors tersely that no one was allowed in. But what Mason always remembered was Kerkorian's response.

"Couldn't we just take a peek?" the mogul pleaded.

♣ ◆ ♥ ♠

When the new MGM Grand Hotel & Theme Park threw open its doors on December 18, 1993, the two things that stood out were its size and the magnitude of its problems.

Kerkorian donned a checked sportcoat and an open shirt. "I think it's a completely new convention across the board for families," he said, joined by Lee Iacocca, chairman of Chrysler and a member of MGM's board of directors.

Alongside the seventy-six-year-old mogul that day was his twenty-seven-year-old girlfriend, Lisa Bonder, a tall former tennis pro with ash-blond hair.

Iacocca toured the theme park and gave it a bigger compliment than it deserved. "It's like a small Disneyland," Iacocca said, but guests that day complained that the seven rides looked cheap, with little attention to detail.

In her first paid concert in twenty-two years, Barbra Streisand stepped onto the stage and belted out such aptly named songs as "Everything's As If We Never Said Goodbye" and "I've Come Home Again." It had been thirty years, Streisand noted, since she had been the opening act for Liberace at the Riviera.

As she sang, picketers amassed outside, protesting the MGM Grand's opposition to an organizing drive by the Culinary Union's housekeepers, restaurant workers, and other casino employees.

From the stage that first night, Barbra Streisand complained to her audience about her room's shortcomings. Hundreds of showers lacked hot water. Key cards didn't work. Phones broke down, leaving guests with busy signals. The pool wasn't finished.

Guests waited two hours and more for room service. People commonly waited forty minutes just to check in.

Its sheer unwieldy size was irritating. One travel writer counted 290 steps to stroll down one hallway of hotel rooms. His hike from the front casino entrance, with its passage through the mouth of an eighty-eight-foot-tall lion, to the theme park and then up to a hotel room took nearly twenty minutes.

Yet the MGM Grand grossed roughly $1.6 million a day.

It turned out that kids are trouble in Las Vegas. Children weaving past slot machines; parents fending off prostitution fliers on Las Vegas Boulevard; babies in strollers while Mommy plays blackjack—or the opposite: parents distracted from gambling by their babies.

Wynn and everyone else figured this out quickly, but it would prove difficult to unravel the misguided kid-friendly push. Even today, several billion dollars' worth of Disney-esque casinos contribute to a widely held public belief that Las Vegas is a family sort of place.

Wynn's flirtation with the pitch for families lasted barely past Treasure Island's opening. From the beginning, he dissembled uncharacteristically.

"We are not specifically pitching anything to people under twenty-one," he said in 1993. "This is a place for big kids."

By 1994, Wynn already seemed to be regretting Treasure Island. "We don't want families," Wynn said. "We want adults who gamble."

Years later, Elaine Wynn would sit in the Wynn Las Vegas casino and glance up at the pirate-themed tower's peach façade—a weirdly enlarged Victorian motif with false balconies. "Now, that's an ugly building," she said. "That was a knee-jerk reaction."

The kid-friendly thing did help legitimize casinos for those on Wall Street. Once so leery of gambling, big investors were now pouring their money into casinos in the mid-1990s. This pressured casino operators to demonstrate steady, predictable growth, like McDonald's or Wal-Mart.

There were two problems with this. One was Kerry Packer and his ilk: gamblers known as "whales."

When Packer arrived in Las Vegas, the whole town got pulsed up. The hefty Australian media and casino magnate would bet millions of dollars in an evening. Packer was Australia's richest man, and he was also a "george," a big tipper, in Vegas parlance. According to lore he once paid off the mortgage of a cocktail waitress who brought him a drink. He would eventually die of kidney failure at home in Sydney the day after Christmas in 2005. But while he was alive and in Las Vegas, casinos' chief financial officers crossed their fingers and prayed for the house. Packer's runs of luck could throw off a company's quarterly earnings by a nickel a share. That kind of thing is awkward to explain to antsy hedge-fund managers. The volatility of casino earnings was cited as the reason why casino companies trade for lower prices than, for instance, hotel companies.

What's more, opening a new casino is tougher than opening a Wal-Mart. New casinos must be approved by state legislators or voters. Fortunately for casinos in the early 1990s, a recession was killing state budgets. Lawmakers began to legalize gambling in places where it had previously been illegal so they could tax the heck out of it.

To make casinos palatable to constituents, many of whom opposed gambling, someone came up with the bright idea of quarantining casinos on riverboats. With many voters envisioning Mark Twain–style paddlewheels churning up and down the Mississippi, riverboats turned out to be the sugar that made the medicine go down. Eventually, the whole thing became a fiction, with "riverboat" casinos built over huge, water-pumping systems on the side of a river or lake.

Many casino operators spent the 1990s desperately sniffing across the United States like bloodhounds for riverboat licenses: New York, Mississippi, Louisiana, Iowa, Florida, and nearly every state in the union other than Utah.

Harrah's did this better than anyone, growing from a small company to a big one as it docked new riverboats all over the country. Kirk Kerkorian never seemed much interested in that small-time stuff; his love was always Las Vegas. Still, he did snare a lucrative casino license in Detroit—an opportunity so golden that Wynn, upon learning he himself hadn't won the license, pitched a temper tantrum so wild that people say they heard glass breaking in his office.

Wynn was enormously powerful in Nevada politics. In addition to making hefty donations, he had created an operation in Las Vegas that polled residents on local issues and elections. He smartly loaned these resources to candidates.

Outside Nevada, though, Wynn's political batting average was nearly nil. Maybe it was his Vegas hair and flamboyant swagger—a personality too flashy for conservative Midwestern or Southern tastes. He spent millions, but failed to win new casino opportunities when he campaigned in places like New Orleans, Missouri, Illinois, Connecticut, Florida, Michigan, Australia, and Vancouver, British Columbia.

Meanwhile, a group of guys at Harrah's Entertainment in Memphis, Tennessee, was snapping up state casino licenses right and left.

The Las Vegas casino elite tended to view Harrah's in the way that many New Yorkers view people from Birmingham, Alabama—as bumpkins from another planet. The Vegas crowd was a clique, alternately bickering and closing ranks against outsiders. Harrah's was snubbed for its pedestrian focus on meeting the American lower classes in their own backyards.

Harrah's offered the convenience of proximity. There was nothing glamorous or even pretty about Harrah's casinos. They tended to be loud, smoky places that appealed to the blue-collar residents nearby and were often full of people who looked like they could barely afford to be there.

Wynn practically sneered at the riverboat casinos.

"The riverboat is preposterous," Wynn said in 1994. "When you build a riverboat, you build a gambling hall. A gambling joint appeals to that small percentage of the public that wants to gamble. If we're looking at a cross-section of the earth, that's the equivalent of the earth's crust. . . . When you talk about a destination resort like Las Vegas, you're talking about a cut that goes down deep into the igneous rock. We build places for folks who don't think of themselves as gamblers."

Wynn wanted bigger and brighter. "My hero was Disney," Wynn said in 1993, again referring to the theme parks that fascinated him. "I would be just as happy building theme parks as casinos, but it's been done already."

chapter six

BLIND

I see just fine.

—STEVE WYNN

teve Wynn steps out of the casino into the bright sunlight of May in Las Vegas. He halts midstep and midsentence and yanks his deeply tinted sunglasses over his eyes. He does not explain this interruption. Two people wait as Wynn's eyes adjust to the blinding sun—about thirty seconds. When he regains his bearing, he proceeds energetically.

Wynn learned he was going blind as a young man.

Retinitis pigmentosa, a genetic disease, has been destroying the photoreceptor cells in Wynn's retinas for most of his adult life. The rod cells around his retinas' outer perimeters are dying, taking with them his ability to convert light into the electrical impulses that are transmitted to the brain to create vision.

Over years, he has gradually lost the ability to see images in his periphery. It is as though he is staring through tubes, only to view objects within a small circle at the end of a dark cylinder. His perception of light and his ability to adjust to dimly lit environments are altered. In a dark room, he can be completely blind.

Wynn can fix his eyes on a person's face with urgency, but he won't see the person's torso and may leave a proffered hand dangling naked in midair. At dinner, he fails to see the waiter who is trying to place a plate before him.

He is a hazard on construction sites. He trips over extension cords,

41

bumps into circular saws, and ricochets off walls without acknowl-edging his fumbles. He is a master of disguise, wrapping his arm around the shoulders of a nearby person in a gesture that seems inti-mate, but turns that person into a seeing-eye guide—and these guides sidestep and duck and veer around obstacles to save them both.

Wynn is unable to drive, but this hasn't stopped him from buy-ing fast cars. He bought a red Enzo Ferrari, valued at $1.4 million, and parked it in his casino's showroom with twenty-seven miles on the odometer. He has enjoyed being ferried around Las Vegas in a Mercedes Maybach, with double-paned windows and reclining backseats, by his driver, Albert, whose salary is paid for by Wynn's company.

Wynn, who is easily tickled, says he dreams of buzzing himself around town in a Volkswagen bug. He gets a vicarious thrill riding shotgun in Elaine's Ferraris. "I like to watch the guys looking at her," he says, grinning. She rolls her eyes.

Wynn loves to keep strict company with creative types. Some say they suspect that his perception doesn't quite match theirs. He might fail to grasp the action occurring across a stage, for instance, or to see the reddish tones in a shade of chocolate. These creatives often com-ment, privately, on the tragedy of a visual man losing his vision.

Sympathy infuriates him. Wynn plows through this obstacle. He peers at every fabric swatch. He critiques the staging of shows and the engineering of a porte cochere. When he is unsure, he leans on Elaine.

Asked about his eyesight one day, Wynn visibly cringes and growls, "I see just fine."

"I see like this," he says, making his hands into conical viewfind-ers in front of his eyes. "You see like this"—taking his hands above his head and below his chin—"almost vertical." A special telephone sits on his desk with enlarged numbers for easier dialing.

People who work with him sense the gradual decline of Wynn's vision, the narrowing path of light in which he lives. At meals, they watch him swallow handfuls of vitamins and herbs. They learn to greet him by announcing their names and touching his arm to iden-tify their location. But they do not mention *it*.

Wynn's diminishing eyesight is a matter of mystery around his company—something widely known but thinly understood, discussed in whispers and code.

"I've never asked him about his eyes," says the political pollster Frank Luntz, who has worked for Wynn for many years. "I'm afraid."

chapter seven

BRASS BALLS

He was kind of loud and a little bit in the pounding-his-own-chest department.

—BOYHOOD FRIEND OF STEVE WYNN

On New Year's Day in 1994, Paul Meloro, who was thirty-one at the time, was alone processing film in the Mirage's photo lab. When the lab phone rang sometime after lunch, the photographer put the receiver to his ear and heard a gruff voice say, "This is Steve Wynn. Send somebody down to the dolphin pool."

The Mirage is one of the few places in the United States with a license from the National Marine Fisheries Service to keep dolphins. This is because Wynn took a trip to Hawaii while he was building the Mirage. There, he swam with dolphins at a resort. "He came back from that trip and said, 'Well, add a dolphin pool to your list of things to do, Bobby,'" says Bobby Baldwin, who at the time was busy attending to the details of constructing the Mirage.

Animal rights activists protested, opposed to keeping dolphins in captivity in the Mojave Desert. "It took hundreds of people three years to get the licenses," Baldwin says. Wynn arranged to be "tipped off" by federal officials about five maltreated bottle-nosed dolphins—four from Florida and one from Texas. He says he offered the owners $20,000 per dolphin. "If they took the deal, they had to sign a paper that they wouldn't apply for another license," Wynn says.

Sigma, Duchess, Merlin, Darla, and Banjo were flown into Las Vegas like any high-roller: in chartered jets outfitted for their comfort.

They were also just about as bad-tempered as any high-roller on a losing streak.

Sigma arrived first, at around four in the morning in October 1990. She rolled off her sling, did one high-speed revolution around the small holding pool where she was intended to settle down for a few hours, and blasted straight through its steel gate at about 30 mph, exiting right into the Mirage's 1.6-million-gallon, 26-foot-deep lagoon.

When Wynn arrived, he demanded to know what had happened. Wet-suited divers were dispatched to inspect the gate with flashlights. They found a frayed hole in the chain link that looked as though a large bullet had shot through. Sigma's nose was scratched. "We learned as we went along," says Baldwin.

When the babies started coming, Wynn learned that pregnant dolphins should be isolated. This required another pool. The budget nearly quadrupled to $14 million from $4 million.

Wynn had promised federal authorities that he would create a research center, and he brought in a trainer to make the nasty-tempered mammals more manageable. The Mirage dolphins eventually participated in so many research projects that they learned to lie still in the water for ultrasounds. They will urinate, defecate, and, if male, ejaculate on command.

On the far side of the dolphin pool, Wynn built a private getaway known among the dolphin habitat employees as "Steve's Room." There was a terrace with a table and phone and inside, a private bathroom and changing area. In a larger room, three walls were hung with photographs of Wynn swimming with the dolphins, and the fourth wall was open, its floor sloping into the water. This was where a wet-suited Wynn slipped into the water to swim with his dolphins.

Wynn spoke in baby talk to them. He watched them give birth through a glass partition. One year, when Darla's baby died unexpectedly, he issued a touching obituary, which ran in the *Las Vegas Review Journal*. He had the baby dolphin buried in a child's casket overlooking the 17th hole on the golf course at Shadow Creek.

So Paul Meloro, the Mirage staff photographer, hung up the phone that New Year's Day in 1994 and ran. "If Steve Wynn calls, you drop everything and close the lab," Meloro said years later when he was driving a taxicab in Las Vegas. He arrived at the pool to find Wynn and Michael Milken clad in wet suits. "They had an entourage. Typical Las Vegas—well dressed," Meloro says.

Wynn wanted Meloro to take photographs of his friends as gifts. "I hung around for an hour and a half, shooting pictures," Meloro says. Meloro says his photos captured the men frolicking with the dolphins, gliding in the water, whiling away a chilly afternoon in the Las Vegas winter.

Wynn had traveled a long road to that pool.

♣ ♦ ♥ ♠

Utica, New York, in the 1950s was a town of leafy green elm trees and Italian immigrants whose streets rang with the mother language. About a quarter of Oneida County's 264,401 residents told their census taker in 1959 that they'd been born in Italy. Most of Utica's Jewish kids lived in the better-off middle-class neighborhood in south Utica known generally as "uptown." That's where the Wynn family lived when Steve Wynn was a teen, on a street called Bonnie Brae. The small Jewish population focused on its Jewish community center.

Mike Wynn, the Wynn family patriarch, ran bingo parlors in Utica, Syracuse, and Binghamton. Work kept him on the road. He was a good earner, according to townspeople, and his wife, Zelma Wynn, was a doting mother. Their spoiled son Steve wanted for little, other than maybe for more of his father's time.

Mike Wynn was born Michael Weinberg, but it's said he changed his name to disguise his Jewish heritage for a job. He was the son of a vaudeville performer who once played Valvino in an act called *Valvino Lamore*. Wynn says his grandfather's act once got second billing to Al Jolson on Broadway.

This seems particularly fitting. It's easy to assume that this grandfather's vaudeville roots made the ancestral voyage to the infant Stephen Alan Wynn. "Maybe there's a gene," Steve Wynn says, nodding.

It was well known around town that Mike Wynn was a heavy gambler. It was also a common belief that the bingo joints he ran, much like those up and down the East Coast, were connected to organized crime. True or not, this was not especially notable in Utica, which served as a Prohibition conduit for Canadian booze.

"I knew that he was involved somehow in quote-unquote gambling. I think I probably heard that from my parents," says Arthur Resnikoff, a childhood friend of Wynn's who is now a San Francisco psychologist and management consultant. "It really wasn't very pejorative. It was like, well, that's what he did. We wouldn't do that, but he did."

Irving Resnikoff, Arthur's father, owned a liquor store and was Steve Wynn's scoutmaster. At age twelve, the boys rode in the back of a butcher's stench-filled cattle truck on a Boy Scout newspaper collection drive. As far as Arthur Resnikoff could tell, "There wasn't a lot of family life." Maybe it was just that Wynn didn't talk much about his folks. Resnikoff was surprised to learn, five decades later, that Steve had a younger brother, Kenneth, ten years his junior.

Wynn was [on] "the border of confidence and swagger and arrogance," Resnikoff says. "I wouldn't call him likeable at that point, but there was something about him that was attractive. He had a sense of humor, always a smile, a very optimistic, I-can-do-anything kind of guy."

Wynn's scout troop made ample use of the wooded Adirondack Mountains nearby. Mike Wynn joined them on a camping trip when the boys were twelve or thirteen. "It was a big deal," Resnikoff says. Steve "was so proud that his father came on that trip." Nearly the entire troop was Jewish, but Mike Wynn arrived with a whole side of bacon.

When Steve was ten, his dad took him to Las Vegas for a weird two-week sojourn. Mike Wynn was attempting—but would fail—to operate a bingo parlor on the second floor of the Silver Slipper casino. In its retelling, this story becomes a dramatic portent of Wynn's future: Mike Wynn gambling at night while his son wanders through casinos in search of him. A powerful yen to be a big shot in Las Vegas grows in the boy's belly. And the Silver Slipper right across the street from the Desert Inn—a parcel of land that fifty years later would be called Wynn Las Vegas, despite his earlier claim that he wouldn't put his name on a property.

At home, Wynn was rambunctious, according to his friends, and in the eighth grade was sent away to Manlius Academy military school, a place of crew cuts and discipline where he spent a great deal of his time avoiding being apprehended for various high jinks.

But summers were the magical opposite of Manlius: full of freedom at his family's summer home on a lake in Old Forge, New York.

Old Forge is a postcard mountain village with a covered bridge and an old Tudor-style manse of a library: Mayberry in the Adirondacks. It's a snowy wonderland in winter, and in summer a boating, hiking paradise dotted with lakes and camps. Wealthy East Coast families have summered there since the nineteenth century.

The Wynns' vacation house was on a channel that ran into one of the region's lakes. Wynn's parents gave him a speedboat as a gift. Toby Daniels Fava, who was Toby Denmark in those days, recalls riding out on Wynn's boat at the age of fourteen, no adults along. "We were all good kids," she says. Wynn and some friends became accomplished enough to water-ski for fifteen miles through lakes and channels.

Wynn was "the kind of kid that if they built a ski jump, he had to jump highest," says Wayne Blank, another boyhood friend, who now owns the Shoshana Wayne Gallery in Santa Monica, California. Back then, Stevie Wynn "was the center of attention," Blank says. "He had the best boat. The ski jump was his."

Those who knew Steve Wynn in Old Forge know a little piece of his soul. Many years later, in the 1990s, Blank took a drive along the north end of Lake Tahoe. His hired driver pointed out the sprawling mansions of billionaires who had lately been pushing out the neighborhood's millionaires. "That's Steve Wynn's place," the driver said as they passed one of these estates, "and it's where the lake scene in *The Godfather* was filmed."

A mile or so down the road, the hired car slid past the imposing gates of another Tahoe estate. Blank could just make out a plaque revealing the name: OLD FORGE.

Blank turned to his wife. "I don't know where *The Godfather* was filmed," he said, "but *this* is where Stevie Wynn lives."

♣ ♦ ♥ ♠

Wynn headed off to the University of Pennsylvania in Philadelphia, where he earned a degree that helped him stand out in Las Vegas. It was in English literature. During a vacation from Penn, Wynn met Elaine Pascal, a former Miss Miami Beach, on a blind date arranged and attended by their parents in the same city where she won her title. "He told me he was nineteen," Elaine Wynn recalls. "He lied. He was nineteen in three months."

Over the next few years, Wynn would lose his father during an open-heart surgery, finish college, and take over running his dad's bingo parlors with his new young wife, Elaine. Savvy, he even paid off his dad's gambling debts to the likes of Charlie Meyerson, a big-time New York bookie.

By the time they'd made the leap to Las Vegas and opened the Mirage in 1989, Wynn was forty-seven years old, with two daughters and the same pretty blond wife. Well, not wife, exactly, as the two had divorced three years earlier. Steve Wynn by this time had honed a wide reputation as a Casanova. A former Mirage executive says the casino boss made little secret among his confidants that he kept keys to several hotel rooms for his personal use.

Still, theirs wasn't much of a divorce. The Wynns continued to share their ranch house at 2020 Bannie Avenue in the Scotch Eighties, a respectable upper-class neighborhood not far from the Las Vegas Strip. Long before vintage kitchenware was fashionable, their yellow kitchen contained original appliances. "Their home was a home, it wasn't a showpiece," says Alan Feldman, the former Mirage spokesman.

The comedian Jerry Lewis resided in a five-bedroom home a couple of blocks away, in the same house where he lives now. Directly across the street lived a Nevada Supreme Court Justice. The Scotch Eighties would soon be abandoned for gated suburbs of mass-produced Tuscan dream homes.

In those days, wealthy casino types were moving into a gated golfing community called Spanish Trails. So, naturally, Wynn looked the other way. It was at this point in his career that Wynn began a troublesome habit. He bundled his personal life in with the publicly traded company. Wynn's idea was to create a forested golf resort and build his dream house smack in the middle. While designing the Mirage, Wynn had the company buy up roughly 230 acres in one of the uglier parts of Clark County, North Las Vegas. The desert there looks bulldozed and industrial. It's a hop and a skip to Nellis Air Force Base.

Elaine balked at the idea of moving to North Las Vegas. "It was out in the middle of nowhere," she said. But Wynn teed up $45 million and named the place Shadow Creek.

To enter Shadow Creek now is to step beyond the proverbial looking glass. The drive out of Las Vegas proper passes by arid automotive repair shops and industrial detritus. Then there is the right turn from Losee Road onto Shadow Creek Drive and the stop at the guard shack. A long, high berm disguised as a hill blocks the view of another climate zone that exists beyond.

"Make me a North Carolina-North Georgia kind of course," Wynn told Tom Fazio, the golf-course designer. Wynn's eyesight was failing, so Fazio gave each golf hole "sides" to help define the target. Crews dug down into the desert floor and created hills alongside the fairways. The hills were planted with pine trees, each watered by its own personal drip nozzle. To avoid sun dazzle, which would hurt Wynn's sensitive eyes, the tree line was brought right to the water's edge, creating dark lagoons.

Wynn and Fazio installed 13,000 trees in three million cubic yards of soil that was hauled in and laid atop the desert floor. This transplanted pine forest left carpets of pine needles in thickets around Shadow Creek. It cooled the air and shaded the clubhouse, which could have been mistaken for a genteel Adirondack hideaway.

They also built a mile-long creek, added waterfalls, and planted wildflowers. It was all irrigated with wild abandon—that is, relative to the water deprivation that existed beyond the berm. All this created shady glens and a nesting habitat for Wynn's imported wildlife. Eight wallabies from Australia lived alongside pheasants and African cranes, which looked so weird on a golf course, Wynn said, "they scared the golfers." Wynn, an inveterate lover of animals, mothered them all, clucking and fussing. ("I'm just this side of PETA," he once told me, referring to the animal rights group.)

Wynn was heartbroken when a wallaby named Speedy sat under the front wheel of a car and was crushed. "He died," Wynn lamented. "I realized I couldn't protect them and they couldn't protect themselves."

Some people joked—and in a way it's true—that Shadow Creek was paid for by the now-late Ken Mizuno. Mizuno was a high-rolling Japanese gambler who flew into Las Vegas on his private DC-9, visiting the Mirage twenty-nine times between December 1989 and October 1991, according to *Yakuza,* a book about the Japanese underworld. He lost as much as $65 million at the Mirage, according to legal filings involved in his later bankruptcy. He left behind as much as $11 million in one visit.

Like Kerry Packer, Mizuno was a serious George—a big tipper. But it turned out that he was playing baccarat with money that he'd bilked from Japanese investors. He and his partners had sold 52,000 memberships in an unbuilt golf club outside of Tokyo that could accommodate only 1,830 members. His scheme collapsed, and he was eventually convicted in Japan of tax evasion and fraud.

Wynn believed Shadow Creek would spark more deluxe development in North Las Vegas. He bought enough land to buffer Shadow Creek and planned to develop further once the area took off. This proved to be one of Wynn's bad bets, like the time he visited Laughlin, Nevada, and announced that he would build a Golden Nugget casino there because Laughlin reminded him of what Vegas was like forty years earlier.

Steve Wynn was Shadow Creek's only official member. To enhance its mystery, he savvily barred photography and personally approved invitations to play. Lockers had magnetic plates for brass name tags, so a guest would arrive and find a personalized locker, possibly one next to Michael Jordan's.

Soon after opening, the 18-hole course won awards as one of the world's best new golf courses from *Golf* magazine and *Golf Digest.*

It was possible to play golf there without seeing another soul all day. But one never knew who might turn up. The boxer James "Buster" Douglas ran on the course to train for an ill-fated 1990 match with Evander Holyfield. Andre Agassi, a favorite son of Las Vegas, once played fifty-two holes of golf at Shadow Creek in one day, just in time to tell *The New York Times* all about it. Willie Nelson lost $55 to Kris Kristofferson there on a Father's Day bet in 1991. They were in town performing at the Mirage along with Waylon Jennings and Johnny Cash.

Wynn wielded Shadow Creek as a political tool. Presidents George H. W. Bush and Bill Clinton played there. While campaigning to expand his casino empire into Connecticut, Wynn flew a contingent of local government officials from that state on the Mirage plane, squired them around Las Vegas, and toured them through Shadow Creek under the noses of the Connecticut press, which duly reported the glamorous tour in daily missives.

Wynn's political reach was expanding to the national level. When he heard that President Clinton was considering a national gambling tax to finance welfare reform, Wynn telephoned Dan Rostenkowski, chairman of the House Ways and Means Committee, at home at eleven p.m. to complain as the U.S. representative dozed through the Academy Awards.

Wynn, who described himself as a moderate Democrat, continued his campaign with a visceral attack on the Democratic administration. "That's the Clinton administration's operating philosophy: ready, fire, aim," Wynn quipped.

In November 1993, Wynn gathered a group of Las Vegas casino executives at Shadow Creek to meet Republican National Chairman Haley Barbour. Wynn asked them each to contribute "a quarter"— $250,000—to the Grand Old Party. Shadow Creek hosted more Republican political fund-raisers in Wynn's battle against Clinton, including a thousand-dollar-a-plate luncheon in 1995 for Senator Bob Dole of Kansas. Clinton's proposed 4 percent national gambling tax was quickly killed.

The Wynns chose their own address as they moved from Bannie

Avenue to Shadow Creek: One Shadow Creek Drive. The romantic Wynn, who had grown up in the woods in Upstate New York, loved it. "It was like going to a cocoon—tranquil," recalls Elaine Wynn. "There was nothing out there, not even a 7-Eleven. I complained to him. He said, 'It's beautiful.'"

Wynn offered home sites to his friends and executives. Only one, a Golden Nugget loyalist named Marc Schorr, was unwise enough to take him up on it. Schorr built a modern house—white and stark like a spaceship. Wynn did not like looking at it as he drove to and from his own home, according to several people close to the company. So he had a forest of trees planted to obscure Schorr's house.

In June 1991, Steve and Elaine Wynn remarried at the Waldorf Towers in New York, on the same date and in the same place as their first marriage twenty-eight years earlier. Since their divorce in 1986, they had never separated. "Steve just never got around to moving out," Elaine said.

"We regret to say that the divorce just didn't work out," Steve Wynn quipped.

♣ ♦ ♥ ♠

Steve Wynn pointed to a vein bulging in his arm.

"This company runs on my adrenaline. It's tapped right into my vein!" he hollered at Daniel R. Lee, his chief financial officer, who was trying to negotiate a new employment contract for himself in the late 1990s.

At the time Lee thought it was a "really egotistical" thing to say. Years later, he realized Wynn had been right.

When Dan Lee was a wee, towheaded child in the 1960s, he lived in Syracuse, New York—roughly the same neck of the woods where Steve Wynn had grown up. Lee didn't have a fancy childhood. His mother raised her children by working as a banquet waitress.

Lee became a self-starter at a young age. He had a friend who managed to get his hands on *Playboy* magazines. Lee snipped out the pictures and sold them to other kids: 10 cents for a whole girl, 25 cents for a "boob," more for a "boob and a butt."

"It was like buying a Mercedes and selling the parts," Lee says.

This entrepreneurial spirit carried Lee through an undergraduate degree in hotel administration as well as Cornell University's MBA program. During a summer internship at the hotel company Marriott, Lee saved money by camping in a tent in a park near Marriott's Bethesda headquarters.

Dan Lee loved minutiae. He read bond indentures late into the night. He pored over offering statements with a clue-seeking relish that most people reserve for a good murder mystery. By the time he was middle-aged, Lee was the chief executive of Pinnacle Gaming, a riverboat casino company, when a hurricane was bearing down on his casino in Lake Charles, Louisiana. From his desk in a Las Vegas high-rise, Lee familiarized himself with nautical charts and studied the stress loads that could be borne by the casino barge. He apprised the remaining staff of where they should hide in the casino for safety and while the winds were still gusting, Lee formulated his plan to pilot his own plane to Lake Charles in the aftermath.

After Marriott, Lee worked as a financial analyst in Boston, where he covered casinos and hotels, including Mirage Resorts. Lee published a report that criticized Mirage for behaving in a surly and amateurish manner with its investors.

Wynn raged, then offered Lee a job in a challenge, as if to say, "You think this is so easy?" Off went the boyish Dan Lee to Las Vegas in 1992 to be Mirage Resorts' chief financial officer.

This was an astounding career decision. Most Wall Streeters in those days wouldn't loan money to casinos, let alone move to Las Vegas to work for one.

Lee moved into an office just down the hall from Wynn's. Soon he was answering to Wynn's hollers of "Danny Boy!"

All the flotsam of casino life—designers, entertainers, gamblers, politicos, salesmen, cops, and old friends made their way through. "My first day, a kangaroo came into my office," Lee says. "I remember thinking, 'That's a kangaroo. I'm not on Wall Street anymore.' That place was fun."

Right before their eldest daughter Gillian's wedding, Elaine Wynn tried out the decorations in the board room, tying the chairs with big bows. Wynn bellowed instructions to his assistants, Joyce Luman and Cindy Mitchum. Smooching sounds emanated from his office as he baby-talked to Toasty and Harry, his dogs.

The journalist Mark Seal, sent to interview Wynn at the time of Treasure Island's opening, included the following description of his office at the Mirage in an essay entitled, "Steve Wynn: King of Wow!"

> I am led by a publicist through rooms that seem to grow increasingly brighter in color, from a merely bright magenta waiting room into Wynn's absolutely electrifying office. The carpet is streaked with rivulets of primary colors. The chairs are such a bright shade of magenta they seem to be floating. And leaning back in a white leather chair with armrests big as hotel pillows, his white tennis shoes kicked up on his desk, wearing blue jeans and a black Donald Duck T-shirt, is Steve Wynn.

The Wynns considered Mirage Resorts to be a family, and Wynn saw himself in the role of father. "Every company needs a dada," he would say.

When the daughter of Mirage spokesman Alan Feldman needed a cochlear implant to allow her to hear, the Wynns approved payment in a single phone call, astounding the hospital.

Once, when Dan Lee's wife lay groggily in a hospital recovery room after a surgery for varicose veins, she overheard the nurses discussing her anxious husband: "Who is this asshole? He thinks we're going to wheel her into a private room? She'll recover here like everyone else." Lee was incensed and mentioned the episode to Wynn.

A day or so later, a senior hospital executive appeared at the Lees' front door to apologize. Wynn had called, offering Mirage Resorts' employee training facilities to train the nurses on customer service.

Dan Lee and Glenn Schaeffer at Circus Circus brought new resources to Las Vegas by pioneering relationships with banks that had previously shunned casinos. Lee also bought up land for Mirage

Resorts' expansion and, perhaps in his most vital role, shielded Wall Street from Steve Wynn's increasing theatrics.

Once a spoiled boy, Wynn was now catered to as a genius. Those who worked closely with him developed a cultish environment.

"When he hates something, he lets you know it. When he loves something, he lets you know it. It's a great thing to leave a 'Good Steve' meeting," says John Schadler, Mirage Resorts' former head of advertising. "Which is why there are people who live from meeting to meeting."

"If you didn't have really thick skin, you didn't know if you were going to last there, but you wanted to because you wanted to be a part of what was happening there," continues Schadler. He left Mirage in 1999 and formed his own ad agency, Schadler Kramer Group, taking on Kirk Kerkorian's company as his primary client.

While choosing photographs for the company's annual report one year, Wynn tossed the photos down the length of the boardroom table and shouted, "Who the fuck chose these?" And there at the table cringed poor Alan Feldman, the PR guy who had chosen them.

"He'd throw [things] against the wall and say, 'This is bullshit. What do I pay you for?'" says another longtime executive. During a negotiation with the wild-haired fight promoter Don King, Wynn got up on his chair and then climbed on his desk to make a point.

Wynn's battle-fatigued executives learned to duck when shrapnel was incoming. His assistants Joyce and Cindy would warn people away, rescheduling his calendar around his temper, but sooner or later, every senior executive had his or her turn. "The first time you have 'The Moment' with Steve, your life is changed," one former executive explained. "From that point, you're more careful, more of an ass-kisser."

In an ugly lawsuit—stemming from years of rivalry with Donald Trump—the Golden Nugget's president, Dennis Gomes, accused Wynn of a litany of abuses. Gomes had been recruited to run Trump's Atlantic City properties in 1991, before his contract with Wynn was due to end. Wynn sued for breach of contract. During the ensuing legal snarl, Gomes accused Wynn of racism, sexism, and financial malfeasance. In interviews and legal papers that included a 660-page deposition, Gomes portrayed Wynn as a womanizer and as a brutal employer who lambasted his staff.

"His face turned completely red and all puffed up and his eyes bulged and he started screaming at the top of his lungs and banging his head on the table," Gomes asserted in one interview.

Gomes said Wynn used the company jet to fly his dog to a surgeon, to vacation in Australia with Elaine, and to travel to New Jersey so Wynn, Gomes, and another casino executive could be fitted for new suits.

Wynn dismissed it all as lies. No court ever ruled on the veracity of Gomes's claims. The civil lawsuits were settled before what had promised to be a juicy trial.

George Mason had sat on Wynn's board of executives since 1973. He joined MGM Grand's board in 2000, and he was a friend of both Wynn and Kerkorian.

"[Wynn's] board meetings were always fun. They were exciting. They'd get you involved," Mason said. "Most board meetings are just boring."

♣ ♦ ♥ ♠

Las Vegas casino titans' ideas about personal security were changed on a Monday night in July 1993 when the Wynns' twenty-six-year-old daughter Kevyn was kidnapped from her home in Spanish Trails.

The kidnappers ordered Kevyn to call her father. She later testified that her father suspected his zany daughter was making a prank call until she began to cry. "Don't worry, honey, I'm gonna take care of this," Wynn told his baby girl.

When the kidnappers demanded he remove $2.5 million from the vault, Wynn gave them a blast of his classic temper, worried that taking so much money from the casino would draw the interest of regulatory authorities. "I said, 'You can't do that, it will cause a complete stir,'" Wynn told the jury when the case went to court.

The kidnappers then asked if taking $1.45 million from the vault would cause a stir. "How the hell do I know?" Wynn replied. "The chairman of the board doesn't come down to the vault every day."

As it turned out, he did withdraw the ransom in hundred-dollar bills from the Mirage's coffers. Wynn called the police after delivering the money with the aid of Mirage security. Kevyn was found, bound but unharmed, at McCarran International Airport where she had been left on the floor of her black Audi, whose license plate read BIONDA—Italian for "blond."

Elaine Wynn was told of the incident when it was over. Wynn said he didn't think she could have handled the stress. "I was terror-stricken, a word I did not appreciate until that happened," Wynn said.

The bumbling kidnappers, who turned out to be amateurs, were captured (after one began spending the cash), tried, and convicted. The FBI advised all casino operators to review their personal security precautions.

Wynn didn't want to travel around with a phalanx of bodyguards like Donald Trump. (Trump has been schooled in such security practices as allowing his bodyguard to exit an elevator in front of him into a public space.) Instead, Wynn's friend Bo Derek recommended a Los Angeles dog trainer, Howard Rodriguez, who once trained narcotics dogs and advertises in the *Robb Report*. Wynn thereafter employed a steady stream of highly trained German "Shutzhund" attack dogs that he cuddles and claims are pets.

♣ ♦ ♥ ♠

There was a secret office. In the Mirage days, it was tucked away on Industrial Road, a mile or so from the Mirage, at the offices of a subsidiary called Atlandia Design.

In this office was a long drafting table and two tall drafting chairs for Wynn and his architect. The table was lit vividly to aid Wynn's failing eyes. There was a bucket full of colored, felt-tip pens that he used to move walls, enlarge hallways, and eliminate staircases. Wynn's designers learned never to give him an original blueprint.

Once, Wynn peered at blueprints for a resort he hoped to build in Atlantic City. He wanted to make a point about human traffic— where people would walk and where the gardens should go. He grabbed at the basket of pens, fumbled, sent them all flying, retrieved one, and began scribbling with bold lines and arrows.

Blind or not, Wynn mentally crawls into blueprints. He envisions what it will feel like to be in that hallway, to turn that corner, to arrive at the top of that stairway. He smells the air and touches the cold marble.

It's here in this other office of his that it's possible to grasp how truly complex these Las Vegas casino resorts have become.

He imagines how long it will take to load a cart with plates, napkins, utensils, salt and pepper shakers, one pink orchid, and an entrée from the room-service assembly line; roll this into the elevator; rise to the correct hotel floor; and proceed down a not-too-long corridor to the room of a guest who will hungrily lift the lid on a plate of scrambled eggs garnished with a sprig of fresh chervil and—if Wynn has put the kitchen close enough to an elevator that is the Lamborghini of its class, and if he has hired a top-notch room-service manager who can turn the Barnum & Bailey of a hotel kitchen into an efficient and organized workspace—then this guest, among eight thousand others, will see steam rise from her still-warm eggs while her butter waits dotted with chilled beads of perspiration.

"We're all funny creatures in the morning," Wynn says. "The sugar, the Sweet'N Low, the jam and butter—it all has to go on the cart. You can't miss the sugar—it screws up the whole breakfast because people can't drink their coffee."

He worries about the front desk. Will guests be appropriately awed and wait no longer than a few minutes in line? He considers the placement of architectural support columns in the porte cochere: They mustn't get in the way of speedy parking valets. The swimming pool should draw the sexy and beautiful, who will in turn draw the old and rich. It should have a wide-open area to entertain parties of conventioneers, wading steps for children, and nooks for romance. There is the casino, with its dealers and pit bosses and floor supervisors and slot machines and coin fillers and cocktail waitresses.

It isn't unusual for the members of Wynn's design team to consider taking a year off or a change of career direction after working on a project with him. At the age of fifty-seven, the architect Joel Bergman conceded that the week that Treasure Island opened, he'd had enough.

"I worked a lot of hours over the fifteen years with Steve, and I think I want to take a rest," Bergman said in a local newspaper interview at the time. "I'm not going to quit working, but I am going to slow my pace down. If you notice, there are two drafting stools at my rather long drawing board. One is Steve Wynn's. Steve and I spent thousands upon thousands of hours there."

Wynn designed the Bellagio at those offices. His original idea for the Dunes site would have been an echo of his youth—a hotel modeled after the Fontainebleau Hotel in Miami Beach, where he and his parents had often stayed. Outside, he planned a fourteen-acre lake for championship water skiing—harkening back to Old Forge.

"I envision a place where we could host the world windsurfing championships and waterskiing championships," Wynn said. Styled in the French architectural mode, he called it Beau Rivage, or "beautiful shore."

Aviation regulators thought the hotel tower was too tall. The county wanted to split the property to make room for a thoroughfare and sewer line. Manmade lakes had been banned in water-starved Clark County.

Wynn dispatched these issues with the efficiency of a politically connected businessman. He lopped twenty feet of the tower, pledged $1 million for local road projects, and convinced local authorities that the Dunes' former golf course used more water than his lake.

In January of 1993, Wynn estimated that Beau Rivage would cost $400 million—more than the Mirage, but not frighteningly so. He expected the new resort to be completed in 1996. Then he scribbled all over the blueprints. By the following fall, the cost had reached $900 million.

Early on, he had described a resort with 3,000 hotel rooms in a 49-story blue-glass hotel tower, fronted on three sides by a 17-acre island in a 50-acre lake. Shops and restaurants would nestle among cliffs and waterfalls. There would be no swimming pool—only a 980-foot beach where guests could rent paddleboats or ski. Wynn dubbed it the "single most extravagant hotel ever built on earth."

In the midst of this, Merlin, the eldest Mirage dolphin, died in

October 1994. He was thirty years old. Wynn sadly issued the same sort of statement he would have made for a relative: "He lived a long life and has left us a wonderful legacy as he fathered three calves at our habitat—Squire, Bugsy, and Picabo."

Even the *Las Vegas Review-Journal* ran an obituary: "Besides his cows and calves, Merlin leaves Sigma and Banjo, his younger companions from Florida."

In those years, Wynn was visited by his past. The old gang from Utica's Jewish Community Center held a reunion at the Mirage, not because Wynn invited them—he didn't—but because Wayne Blank dropped Wynn's name with the sales office and negotiated a better price than the offer from Caesars Palace.

About seventy people showed up, and so did Wynn. "I've never been invited to a party at my own place before," Wynn chuckled. He escorted his old friends backstage at the Siegfried & Roy show and even invited a group to lunch at the club at Shadow Creek.

Arthur Resnikoff found his old Boy Scout friend little changed in middle age: "Same brass balls, but more polish."

chapter eight

THE OUTSIDERS

We do not get intoxicated with Las Vegas.

—JOHN BOUSHY, HARRAH'S EXECUTIVE IN 2005

There was a time in Las Vegas when casino moguls were known for their big appetites. They were gamblers and poster boys for failed marriages, fast living, and self-destruction. Jay Sarno died after a night at Caesars' tables. Bill Bennett built the Luxor and Excalibur but struggled with addiction. Thrice-married Kerkorian played craps and bet on sports. Wynn—well, we'll soon see what his thing was.

Phil Satre's only known vice is fly-fishing. Which helps explain why Harrah's Entertainment zigged while the others zagged.

For many years, it looked as though Harrah's Entertainment would always operate in a separate universe. As Kerkorian and Wynn tried to out-fantasize each other, Harrah's ran a pitiable joint in Las Vegas that was once a Holiday Inn. Choked with cigarette smoke, its ceilings were low and its hotel rooms exactly what one would expect for a Holiday Inn on the Las Vegas Strip. Harrah's was primarily a riverboat company, with dinky joints spread all over.

Satre doesn't even look like a Vegas type. The jewel on his finger is a Stanford class ring—1971, with a degree in psychology. There is, even in his later years, a fresh, coed air of "Go Cardinals!" about him.

In the 1990s, when Satre was Harrah's chairman and chief executive, the riverboat company's headquarters sat in a bucolic corporate park in Memphis, Tennessee. Satre's office was a former bedroom in a refurbished nineteenth-century home attached to a modern office building. The executive offices were furnished with antiques. Outside, trees shaded the long drive and grounds.

Wall Street shared Las Vegas operators' condescension toward Harrah's. This ate at Harrah's executives, though there was some sense to the Street's logic. Harrah's growth came as states were legalizing casino gambling during the 1990s in pursuit of new tax revenues. Harrah's beat its competitors to market with cheap, generic casinos.

By the late 1990s, when most any state that was going to legalize gambling had already done so, rivals began newer, nicer casinos right next door to Harrah's places. Harrah's had been proud of itself for beating the competition to market with a $40-million casino in Tunica, Mississippi, but then got slammed a couple years later when a couple of nicer, $80-million casinos opened up there.

"We were fed up with running our business as a victim," said Colin Reed, who was then Harrah's chief financial officer. "You build a property and someone else builds next to you, and you put up the white flag."

Rather than tearing down all the old casinos and building new, fancier ones, Satre figured he might find a solution outside the gambling industry. It's hard to emphasize how revolutionary this was. Casinos grew their own—raising executives from the casino floor, often without the benefit of a college education. They saw their business as different from drug stores and banks and clothing retailers.

But Satre wanted to be the Procter & Gamble of riverboat casino operators. People buy toothpaste from P&G because they believe Crest is better than Colgate. So he began to look at brands like Coca-Cola and Nike. "We don't have a facility-based strategy," Satre said in a 1997 interview. "We are trying to compete based upon a higher level of relationship with our customers."

In 1990, a Harrah's executive named John Boushy had begun doing something known as "longitudinal tracking" studies. Boushy came to Harrah's by way of Holiday Inns, and his parents were college professors, not numbers runners. As vice president of strategic marketing, Boushy wanted to glean more information about what made gamblers tick. He buried the $100,000 cost of the studies in his budget. Each month thereafter, he surveyed 10,000 customers about who they were and where they gambled.

Unlike many Las Vegas executives, Boushy is still married to his first wife, Lisa, whom he met in 1970 in the hallway of their Fayetteville, North Carolina, high school. Boushy can still describe his first glimpse of sixteen-year-old Lisa in the summer after their sophomore year. "She was wearing a lavender skirt, a purple and black and white blouse with sort of fluffy sleeves, and she had long dark hair down to her waist," Boushy says. "I was with my best friend, and I turned to him and said, 'I think I just met my wife.'" Four weeks later, at a football game, he kissed her and said, "I love you." The Boushys have six kids.

Also, Boushy has a master's degree in applied mathematics from North Carolina State. So he can read a longitudinal tracking study. Armed with his data, Boushy convinced Satre that Harrah's needed a customer-rewards program like those cropping up at airlines and credit card companies. So Harrah's came up with a loyalty program called Total Gold (later changed to Total Rewards). In 1992, it became the beneficiary of all that customer data that Boushy had been squirreling away.

Total Gold was what was known as a "slot club." Gamblers enrolled and received a magnetic membership card to insert into a slot machine to earn points that could be spent on freebies, or "comps." Once gamblers stuck their card into a slot machine, they might as well have been having a brain scan. Every bet they placed, how fast, how frequently, on what odds, for how long, in what pattern—all that information was fed into the casino's database.

Pretty soon, Harrah's was the repository of powerful information on how people behave while gambling. Other casinos were launching slot clubs too, but Harrah's wrestled harder with how to make use of its customer data.

In 1994, Satre reached outside the gambling business to hire a chief marketing officer, Brad Morgan, who had previously worked at Visa and Procter & Gamble. When a headhunter first approached Morgan about the job, Morgan said he wasn't interested. "I'm a Midwestern-values kinda guy," he said.

But he reconsidered, and soon Morgan was in Memphis, sizing up gamblers "psychographically"—rating and segmenting them according to characteristics such as their careers, interests, attitudes, and where they lived. His approach was foreign to his colleagues at Harrah's. "I was the Visa guy," Morgan said. "I was the only guy on the management team who hadn't spent their entire life in the casino business."

Morgan and Boushy identified a small group of customers who produced most of Harrah's profits. It turned out that they weren't the flashy high-rollers. They were low-rollers—average Americans who spent between $100 and $499 on a gambling trip. These people made up only about 30 percent of gamblers, but they gambled so frequently that they accounted for 80 percent of Harrah's revenue and nearly 100 percent of its profits!

Harrah's decided to make these highly profitable customers its core audience, calling them "avid experienced players" or AEPs. "I felt like I'd discovered the Rosetta Stone of casinos," Morgan said several years later.

Although Satre didn't fully grasp it at the time, the electronic card was generating some other key marketing intelligence. It helped the company to identify where the gamblers were coming from, and it turned out that many of them visited other Harrah's casinos in addition to their hometown riverboats. Eventually, this provided a key new strategy.

In 1992, when the option to legally gamble was pretty much either Las Vegas or Atlantic City, Harrah's found that the average gambler made three trips a year to a casino. By 1997, with casinos all over the heartland, the average gambler was making five trips a year. To take advantage of its national casino network, Harrah's began to encourage its six million slot-club members to visit Harrah's casinos while on business trips and vacations. Harrah's called this "cross-market visitation" and figured it would revolutionize the company as gamblers became "brand-loyal" to Harrah's.

This worked all over the country, but it didn't work in Las Vegas. Top customers disappeared from Harrah's data map when they traveled to Las Vegas. "I wasn't getting their Las Vegas business," Satre said. "I went through a period of frustration. I said, 'Why isn't any of this stuff working?'"

Satre got a jolt during a mid-1990s fishing trip to Alaska—an annual trip he made with his best customers from Atlantic City. His guests said they got treated better elsewhere in Las Vegas. While they were recognized as high-rollers at the Harrah's near their home, they were just another face in the crowd in the gambling mecca.

Satre contended that Total Gold needed a giant, nationwide database that could be used by any Harrah's property anywhere, so the casino president in Las Vegas knew when he had a lady worth $20,000 in video poker walking in the door from Vicksburg, Mississippi.

♣ ◆ ♥ ♠

Constantly on the hunt for new talent, Satre had started a management development program as far back as the 1980s. He brought in two professors from the Harvard Business School, Stephen Bradley and Earl Sasser, because they argued that great customer service leads to greater profits. In 1992, Drs. Bradley and Sasser invited a popular young business school professor named Gary Loveman to join them.

"We decided to include Gary Loveman in the program because he was a terrific teacher and would benefit from the involvement with Harrah's management," says Bradley.

Loveman didn't know a thing about gambling, though he'd once visited Monte Carlo in Europe. "Gary was the hottest labor economist on the market the year he came to Harvard," says Jack Gabarro, a Harvard Business School professor who was then Loveman's department head.

At Harvard, Loveman had been gathering case studies on businesses as diverse as the Merry Maids cleaning service, Kumon Educational Institute, and a Polish shipyard. He became interested in research spearheaded by a Harvard professorial triumvirate of Earl Sasser, James Heskett, and Leonard Schlesinger. They would later coauthor a groundbreaking business-strategy book called *The Service Profit Chain: How Leading Companies Link Profit and Growth to*

Loyalty, Satisfaction, and Value. It wasn't long before Schlesinger would "go native"—in Gabarro's words—abandoning Harvard to join Limited Brands as its chief operating officer.

Loveman's introduction to Harrah's emboldened him to write Satre an unsolicited letter, suggesting how the gambling executive might grow his company's business without spending money to build new casinos. Virtually on the spot, Satre hired Loveman as a consultant, hoping he could help refine rudimentary marketing programs like Total Rewards.

Loveman's being at Harrah's was weirder than Brad Morgan. He applied foreign concepts, such as "same-store sales"—a retailing concept that quantifies business in existing stores without being diluted by new store openings. He pushed Satre to segment customers: "Some customers are worth very little to you, while other customers are very valuable. This is not something that has been pursued very well at all," Loveman said in August 1997.

The untenured associate professor began using Harrah's data to test theories about how customers behave. The idea was to offer large numbers of customers the goodies they wanted so they would come more often and gamble longer—like rats in a maze.

This is one thing when selling airline tickets, but with gambling, it was a ticklish concept. Encouraging people to gamble more introduces the thorny subject of gambling addiction. Is it fair to entice people to make a bet they otherwise would not have? Loveman said Harrah's wasn't trying to entice people to gamble more than they otherwise might. It was looking to take customers away from rivals.

"For most customers, this is about switching from one property to another," Professor Loveman said in 1997. "But there will be some customers who will do more gambling as a result of this."

♣ ♦ ♥ ♠

In 1997, Phil Satre told Morgan it was time to part ways. To replace him, Satre hired an executive search firm.

"I didn't want a traditional marketing chief who had come up through the casino, knows all the games, that sort of stuff," Satre said. He interviewed people from banking and retail, but couldn't find anyone, he said, who "got the strategy."

A few weeks before Christmas, Satre says he made a pilgrimage to Atlanta to see Sergio Zyman, Coca-Cola's marketing guru at the time. The two men talked for two hours in an executive lounge at the airport—or, actually, Zyman talked while Satre scribbled notes. Zyman suggested that instead of a marketing executive, Satre needed a chief operating officer with a marketing background. With that broad authority, the executive could make marketing the driving force at Harrah's.

Not long after that, Loveman invited Satre up to Cambridge to spend a weekend talking about the connection between good service and higher profits. Satre figured it was a sales pitch to get him to hire more Harvard consultants. He went anyway.

It would be too dramatic to say that Satre slapped his forehead and shouted "Eureka!" on this visit. But it was in Cambridge that he decided Gary Loveman was his guru. "It was like an epiphany—I thought, 'I've got the guy,'" Satre said later. "'He doesn't know it, but he's right under my nose.'"

Satre didn't bother to consult with his board of directors. "I was afraid they might try to talk me out of it."

That February, Satre invited Loveman to Atlantic City. There, as they exited the casino after a meeting, Satre asked if Loveman would consider becoming Harrah's chief operating officer. "I was absolutely dumbstruck," Loveman later recalled. But he was quick-witted enough to make it clear that his family wouldn't relocate from Boston.

Loveman was a year away from being eligible for tenure at Harvard. According to his colleagues there, he was likely to get it. He says he discussed the job offer with his wife, Kathy, although he concedes, "There is a dispute between my wife and myself about how much we actually talked about it."

Loveman finished teaching the spring semester. He arranged his departure from Harvard as a two-year leave of absence—keeping one foot in the door, just in case. Satre informed Harrah's board later that month, wondering, "Am I out of my mind?"

"I've made a very unconventional decision," Satre told his directors. And of course, they did think Satre was out of his mind.

chapter nine

HIGH LIFE

Elaine and I had dinner with her. She's a great girl.
—STEVE WYNN, REFERRING TO HER MAJESTY
QUEEN NOOR OF JORDAN

Kirk Kerkorian had once been mistaken for a car valet. His primary home has, at times, been the one-bedroom guesthouse of his Beverly Hills estate, where a painting of Jack Dempsey fighting Gene Tunney hung over the mantel, a gift from Frank Sinatra.

In the years that the Wynns were establishing themselves as Las Vegas moguls, Kerkorian was cozying up with his young girlfriend, the tennis-playing Lisa Bonder. He spent a lot of time in California, invested again in the movie business, and launched a hostile takeover of Chrysler Corp. It wasn't that he'd lost interest in Las Vegas. It was just that he had others to manage it for him—his preferred style after leaving the airline business—and he hadn't adopted "casino titan" as a lifestyle.

It would be impossible to mistake the swaggering Steve Wynn for a valet. Luminaries were drawn to the Mirage, and the Wynns courted many of them as friends. Their lives took on an aspect of fantasy. "Bibi Netanyahu did his honeymoon at the Mirage with Sarah," Wynn once blurted out. "I didn't know he was going to be prime minister."

George and Barbara Bush were frequently spotted with the Wynns—jetting in to Lake Tahoe on Steve Wynn's speedboat, for instance, or golfing together. During a 1995 golf game at Shadow Creek, six U.S. Air Force Thunderbirds descended at high noon and dipped their wings in homage to the onetime commander in chief while Wynn giggled.

The Bushes were such frequent visitors that George Bush had learned to make his own coffee at the Wynns' homes and was a favorite visitor among the household staff, according to a person who worked for the Wynns.

Wynn, acutely aware of what Kerkorian was doing, sniffed around Hollywood and made forays into other businesses. Unlike Kerkorian's forays, however, they were rarely successful. Wynn toyed with and dropped takeovers of the Music Corporation of America, Hilton Hotels, and even the Walt Disney Company. He joined movie producers Steven Spielberg and Jeffrey Katzenberg as investors in DIVE!, a Los Angeles eatery.

At home, the Wynns had a butler, Pierre, and a driver, Albert, as well as several other household staff. There were Bentleys, Rolls Royces, and Ferraris. Mirage Resorts owned some of the nicest planes around.

Mirage bought a new Gulfstream jet that could make the long haul to Australia—a trip the Wynns made annually, according to people close to them. Elaine Wynn preferred the company's MD87, it was said, because they could put the whole family in it to fly to Sun Valley. "It was like a flying house," said one former Mirage executive. While Wynn flew around in the newest planes, the company also kept an older Gulfstream III, which this same former executive referred to as "the beat-up old one that we used for customers."

Wynn has said that he wishes his father could have seen his planes. He boasts that he hasn't flown commercial since 1974. Almost. "Well, I flew the Concorde. Twice," he says with a broad grin.

The Wynns traveled annually to Australia to vacation and check out casinos in that gambling-crazed country, often stopping off in Hawaii or Tahiti to refuel, Dan Lee said in a 2001 interview. At an estimated $3,000 an hour for fuel and operations, Lee estimated the cost to the company of each round-trip flight at $100,000. That was enough, at the time, to buy a nice middle-class house in Las Vegas.

There were regular trips to Sun Valley, Idaho, where the Wynns keep a vacation home. There was, for several years, the home at Lake Tahoe near the Milkens' place. There was a company-owned apartment in New York—first in the Waldorf Towers, later on Fifth Avenue by Central Park. There were regular jaunts to Los Angeles for business, fun, and cosmetic surgery.

The Wynns traded valuable gifts with their jet-set friends. They received an early plasma-screen television valued at $10,000, which they installed at Shadow Creek. Stewart and Lynda Resnick, owners of the Franklin Mint, gave them a "Great Books" library, including a set of Franklin Mint encyclopedias, for their home at Shadow Creek.

Wynn also used his new wealth to make a name for himself back at his alma mater. He pledged $2.5 million to the University of Pennsylvania in 1995 to fund a new project, the Therapeutic Initiative for Hereditary Retinal Degeneration. Wynn made it clear that he didn't want the initiative named for him, according to a thank-you letter from the school.

The thing he wanted named for him was Wynn Commons—part of Penn's student union quadrangle—for which he pledged $7.5 million in July 1995. Although it is named for him, and the school credits Wynn with a picture of him on its Web site, it was Mirage Resorts shareholders who actually paid for the bulk of Wynn's $10 million in pledges to Penn—$6.6 million, according to the company's records.

Mirage's SEC filings show that among the plane rides, hotel suites, meals, and other goodies allowed to certain executives was the use of Mirage employees for "personal services." The Wynns' home at Shadow Creek, for example, was designed with help of Atlandia, Mirage's design subsidiary, which kept detailed records on the entire project—every tchotchke, faucet, electrical fixture, and lamp purchased for the home.

The Wynns' home at Shadow Creek became a Mediterranean showpiece, with two swimming pools—one a lap pool—overlooking expansive gardens.

The three-bedroom, 12,000-square-foot house was built in a semicircle that opened onto a circular court and a water fountain. The vistas from the windows were of the golf course beyond the gardens. A wide, circular hallway connected the rooms.

The master bedroom faced the golf course's 18th hole. In one direction lay Elaine Wynn's elaborate suite of closets and her bath. This boudoir consisted of five smaller rooms with elaborate wood millwork, drawers for jewels, racks for gowns. There was a central dressing area. To one side lay a cosmetic room with a television and stereo system, leading out to a private spa with a tiled hot tub and sitting area. Her bath opened onto an outdoor terrace.

In the other direction lay Steve Wynn's closet—the size of a large bedroom itself—elaborately lit to aid his failing eyes. That closet led to a curious small oval room. It's easy to imagine this oval room tickling Wynn's funny bone. At times, it was adorned with two flags on floor poles—a U.S. flag and a presidential seal flag—gifts from George Bush, according to a Wynn executive. The room became George Bush's tiny oval office during his visits to Shadow Creek.

Later, the oval room contained Elaine's Pilates machine, says a person who worked there.

Steve Wynn's boyish playful nature also showed in his round, two-story library. It is the sort of room that people who dream of being outlandishly rich dream up. Its walls are lined with fine books to the high ceiling. Tall brass ladders travel around on rails.

The library held a secret: a small hidden door, masked by an antique collection of works by Dante. The poor old volumes had had their guts replaced with Styrofoam to reduce their weight on the door. Anyone with the knowledge of where to press could open this door and make his or her way into the small oval room and beyond to Wynn's closet.

♣ ♦ ♥ ♠

Dan Lee was not as fussy about riverboat casinos as his boss in the early 1990s. Lee headed to Biloxi, Mississippi—a beach town with Southern romance, live oaks, and antebellum mansions along the strand tucked among honky-tonk motels and casinos.

Forty-three million people lived within six hundred miles of

Biloxi, including population centers like Memphis, Orlando, and Dallas. The region offered low taxes, high population growth, a plentiful supply of labor, and highly cooperative state officials who were keen for commercial investment. To Dan Lee, this looked like unmined gold.

Lee urged Wynn to buy a countrified casino called the Boomtown that sat on Biloxi Bay. But Wynn wasn't interested in running a Harrah's-style riverboat. He put another Golden Nugget veteran, Barry Shier, in charge of the project and found a glorious 18.2 acre site just off of Interstate 110, down the road from downtown Biloxi. They bought the property for $27 million—more than the entire cost of the state's first casino in Tunica.

Legally, the casino had to be a riverboat, but it wouldn't look or behave like one. Wynn wanted to do for Mississippi what the Mirage had done for Nevada. He called the place the Golden Nugget when he announced the plans in November 1995.

Early discussions with the head of the Mississippi casino-regulatory commission, General Paul Harvey, left the Mississippians with the impression that the project would cost around $110 million. By the time the plans were announced publicly, the cost was already $200 million—paltry by Vegas standards, but a shocking price tag in Mississippi. "Nobody's ever spent that kinda money here," General Harvey said in a 1999 interview.

Wynn, unwilling to spend much time in Mississippi, left Shier to get busy there while Wynn focused on his next new casino in Las Vegas, the Beau Rivage.

It was another vacation that changed the destiny of that resort. While the Wynns were on holiday with their friends Paul Anka and his wife, the group took the singer's boat out onto Lake Como in Italy. Wynn became captivated by the vista of a village called Bellagio, where hotels and houses nestled romatically against the banks.

The giggling group looked up the word *Bellagio* in an Italian dictionary: "A place of elegant relaxation," it said. The way Wynn tells it, they all cheered, "That's the name of the new hotel!"

So the Beau Rivage in Las Vegas became the Bellagio. Eventually, the Biloxi casino would inherit the castoff name of Beau Rivage. In Las Vegas, the planned water skiers and beaches and French architecture were replaced by a splendorous Italianate theme. "Ten months' worth of architectural drawings hit the trash can," says Bobby Baldwin.

The world had become accustomed to a Las Vegas of themes—pirates, Egypt, Oz. Wynn wanted a new kind of theme: luxury. Marble bathrooms, peaceful gardens, classical music.

Wynn couldn't contain his excitement. Dan Lee recalls dining one evening at the Mirage with Larry Haverty, then a managing director with State Street Research. Wynn ran into them and settled right in to give the full spiel, to Haverty's joy. "He was like a kid in a candy store," says Haverty. "Two huge strips on either side of Caesars. It was almost like monopoly. He had [reached] critical mass."

Since the stock market was closed at the time of his meeting with Wynn, Haverty waited until five a.m. Las Vegas time to get on the phone and order his team in Boston to start buying Mirage shares. "We knew enough about the Las Vegas market that one and one equal three," he says. "This was just one of the amazing opportunities that happen once in a lifetime. I thought [Steve Wynn] had a vision of how to extract money from people, by building edifices that [are] unparalleled."

By mid-1995, the Bellagio's price tag had climbed to $1 billion. It continued upward. Within two years, the grapevine—a line that traveled in mere seconds from Las Vegas to Wall Street—was abuzz with Bellagio gossip.

Wynn was lining up an extraordinary list of restaurants and shops. Armani! Le Cirque!—or so the rumors said. This sounded unbelievable to many people. They scoffed. But it turned out that Wynn's track record of success at high-end gambling was alluring to luxury retailers.

Wynn's idea wasn't entirely original. The Forum Shops at Caesars had introduced high-end shopping to casinos. And Wynn had been watching his construction contractor, Tony Marnell, turn an off-the-Strip casino into a hot spot by offering, among other things, fine food in Las Vegas.

Tony Marnell is the son of a bricklayer. A tall, exacting man with tight curls that were once black but are now graying, Marnell's rugged face looks as though it might have met its share of knuckles. This and his size would suggest a tough manner and a deep voice, but when Marnell opens his mouth, what emerges is gentle and high-pitched. He is shy. To relax, he loves to cook.

Marnell and his construction company, Marnell Corrao Associates, profited mightily from the Las Vegas boom in the 1990s. He built the Mirage and Excalibur, and built or expanded the Forum Shops at Caesars and other Las Vegas landmarks. Then he got the bug himself.

In 1990, Marnell opened a tropic-themed casino and 500-room hotel off the Strip. He called it the Rio. No one on the Strip paid much attention to this locals' joint, but it became more than a hobby to Marnell. In his spare time, he would head to the Rio's kitchens, shrug off his designer suit jacket, and slice ingredients for a good marinara like his Italian mama made. "No dish is served in this hotel without me tasting it," he said in 1997.

When the tourists heard about the Rio's food, they left the Strip and made their way across Interstate 15 for seafood, French, and astoundingly authentic Chinese cuisine. Marnell expanded, building a second hotel tower—all suites—and more restaurants, slots, and stores. He imported ovens from Europe to bake bread. He put an aquarium in the basement for fresh seafood.

Marnell brought in Jean-Louis Palladin—a Michelin-starred chef who had been running Jean-Louis at the Watergate Hotel in Washington, D.C.—to run a restaurant called Napa. Palladin's arrival astonished foodies everywhere. Las Vegas patrons required some education. "Even foie gras is considered exotic here," Palladin told *USA Today* in 1997.

When he was growing up, Marnell's family drank wine with dinner—usually the bottle came with a screw top. At the Rio, Marnell hired Barrie Larvin, a pudgy British master sommelier from the Ritz Hotel in London. The wine world gasped. Fritz Hatton, then director of the auctioneer Christie's wine department in New

York, described the general response among oenophiles as "wondrous horror."

The jolly Larvin, afloat with $6 million to build a wine cellar, scoffed, "People come to Las Vegas and think they're going to be met at the airport by a prostitute." He put a stop to cocktail waitresses serving white zinfandel over ice, but he also took pains to puncture snobbish wine myths. When Marnell invited him to a party at his house, Larvin was asked by a guest why waiters often hand the cork to a diner to sniff. "Because he's full of shit," Larvin replied with a laugh.

Larvin quickly became the toast of wine auctions all over the world. He bought all but nine vintages produced by the legendary Chateau d'Yquem from 1859 until 1989. Francis Ford Coppola launched his prized 1992 Rubicon at the Rio in March 1997. The director of *The Godfather* and *Apocalypse Now,* who was lately devoting his attentions to developing the Niebaum-Coppola winery in Napa Valley, brightened with surprise when he took a peek at the Rio's wine cellar. Coppola, his hair streaked with gray, announced with a glass of a grand cru Champagne in one hand, "You can see that he's been given carte blanche."

Coppola's winemaker, Scott Mcleod, threw the party at the Rio because he saw the vast potential of millions of visitors. Big-city retailers and restaurateurs, unimpressed by Las Vegas's 1.1 million residents, had long written the town off as backwater. But at the time, thirty million high-spending tourists were visiting Las Vegas each year—a potential that other retailers and restaurants had been inexcusably slow to grasp.

Next thing you know, business travelers started heading to the Rio to stay in its suites, eat its food, and drink its wine. Soon even the high-rollers were making their way across I-15 to play baccarat there.

Even the Rio's cocktail waitress uniforms were innovative— confetti-colored bathing suits and heels an inch higher than those worn at most other casinos. Babe-a-licious cocktail waitresses played a big role in the hotel's success with businessmen.

One reason they were such babes was that they weren't represented by the Culinary Union. Some cocktail "goddesses" at unionized Caesars

Palace had been working there since the place opened in 1966, protected by seniority rules. The Rio on the other hand had a reputation for firing waitresses who gained weight. Casino owners pay a lot of attention to the appearance of their cocktail waitresses—and with good reason: they're an important part of the food chain in Las Vegas.

When Steve Wynn noticed that a dozen of the Mirage's servers were growing out of their blue uniforms, he offered to build them a gym. "He said, 'You're too fat, and I'm embarrassed to have you working here,'" one of the waitresses told the *Las Vegas Review-Journal*.

Wynn conceded he had been frank. "We've got a couple girls who have let themselves go, and it is unattractive. I tried to use my personal persuasion to get them to take care of themselves," he said. The waitresses, most of them older than forty, sued Mirage Resorts, claiming they were forced to wear one-and-a-half-inch heels and to sign contracts requiring them to have no more than a six-pound weight variance from their weight at hiring, or they would be placed on "weight probation" and face potential termination. It took six years to settle most of the lawsuits.

All these years later, Tony Marnell is rarely credited with his influence on Las Vegas. While Jean-Louis Palladin was serving up foie gras at the Rio, Wynn was chasing down Sirio Maccioni. Maccioni opened New York's elite Le Cirque restaurant with five kilos of the finest white truffles, setting New York on its ear, food-wise, in 1974, back before New York was a food sophisticate.

Wynn wanted Maccioni to run a restaurant at Bellagio. The restaurateur's first response was to laugh. He is an old-world gentleman who expects his restaurant guests to come dressed for the occasion. Elitism, to Maccioni, is an aspiration. "Elite? Of course I believe in elite," he says.

Maccioni lives on Fifty-third Street in Manhattan, and two of his sons live within two blocks. When Wynn came calling, he had been to Las Vegas once—he stayed at Caesars Palace—and the visit wasn't a high point. "I swore to myself I'd never go back," Maccioni recalls.

But Wynn sent his plane. He put Maccioni up in a villa at the Mirage. He did this five times, Maccioni says. Maccioni had a hard time understanding what Wynn was talking about as they toured the site of the old Dunes. But Maccioni's son Mario understood. So did Elizabeth Blau, Le Cirque's manager and a friend of Wynn's daughter Gillian.

It took a year to cut the deal. Wynn promised to build the restaurant, but give Maccioni the right to approve everything. It was the kind of offer that only a casino could afford to make. Sirio Maccioni agreed, but only because Mario wanted to do it.

"People were making fun of me," Maccioni recalls. "They'd say, 'Oh, you're going to Las Vegas? To do what?'"

A few years later, people would forget that they'd gasped at the idea of great food in Las Vegas. There would be so many people trying to choose among great restaurants that there would even be a special Las Vegas restaurants guide.

It dawned on Wynn that he could fill his new place with celebrity chefs and that they could become a draw, like the volcano and the pirate show.

"Executives in food and beverage are like tits on a bull," Wynn said once. "They're unnecessary."

He dived headlong after the most famous chefs he could get his hands on. He offered Jean-Georges Vongerichten 5 percent of the gross, and 10 percent of the net to bring Prime to Bellagio—numbers that could make a chef rich beyond his dreams with the kind of traffic Las Vegas provides, numbers equaled only in cities like New York. And Mirage Resorts was footing the bill. Wynn pursued Julian Serrano, Todd English, Nobu Matsuhisa. He cut a deal with Petrossian to have caviar 365 days a year.

One weekend, at Gillian's wedding, Wynn tried another coup—to hire away Elizabeth Blau from Maccioni. Because of her job, the statuesque Blau knew most of the big names in the chef business. Shocked at the offer, she went for a hike to consider it. When she returned, she signed on for the revolution.

Blau got busy pursuing famous chefs who looked at Las Vegas as though it was Green Acres. "The first question Jean-Georges asked is, 'Where am I going to get my bread?'" Blau says.

Wynn's basic negotiating stance with the chefs was the same one he took with other artists: "I'll give you what you want. I want you here."

Nobu Matsuhisa slipped through Wynn's fingers, choosing instead to open a sushi restaurant at the Hard Rock Hotel & Casino. But for bread, Wynn brought in Nancy Silverton, the award-winning Los Angeles owner of La Brea Bakery, and built her a satellite bakery. He hired Jean Philippe Maury to be Bellagio's top pastry chef. Maury in 1997 was presented with a gold medal from French president Jacques Chirac for winning a competition that crowned him Meilleur Ouvrier de France—Best Pastry Chef in France.

"He made a revolution," Maccioni says. "What Steve Wynn brought to Las Vegas, nobody brought before."

At Bellagio, there was to be shopping for the likes of the Wynns' new social set. Wynn sat down with his retail executive, Frank Visconti, who had come to Mirage Resorts by way of Neiman Marcus and Saks. They identified seven luxury retailers who they deemed essential to the Bellagio's success: Chanel, Gucci, Prada, Hermès, Fred Leighton, Armani, and Tiffany.

The folks at Chanel responded with lip-curling skepticism. Haute couture in the land of sequins and fanny-packs? One high-level Chanel executive told Visconti, "You know, I love the idea but I can't bear the idea of having 'Las Vegas' on our brass plaques: 'Paris, London, Las Vegas.'"

"Well, then don't put it on the plaques," Visconti responded.

While visiting Wynn's Old Forge home one weekend in 1996, Visconti confessed that he had no contacts at Armani and didn't know how to open doors there. "Do you have any ideas?" Visconti asked.

Wynn, Visconti recalls, pursed his lips and scrunched his eyes. "I'll see what I can do."

Two weeks later, Visconti says, Wynn was having dinner with Giorgio Armani himself at Armani's home in Italy. Wynn had called Lee Radziwill for an introduction to the designer.

Wynn even broke his cardinal rule of owning everything down to the photo services in his casinos. "I've never given a lease in twenty-six years, but there are seven. I need the cachet," he said. To get them signed, Visconti had to fudge. No one wanted to sign before the others. Finally, someone asked if Chanel had signed. "I said, 'Yeah, I'm looking at his signature,'" Visconti says. "I had to lie to get the first guy."

Bellagio couldn't draw the numbers of people necessary to support it without a very special show in its showroom six nights a week. What with *Mystere*'s success at Treasure Island, Wynn went back to that well, asking for a new specially created Cirque du Soleil show. Still harkening back to his boyhood days on the lake, he asked for a show based on water. At first, it was to be called *Eau*—the French word for water. But people feared that Americans would mistake it for "Eww," according to people involved in the discussions. So they lit on something appropriately surreal: *O*.

Outside Bellagio would be more water. Not waterskiing, as Wynn had originally imagined, because he needed the space for a convention center and theater. Instead, he would build an eight-acre lake with water fountains that would be choreographed to perform like dancers.

Wynn hired a Southern California company called Wet Design that had been founded by three Disney alumni. Naturally, he threw himself into the technology. He became an overnight expert in fountains. He wanted the tallest, fastest, most graceful water fountains in the world.

He brought in Kenny Ortega, the Emmy Award–winning choreographer of *Dirty Dancing,* who would later go on to direct *High School Musical*. So the fountains danced to "Singin' in the Rain," an aria by Luciano Pavarotti, "Luck Be a Lady," "Hey Big Spender," "Fly Me to the Moon," and a Rachmaninoff rhapsody.

To make water dance, streams must jet high for a crescendo. Spurts must leap and stop for a staccato movement. Water must sweep horizontally and in circles, and it must halt instantly and then fall back to the lake on tempo.

All this wasn't possible with existing technology. Wet Design set about inventing new machinery. There were robotic nozzles capable of moving water 180 degrees in any direction. There was a controller to send water at 698 miles per hour along an arc of the circles. There were "hypershooters" that could shoot water 250 feet in the air using air pressure at 200 pounds per square inch. And the hardware had to disappear into the lake so it would be invisible between performances.

The robotic nozzles came to be called "oarsmen" because of the way they could swish water from side to side, causing it to swing and twist in the air.

A scientist from the California Institute of Technology was brought in to figure out why the "hypershooters" were firing wildly and inconsistently. It turned out that compressed air was chilling to fifty degrees below zero Fahrenheit when the jets fired, clogging the works with ice balls.

Ultimately, Bellagio's fountains would operate with 1,203 nozzles, 4,500 submersed lights, five miles of piping, and enough electrical wire to run from Las Vegas to Los Angeles—all built in two concentric rings and settled in 25 million gallons of water. The water could be blasted 240 feet in the air, with as much as 17,000 gallons of water in the air at any time. It's enough to cool a Mojave summer's day, if you're standing close enough.

The fountains were tested on Bellagio's dry construction site, the tower rising behind, on a vast expanse of flattened dirt that would one day fill with water. Wynn fussed and fumed. He changed the color of the lights from multicolored to white, which he said seemed classier.

Bellagio's price tag was rising so fast that even Wynn was shocked. He asked Dan Lee, his financial ferret, to look into things. Lee hired the accounting firm Arthur Andersen, at a cost of $80,000, to take a look at Marnell's books. They wanted to compare the prices Marnell was charging for Bellagio and the Rio. "If we were getting screwed somewhere, we knew it would show up at the Rio," Lee explained in 1997, about a year and a half after the audit.

Lee didn't want to appear to question Marnell's honesty, so he claimed that Wynn wanted to compare Bellagio's costs to the Monte Carlo—a 1996 casino joint venture between Mirage Resorts and Circus Circus that Marnell had also constructed. "If [Marnell] was getting kickbacks, the subcontractors would have factored the cost of the kickbacks into the price of their bids," Lee said. But the subcontractors' prices were basically the same for the Monte Carlo and for Bellagio. "We found nothing," Lee said.

Bellagio was simply bigger, more deluxe, more complicated.

Was the world ready for it?

♣ ♦ ♥ ♠

Two years before Bellagio was due to open, Alan Feldman launched an education project for the national media. National magazines and newspapers saw Las Vegas for what it had always been: a tacky home to has-been entertainers and drunken bachelor parties. Wynn, meanwhile, wanted onto the pages of fashion and high culture outlets.

Feldman started making the rounds in New York in 1996, approaching the editors of publications like *Travel & Leisure, Conde Nast Traveler,* and *Vanity Fair.* He went with his head down, hat in his hand: "I know we're Las Vegas, and we're not really on your radar . . ."

chapter ten

CRUSHED VELVET WORLD

Las Vegas allows people to try things outside their comfort zones.
—Tony Marnell, casino architect and builder

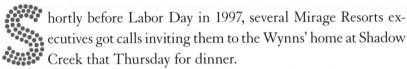hortly before Labor Day in 1997, several Mirage Resorts executives got calls inviting them to the Wynns' home at Shadow Creek that Thursday for dinner.

"It was a very odd invitation because Steve and Elaine weren't known to have you over," says John Schadler, one of the attendees. Others included Marc Schorr; Arte Nathan, head of human resources (who had been the little brother of one of Wynn's boyhood friends in Utica); Alan Feldman, his public relations guru; and the executives' wives.

Wynn appeared to want to introduce them to a new idea. Bellagio was due to open in a little more than a year. "Because this place is so elaborate, it needs to have a masterpiece," Wynn told his guests. He proposed buying one piece of rare art to serve as the hotel's center attraction. Like the volcano, only classier.

"We'll buy a Caravaggio, we'll buy a Titian, and we'll put it behind the front desk at Bellagio," Wynn said.

It occurred to Schadler that this could be like buying the *Mona Lisa*: lines out the door to see it. With an initial art acquisition budget of $10 million, according to one knowledgeable person, Wynn set the plan in motion. This reflected Wynn's attempt to draw yet another crowd that had avoided Las Vegas in the past. With the Mirage, he had introduced middle-class vacationers to Sin City, and they had spent less money on gambling than any group of visitors before. With Bellagio, Wynn was aiming to move up the social ladder to the upper- and upper-middle-classes—educated professionals with more expensive spending habits—the kind who shop at Chanel and Prada, and would spend money on a very expensive dinner. These people's sensibilities had been insulted by Las Vegas in the 1980s and early 1990s, but Wynn was betting that they'd respond favorably to a little well-publicized culture.

Wynn later told the interviewer Charlie Rose about the germination of his interest in art:

> I was building Bellagio, and I was thinking, like, gardens. What could be another qualitative statement about this hotel? Not quantitative. I wasn't trying to attract a crowd. At a billion seven, I thought I—if I hadn't attracted a crowd at a billion seven, not likely a picture would help.
>
> But I thought what—what could tell people that we understand you come to Las Vegas for all kinds of stimulation, the animation of a casino, the restaurants and all the rest, but we know that people care for quiet moments of reflective beauty. So if there were paintings in Bellagio, it would make a statement that we understand who you are, and we intend to stimulate you on all levels. And if you want a quiet hour with wonderful paintings by great masters, there's also that here. That was my qualitative statement of the art.

By some accounts, Wynn had been out buying art for himself for nearly a year by the time of his Labor Day dinner. According to Bellagio's own records, he was actively buying and selling major pieces of art as early as October 1997—a month after the dinner at Shadow Creek.

There is no neatly laid-out account of Wynn's art trades, which were sometimes made with Mirage Resorts money, other times with his own, and sometimes involved trades between himself and Mirage. The art world is secretive, and trades among wealthy collectors are often cloaked behind nondisclosure agreements. The details of Wynn's art career can be pieced together from interviews, reports in the art press, and from a series of lucrative contracts he made with the Bellagio to buy, sell, or lease the art.

Also, Steve Wynn, with his vaudeville genes, sometimes couldn't resist showing off. As he had with the dolphins, Wynn studied his subject closely. He consulted art experts. He traveled around looking at art. He bought art. He got himself a dealer's license.

Caravaggios and Titians, dating from the sixteenth century high Renaissance, are extremely rare. So Wynn turned from his original concept to nineteenth-century Impressionists and embarked upon an extraordinary buying spree that lasted for several years and eventually contributed to one of the most dramatic events in his life.

He bought for $12 million Edgar Degas's *Dancer, Taking Her Bow*—a fine but largely unknown work that had been displayed publicly only twice, in 1924 and 1948.

In the same month, for $1,650,000 he picked up a painting by Pablo Picasso called *Seated Woman*. It was based on Françoise Gilot, the mother of Claude and Paloma Picasso.

On December 5, he bought a sculpture by Alberto Giacometti, *Pointing Man*, for $7,350,000.

Five days later came a Henri Matisse still life, for $4,562,812.

Then a real masterpiece, on December 19: Vincent van Gogh's *Woman in a Blue Dress*. The stunning price was $47.5 million—a handful more than the cost of the entire Shadow Creek Golf Resort.

Wynn soon became enamored with contemporary artists.

In March 1998, he paid $50 million for seven works by Jasper Johns (*Highway*), Franz Kline (*August Day*), Willem de Kooning (*Police Gazette*), Roy Lichtenstein (*Torpedo . . . Los!*), Robert Rauschenberg (*Small Red Painting*), and Cy Twombly (*Untitled*).

Wynn let it slip right from the auction tables that the art he was buying would be hung on the walls of a Las Vegas casino. The response resembled the oenophiles' horror of fine wine in Las Vegas, only louder. Masterpieces for philistines and sexpots? The gasps were audible.

But a few people in Las Vegas began to stand a little taller. Like Roger Thomas, the son of Wynn's former banker, Parry Thomas.

Thomas had been Wynn's head designer for nearly twenty years. He is responsible in one way or another for most of the fabrics and carpets, furnishings, and other decor of Wynn's casinos. Thomas grew up with his nose in art books and then hustled off to art school. It was Roger Thomas who arranged, in 1983, for Wynn to be invited to lunch with the artist Andy Warhol at his studio in Union Square in Manhattan. According to Wynn, who wrote about the meeting years later in one of his self-published art catalogs, Warhol put a tape recorder on a table in his office and asked to speak with Wynn for his magazine, *Interview.* Wynn at the time was a fledgling celebrity for his ads with Frank Sinatra for the Golden Nugget in Atlantic City. At the end of their conversation, Warhol snapped three Polaroid photos of Wynn seated backward on a chair, unsmiling, but with the intense gaze of someone who likes being the focus of the camera's attention.

Warhol tossed two photos on the floor, stepping on them as they left. One day, back in Las Vegas, three silk-screen Warhol portraits arrived—one in white, one in blue, and one in gold with diamond dust. Four years later, Warhol was dead.

The portraits wound up in the collection Wynn was amassing.

Like many well-educated Las Vegans, Roger Thomas felt affection and shame for his hometown. "I grew up in Las Vegas. I was embarrassed by Las Vegas," Thomas said in April 1998. "I always aspired to fine art. I thought this was kitsch."

"The world wants Las Vegas to be a sinful place of tasteless glamour," Thomas continued. "They consume it at an incredible rate. People don't think of Las Vegas as a place where children are being educated and adults have discussions about minimalist art.

"People envision Las Vegas as a place with a craps dealer talking to a hooker about a gambler. I don't think they want to allow us membership in the real world, the normal world.

"Crushed velvet has its place in the world," Thomas concluded, "but Las Vegas doesn't have to be a crushed-velvet world."

It was cash from that crushed-velvet world that allowed Wynn to hang out at New York art hot spots like Mary Boone's gallery. He spent so much time and money at Sotheby's that rumors would one day circulate that he wanted to buy the auction house. He outbid the world's biggest art buyers, such as Ronald Lauder and Si Newhouse. He carried enough weight at Sotheby's that when he was bidding on a Cézanne still life in May 1999, Sotheby's chairman Diana D. Brooks personally took Wynn's bids by telephone.

Wynn was adopted by Bill Acquavella, one of the art world's most prestigious art dealers. As he ushered them around, the Wynns began to appear in gossip columns alongside Wendy Vanderbilt, Count and Countess von Berckheim, Marie-Josée and Henry Kravis, and Eugenie and John Radziwill—socialites of the Acquavellas' acquaintance.

Wynn, or rather Mirage Resorts, hired a curator—Libby Lumpkin, wife of Las Vegas–based art critic Dave Hickey.

When Wynn started competing with renowned museums, it became apparent that he was amassing a major collection. When Wynn picked up a Georges Seurat, *Paysage, L'ile de la Grande-Jatte*, in May 1999 for a reported $35.2 million, *Los Angeles Times* art critic Christopher Knight criticized the Getty Trust for missing out.

Wynn became obsessed with Picasso, another man of enormous appetites. He flew off to meet Picasso's children. He flew to Europe in pursuit of Picasso's former mistresses. He created a restaurant at Bellagio called Picasso and decorated it with Picassos and photos of Picasso by Man Ray. He hired Picasso's son Claude to design the restaurant's furnishings. Wynn put himself on a first-name basis with the long-dead artist. "Pablo," Wynn called him.

The Mirage jets were now ferrying art back to Las Vegas. Works arrived at the Mirage casino in crates.

At first, the pieces were stored in Wynn's office. Then they were stacked in the boardroom. For a time, the thin Giacometti sculpture propped open the door to Wynn's office, according to a person who worked for the company. (Later, the Wynns' home at Shadow Creek, with its full bar in the living room, became a depository for art. The walls were wired for security as paintings were hung. Extra art went into the bay of the three-car garage which was converted, according to security staff at Shadow Creek, into a giant safe.)

Mirage officials and the company's insurers began to fret about art storage. "I can't stick it in the warehouse, because I'd have to put a guard on it twenty-four hours," Dan Lee griped in January 1998. "So Steve says, 'Stick it in the salon privé.'"

So off went the art to decorate the salon privé—Mirage's baccarat pit, which consisted of several rooms separated by a balustrade from the sea of slot machines.

The art was expensive, but the publicity was priceless.

"We decided to build the single most elegant place ever created—regardless of whether you're talking about Paris or London or anywhere else," Wynn said of Bellagio. "Now, this is a very lofty goal."

Gastronomy at the Rio. Art at Mirage. Other casinos began to enter a dialogue with the higher classes. Sheldon Adelson, the would-be mogul who bought the Sands from Kerkorian, announced he would build a high-quality replica of Venice—from the Doge's Palace to the canals. Adelson irked Wynn by claiming he would have the biggest, nicest all-suite hotel rooms in Las Vegas. While dividing his time between Israel and Las Vegas, Adelson sent his executives around the world to find Italian artisans, fine marble, and even plump curtain tassels at bargain prices.

Suddenly, Las Vegas was generating buzz, drawing people who had never before deigned to visit. Tim and Nina Zagat went just in time to catch Wynn's act with his art. The founders of Zagat restaurant guides say they find the city disturbing, but they had to see what the chatter was about.

The Zagats are a pair of New York lawyers who hit upon a better thing. Tim Zagat is a gregarious fellow, Nina is more organized. Years ago, they and their friends began to compare notes about restaurants in New York City, where they live. They began to scribble their notes and to share them collectively, voting on the restaurants' qualities. Next thing you know, the thin, red, pocket-size dining-out guides were born. The Zagats, pronounced Zeh-GAHTs, just liked to eat, but they became famous food aficionados.

In Las Vegas, the Zagats booked themselves into the place they'd heard was the best. All their preconceptions about Las Vegas were confirmed. "We stayed at the Rio," Nina Zagat recalls over tea in her breezy suite at the Hotel Bel-Air in Los Angeles. "It was supposed to be the nicest place in Las Vegas at the time. It was unbelievable. Going up in the elevator, there were people with alcohol in paper bags!

"They upgraded us to a suite. It was so big, Tim and I couldn't find each other," she says. "In the bathroom, the soap dish and tissue box were nailed down."

Steve Wynn heard the Zagats were in town and invited them over to the Mirage. It happened to be the day he was hanging some of his art in the baccarat pit.

When the Zagats arrived at the appointed hour of 12:30 p.m., they found Bill Acquavella and a crew of professional picture hangers in the salon privé. Wynn gave them the full blast of Steve Wynn-ness. But the Zagats were hungry.

"I thought we were being invited to lunch at twelve thirty," says Tim Zagat. "But it turned out we were there to consult on where to hang the paintings. I knew he had vision problems. He was asking us, 'What do you think about here—and here—and here?' I don't know anything about that."

"It was weird," says Nina Zagat, widening her eyes.

Wynn was now planning on putting the art in a gallery at Bellagio and charging admission. This meant he hadn't solved the problem of decorating the front desk and lobby after all. So he lit upon the glass artist Dale Chihuly, who creates swirly colorful blown-glass sculptures.

Chihuly and Wynn faxed designs back and forth for a lobby piece that would be worthy of the most beautiful hotel in the world, as Wynn saw it. Wynn visited Chihuly's Seattle studio three times. They agreed that Chihuly would create a piece with 1,000 glass flowers in a sea of brilliantly colored glass, abstract in its design, which would hang from the ceiling above the lobby floor. Chihuly designed a new type of armature strong enough to hold the pieces. Every petal in the seventy-by-thirty-foot sculpture was hand blown at the studio, assembled, then disassembled and shipped to Bellagio, where it was re-assembled.

When it arrived, Wynn wasn't satisfied with 1,000 flowers, and he wanted more orange colors, despite Chihuly's objections (and Elaine's—she doesn't like the color orange). Chihuly finally added orange lights behind the sculpture. "It was the only way we could figure out how to do it," Chihuly says.

Ultimately, the Chihuly sculpture contained 2,000 glass elements and weighed more than 50,000 pounds in glass and steel. They called it *Fiori di Como*—"Flowers of Como"—in honor of the city of Bellagio.

By the spring of 1998, Wynn was one of the top art buyers on the planet. "What we're doing is going to be better than the Getty," he said that April, referring to the Los Angeles museum with a $5-billion endowment.

Wall Street analysts and investors began asking how much this was costing. The dolphins and their habitat at the Mirage had cost $30 million. Shadow Creek had cost $40 million. The art started looking outlandishly expensive at $165 million, and Wynn was still out raising his paddle at auctions.

Investors were getting angry, but few had the guts to ask Steve Wynn about his spending. The person they nailed to the cross instead was Dan Lee.

Bellagio was fast approaching a new and frightening threshold—the $2-billion mark. Applying some of the same creative talents he had displayed as a boy selling cut-up *Playboy* photographs, Lee began to describe the cost of Bellagio "excluding art."

This created confusion about the cost of Bellagio that has never been cleared up. Eventually, Lee would place the property's cost at "One point seven billion . . . plus art"—which means it cost about two billion dollars.

Mirage Resorts would later reveal in a January 2000 conference call that the art was the most costly attraction of any of its casinos. The pirate battle at Treasure Island cost roughly $2 per patron; the dolphins and Siegfried and Roy's tigers at the Mirage cost $3.70 per head; and the Bellagio art gallery cost $4.75 per customer.

So, whose art was it anyway?

Much of it was Wynn's. Lee estimated that of $300 million worth of art, Wynn personally owned about $125 million—or slightly less than half. Shareholders paid for the rest. Wynn and Mirage Resorts forged an agreement in 1998, approved by the board of directors, obligating Bellagio to pay Wynn $4.8 million a year to lease the art he owned personally. It cost Mirage Resorts shareholders roughly 2.5 cents per share, before taxes.

Overseeing Bellagio's end of this deal with Wynn was his old friend and right-hand-man, Bobby Baldwin, who was president of Bellagio. One of Baldwin's roles at Mirage Resorts was to give Wynn bad news. His chosen method was to walk into Wynn's office, blurt it out, and survive the ensuing storm. Baldwin says he once watched Wynn throw a phone book at his brother Ken Wynn. "It was painful, but we recovered quickly," he says.

There is no evidence that Baldwin seriously challenged Wynn on the art habit he was feeding at Bellagio's expense. As Dan Lee tap-danced around the topic, Baldwin approved contract after contract for Wynn's personal trades and leases with Bellagio.

Using the company's money to buy and lease art enabled Wynn to behave like a much bigger player in the art world than he could personally afford. Art changed Steve and Elaine Wynn's lives. For the opening of Bellagio, the Wynns were going to be on the cover of *Vanity Fair*—a publication that their public relations man, Alan Feldman, had groveled to several years earlier.

"I never thought as a humble student that I would ever be in a position to own masterworks of art," Wynn told the television interviewer Charlie Rose. "That was for the Rockefellers and the Whitneys and the Vanderbilts and the likes of that. . . . And then, life went by, and opportunity was very kind."

Wynn was willing to give up a lot to finance his art habit, including diluting his control of Mirage Resorts. Starting in February 1998, Wynn began to sell off his shares in Mirage, three million shares in tranches of $24 and $24.75 a share. That month alone, his stake in the company fell from 15.8 percent to 14.2 percent.

From the perspective of Wall Street, a chief executive's sale of shares is a yellow caution light—a signal that he believes his shares are overvalued. Then investors were further startled when construction delays forced Wynn to push back Bellagio's opening from March 1998 to October. Mirage's stock price began to fall.

Joseph Coccimiglio, an analyst with Prudential Securities, published a report entitled "Bellagio: Titanic or Waterworld?" in April 1998. He compared Bellagio to two big-spending movies of the time, James Cameron's *Titanic*, which won an Academy Award after predictions of failure, and *Waterworld*, a famously expensive Kevin Costner box-office bust.

"The market is pricing Mirage's stock as if Bellagio is going to turn out to be the hotel/casino equivalent of Waterworld!" Coccimiglio wrote.

The Mirage's return on invested capital at that point was 29 percent, Coccimiglio noted, while Treasure Island's was 23 percent. He predicted Bellagio's would be 17 percent.

New casinos were putting pressure on returns as gamblers had more choices about where to place their bets. Hilton Hotels was building Paris Las Vegas. Sheldon Adelson was building the Venetian on the old Sands property he'd bought from Kerkorian and warring with Wynn over whose rooms would be nicest. Circus Circus was building a gold-towered Mirage knockoff called Mandalay Bay at the far southern end of the Strip. Suddenly, everybody was putting in marble baths.

Wynn continued selling off assets that had once been dear to him. During his six years at Lake Tahoe, he had become a director of the Tahoe Regional Planning Agency and had even developed a green streak, convincing the agency to ban Jet Skis to protect the lake from leaked fuel. Old Forge, the Wynns' five-acre Tahoe estate, was separated from the Milkens' estate by only one piece of land, and the two families had a close circle of friends at Tahoe. But Wynn sold the 12,000-square-foot house and grounds of Old Forge, including its private beach and pier, in April 1998 for $25 million.

Wynn sold another three million shares of Mirage stock in August 1998. This time, he had to take a significantly lower price—$21.50 a share. His stake in Mirage Resorts dwindled to 11 percent. He later said he believed his company was too big to be vulnerable.

Kerkorian, who controlled his own destiny with a stake of more than half of MGM Grand's stock, watched Mirage Resorts' share price tumble. Wynn's options dived "underwater"—which in finance lingo meant they were worthless until the share price rose substantially. Conveniently for Wynn, the Mirage board decided to re-price Wynn's options in December 1998, shortly after Bellagio opened. This gave Wynn the opportunity to buy 1.8 million shares at a bargain-basement price of $14.375 per share. It was an astoundingly low price and an inexcusably generous reward for a chief executive whose stewardship had overseen such a dramatic decline in share price in the preceding months.

Even with storms blowing around him, there seemed to be no compromises in Wynn. For Bellagio's art catalog, Wynn insisted on using the same printer as used by Sotheby's and Christie's—Arti Grafiche Amilcare Pizzii S.p.a. in Milan, Italy—requiring numerous transatlantic flights for everyone.

♣ ♦ ♥ ♠

Wynn seemed giggly with anticipation of Bellagio's opening. He made a mischievous pitch on the hotel's huge sign: COMING SOON: VAN GOGH. MONET. RENOIR AND CÉZANNE! WITH SPECIAL GUESTS PICASSO AND MATISSE.

The invitations to Bellagio's opening arrived in black velvet boxes measuring nine inches high by thirteen inches across by two and a half inches deep. The velvet was imprinted with a gold Edwardian script "B." The invitation that lay inside was more of a booklet—a dozen pages encased in a spectacularly beautiful Japanese paper that was laced with fine copper-colored threads, chosen personally by Wynn. *"And so it begins,"* it began.

The booklet contained an invitation from "Stephen and Elaine Wynn" to four days of celebratory activities, from Sunday through

Wednesday, October 18–21. Sunday was for "Arrival," Monday and Tuesday for "Relaxation and Discovery," Monday evening was the opening of the show *O* followed by a dinner, and Tuesday evening was for "Culinary Discovery" at one of Bellagio's restaurants. On Wednesday, there was "Brunch and Farewells."

Beneath this invitation in a special cavity in the black velvet box lay a video, encased in the same copper-threaded paper. YOUR PERSONAL INTRODUCTION TO BELLAGIO the case read. The tape held a short, romantic film accompanied by the opera singer Andrea Boccelli singing *"Con Te Partiro."*

This Bellagio romance was of a *Harlequin* nature. It began with a handsome, middle-aged man in a dark suit. He stood alone, staring sternly across the mists of Bellagio's lake. From afar, a beautiful young woman in a dark evening gown spotted him and approached, descending from one of Bellagio's stone terraces. The camera rested momentarily on her chest as she ran. She flashed a coy smile and cast her eyes downward—inviting, shy, and flirtatious.

The image flashed to the shooting fountains of Bellagio. Streams of white, frothing water cascaded into the air as Boccelli's aria came to a crescendo in full coital eruption. In a parting shot, the woman's hand caressed the man's. Both were dripping wet.

It wasn't as crass as strippers.

♣ ◆ ♥ ♠

Wynn moved his offices right over to Bellagio from the now-dated Mirage. The blazing colors of his Mirage office were traded for a sea of cream, with glass walls looking out onto a private lawn for his dogs.

A long wall of fine, burled elm flanked one of two wings. The blond and chocolate swirls in the millwork concealed cabinetry that contained, among other things, a state-of-the art television and stereo system. Two baseball bats hung from the millwork to the right of the door. One of these bats had once belonged to Babe Ruth, according to people in the office.

At times, the executive suite was like a kennel. There were almost always dogs there—Wynn's German shepherds and smaller lap dogs;

Bobby Baldwin's dogs; other canine visitors belonging to his assistants and others working there. It was entirely commonplace to hear barking during telephone conversations—and even during the quarterly conference calls at which the company discussed its financial results.

Wynn's personal driveway to his Bellagio offices was hidden by a high wall and could be entered via an electronically operated gate. This gate could be accessed from the executive parking area, which was also hidden behind a high wall and entered by passing through an electronic gate. And this gate, too, was hidden behind a third long high wall, which was reached through yet another electronic gate, which was also watched by a uniformed guard. Thus, reaching Wynn required passing the scrutiny of one guard, three electronic gates, a state-of-the-art surveillance system, and two highly trained German attack dogs.

On the Monday two weeks before Bellagio's opening, Wynn emerged from this cocoon to begin a series of employee pep rallies at the Golden Nugget, the Mirage, Treasure Island, and Bellagio. He began with four hundred employees in a Golden Nugget conference room. Increasingly blind, Wynn walked toward the platform alone, knocked his foot against the bottom stair to identify its location, stepped up two stairs, and headed for the lectern.

"Hi," he began, wanting to draw a link between his dreams and theirs. "I know who you are," Wynn told the crowd. "And I know why you're here."

He entertained them with his great life story. He called his friend Clint Eastwood—his neighbor at Sun Valley for sixteen years—a "closet intellectual." He did an impression of Eastwood addressing his son Kyle, home from school after months away. "Hi, son, wanna beer?"

He continued, "I came from the Golden Nugget. This is the base of it all." Bellagio is the "latest addition to this family of hotels that springs from here."

After the rally, Wynn headed back to Bellagio to see his friend Barbara Walters. She was in Nevada to interview Jeremy Strohmeyer, a young man who had been convicted of raping and killing seven-year-old Sherrice Iverson at a Primm, Nevada, casino. The case brought sadly into focus one of the ugliest outcomes of gambling addiction—children being left unaccompanied in casinos while their parents wager.

This was a problem that ate at Wynn. He had come so far from his original concept for Treasure Island that, at Bellagio, he had decided to ban children unless they were staying in the hotel. "Children don't belong in casinos," he said flatly.

Barbara Walters and Wynn met under the Chihuly sculpture and moved on together, dropping names throughout their tour of future restaurants and shops. Wynn ricocheted through the construction zone, tripping over an electric cord and banging into a low partition. Walters was happy to learn that her friend Fred Leighton was opening a jewelry shop at Bellagio. Wynn told her he'd sold a Picasso to Henry Kravis, the king of leveraged buyouts. He told her in a stage whisper that Françoise Gilot, Picasso's lover, was coming to Bellagio's opening!

In the baccarat salon, Wynn pointed to the carpet and said it had been woven by hand in Shanghai and imported in one piece.

After the newscaster left for the airport, Wynn stood in a hallway and puzzled over where to place a Viola Frey sculpture. "Will more people come here or to the other end?" he asked his designer, Roger Thomas. Wynn pondered for several seconds. "Here," he said finally, pointing to the entrance of the shopping esplanade.

Wynn then moved on to the Picasso Restaurant, where a photo of Picasso by Man Ray was being hung. Wynn wanted to inspect the photograph, which was an art object itself.

Libby Lumpkin, Wynn's curator, awaited him along with Thomas. They stood beside a table that was covered with Man Ray original photographs.

Wynn announced that he wanted to check the Man Ray seal on the back of one picture. With his bare, unwashed hands, he pulled the photo out of its matting. Lumpkin reached out to hand him a pair of white cotton gloves. Wynn ignored her.

Oils and acids on the skin can do irreparable harm to art. "Yes, you really should wear gloves," Thomas interjected, squirming.

"It's okay," Wynn said dismissively. He flipped the photo over to see the stamp—MAN RAY IN PARIS—as Lumpkin and Thomas inhaled sharply.

Barehanded, Wynn flipped undaunted through more photos. Lumpkin handed him one of Picasso at a bullfight.

"Stinking sport," erupted Wynn, the animal lover. "Rotten chickenshits. What a sport. . . . How much courage does that take?"

Rumors that Wynn was touching his amazing artworks—he once waxed poetic on the sensation of touching Van Gogh's brushstrokes—eventually reached Charlie Rose, who asked him about it in a televised interview on July 11, 2005. Wynn conceded equably that he'd done it, and that it was "a no-no under most circumstances."

Earlier that afternoon, before Bellagio opened, Thomas and Wynn reminisced about their first meeting. The moment contained worlds of information about Wynn's forceful character.

> THOMAS: *I was twelve. We met in an elevator in Tahoe.*
>   *You were skiing.*
> WYNN: *You were fourteen.*
> THOMAS: *I was twelve.*
> WYNN: *You were fourteen.*
> THOMAS: *My math must not be so good.*
> WYNN: *You were fourteen.*

Having vanquished Thomas, Wynn headed to Sam's American Restaurant to lay into the poor young chef, Sam DeMarco. DeMarco's menu included dishes like s'mores, black beans, and fried eggs. Wynn didn't like the décor or the food. Then he banged his shin and got caught in a billowing curtain that hung from the ceiling as a room divider.

DeMarco flinched as Wynn scowled at his plans to hang sculptures on the wall. "You're just going to mount these from the wall?" Wynn demanded. "How you gonna light 'em? . . . You're gonna get a halo effect. This is the kind of thing that I'd have to see with a model. I don't have the guts to do that without seeing it. It's too avant garde—it's too risky."

DeMarco looked sick as Wynn stomped out. But Wynn's instincts proved correct: the restaurant was not a success and closed quickly.

Wynn led his entourage to the hotel's front desk. The Chihuly sculpture on the ceiling was unlit. Behind the long desk, where he had once imagined a Titian or Caravaggio, was the façade of an Italianate building and garden—oddly plain in the ornate palace of the Bellagio.

"What I need is pots," Wynn announced. His brother Kenny, who had met up with him at DeMarco's restaurant, and three others grabbed a three-foot pot of plants and struggled to bring it over. "Now, that's what you don't expect to see behind the front desk," Wynn said, pleased.

Wynn decided he wanted to rehearse the dancing fountains. He marched through Bellagio's porte cochere, where the drive was littered with construction equipment. "When are these guys going to get this shit out of here?" Wynn demanded.

The sidewalk in front of Bellagio had been wired for sound. There were woofers in the base of the streetlights and tweeters under the lanterns, so when the music started, it came from nowhere and everywhere. Wynn declined to divulge the cost of all that. "That's about money. We're artists here," he said coolly.

Mist, created by ultrasonic vibration, covered the lake and spread like a fog. Music poured from the streetlights: Aaron Copeland's *Appalachian Spring* (a piece that was later cut from the lineup). Wynn raised his arms and began to direct the fountains as if they were an orchestra.

Passersby stopped to watch and to point. Wynn danced. "It's all a balance thing, isn't it?" he asked. "It was appropriate to the place, just like the volcano."

The next piece, Wynn said, represented Las Vegas to him. An aria by Pavarotti, "Rondine al Nido." "Remember this—you're in Las Vegas!" he said with a grin, lifting his arms to the music. "Entertainment and good taste can go hand in hand here. They're not just for effete snobs—they're for everybody."

He went on. "It's a terrible mistake to underestimate the taste of the public. These kinds of spectacles stir people much more deeply than things that are superficial." He threw back his head.

"People will dig an orchestra and a glass of wine," he said. And then he revealed the strategy behind Bellagio and also of his entire career: "There's a tremendous population in the world that does not come here. That's critical to us."

The fountains launched into "Singin' in the Rain." Wynn did a little soft-shoe. He hopped. He swayed. He tiptoed. The oarsmen—his fountain oarsmen—danced on the water. He smiled serenely and opened his mouth to sing, *"I'm siiiingin' in the rain. . . . I'm haaaappy again."*

It seemed appropriate to ask how Wynn would like to be remembered in Las Vegas.

"WHO CARES?" Wynn shouted, arms akimbo, as the tourists watched. He grinned wickedly. "You can be damn sure they won't forget me!"

chapter eleven

HUNGRY ALLIGATOR

February 1998, 11:00 a.m. A half-dozen men exited the small boardroom at the executive offices at the MGM Grand Hotel and Casino in Las Vegas.

The decor was bland as far as corporate offices go. Beyond the office walls, the resort offered gamblers preposterous hotel suites and thickly carpeted baccarat salons. Here, though, the rows of utilitarian rooms fronted by the gray cubicles of assistants could have furnished an insurance brokerage or mortgage lender.

Two of the men paused by the boardroom door. One was wizened, with a long upper lip, wavy gray hair, and an air of quiet. He was Kirk Kerkorian. The other was taller but forty-five years his junior, button-nosed and obsequious.

"It's an honor to meet you," stammered the younger man. His name was Jim Murren. He had recently come to work as the chief financial officer of MGM Grand Inc. The job was merely a taking-off point for Murren, who was transitioning into the Las Vegas action after an early career as a Wall Street analyst. The key to his aspirations was standing right in front of him.

Skin folded in deep wrinkles around the old man's weathered mouth, but his eyes were sharp and alive. Quietly, he began to recite a tale about a hungry alligator:

An alligator rested on the riverbank, unmoving and invisible, watching small fish swim by. The alligator was hungry, but it didn't go after the small fry. The creature waited so calmly that the river's inhabitants became busy with their own interests and stopped noticing the alligator. After a long while, a particularly big, succulent-looking fish swam by.

That's when the beast opened its maw. The alligator gulped the big fish whole.

"I'd like to think," Kerkorian suggested, "that we can be like the hungry alligator."

chapter twelve

TAA-DAAAAH!

It's fun.

—ELAINE WYNN

There is a great tradition of gala casino openings in Las Vegas. One of the most infamous was the Flamingo's in 1946, when bad weather in Los Angeles had grounded flights, leaving only a smattering of Hollywood celebrities willing to drive to Bugsy Siegel's ill-planned party. George Raft, Charles Coburn, and Vivian Blaine arrived to find the place still under construction and their hotel rooms uninhabitable—an opening-night disaster that wasn't matched until the Venetian "opened" its unfinished hotel in 1998. (At least the Flamingo's entertainment was good: Xavier Cugat and Jimmy Durante played.)

Four years after the Flamingo, in 1950, Wilbur Clark opened the Desert Inn with an evening of black-tie glamour. The Desert Inn had cost $4.5 million to build—roughly the price of advertising for Bellagio's opening. Clark's wife, Toni, recalled the fete nearly fifty years later. Jimmy Durante was there again, as were Donald O'Connor, William Powell, Alice Faye, and three hundred other guests. The evening included dinner, a show with the Ray Noble Orchestra, and a pool party. "All the stars were there and everybody looked beautiful," Toni Clark said in 1998, when she was a frail eighty-three years old.

In this tradition, Bellagio's October 15, 1998, opening was anticipated in some circles as if it were a royal wedding. "Steve Wynn does everything beautifully," Clark rhapsodized.

To manage it all, Wynn had taken on labor ballast, hiring 1,000 more employees than the 8,500 that Bellagio would need on a running basis. Elaine Wynn planned the parties—from seating charts to taste-testing the menus. The opening was "an opportunity to make a first impression," Steve Wynn said. "It's like a symphony. All the movements have to be right."

Over the coming months, the worst performers among the employees would quit or be fired, bringing the employment levels down drastically. But in the final week before opening, Bellagio employees were the hotel's first guests, sleeping and eating there as they simultaneously learned their jobs and put the resort through practice laps.

The celebrating was to begin on Thursday with a private black-tie charity gala. Paying $1,000 each for the event only, or $3,500 for a suite overnight, 1,000 guests would enjoy Bellagio without the crowds for a few hours, and proceeds would go to retinitis pigmentosa research.

At the end of this evening, Wynn would find a place with a view of the doors and, walkie-talkie in hand, give the order to throw them wide. Outside, a horde in T-shirts, waving cameras, would race to the slot machines, watched by the glamorous crowd within with a tinge of horror.

The following day, as Bellagio's slot machines steadily cha-chinged, 1,200 of the Wynns' closest friends would arrive for the weekend. For them, there would be no charge.

On Sunday, the media would arrive just in time to not annoy these invited guests on their way out the door. Over three more days—paid for by Mirage Resorts for any media whose rules would permit accepting such goodies (mostly the foreign press)—reporters and their crews would be toured through the art collection, the conservatory, the fountains, and the shops of Giorgio Armani, Prada, Chanel, Tiffany, Gucci, and Hermès.

Press were flying in from overseas to cover the event for the Paris daily *Le Figaro, Le Monde, Femme Actuelle,* the *Frankfurter Allegemeine, Bild,* the *Evening Standard*—roughly 350 news organizations from around the world, excluding the food press and the art press, who would follow in November. Mirage Resorts set up a satellite broadcast service, providing a satellite truck and a half-dozen news crews for television stations that couldn't afford to send more than one reporter.

The whole gambling world was in a frenzy.

The Venetian, not yet open and horribly behind schedule, had hired an outside public relations agency to call around to *The New York Times, Newsweek, The Wall Street Journal*, and the morning television shows. Were journalists working on a Bellagio story, by any chance? If so, would they like to come by and see the Venetian?

"I hear everybody else talking about going, and I think there are going to be some big games," said Phil Hellmuth, then a rising professional poker player who figured Bellagio would be chock full of rich suckers.

Wall Street was as caught up as anyone.

"The pre-opening excitement is as high as I've ever seen in the gaming industry," said Jason Ader of Bear Stearns, one of the gambling industry's top analysts.

Ader's wife at the time, Lori, spent weeks shopping for the right gown in New York. She finally settled on a $1,050 Heidi Weisel creation from Saks Fifth Avenue. It was a minimalist brown knit with cutouts to display cleavage.

"It's been hanging over my head. I waited for the invitation," Lori Ader said three weeks before the opening. "Steve Wynn. Everything he does is just so big."

In what had to be both an ominously telling oversight and a snub, the Wynns had forgotten to invite Wall Street. It was Dan Lee who realized that so many analysts, investors, and bankers—so important in Mirage Resorts' financing—had been forgotten. At the last minute, Lee scrambled to find $204,000 to throw a party for three hundred and forty Wall Streeters, piling them into one of the ballrooms on Monday night. He persuaded Wynn, exhausted by nearly a week of celebrating, to stop by.

The Wall Street guests, of course, were never told they'd been forgotten. As far as they were concerned, their invitations had simply arrived later than expected.

chapter thirteen

SOUTHERN BLUES

*I thought it was terrible! It's heavy. It's too heavy. He did marble
in every cranny. . . . They walk in there with their Bermuda shorts
and they're not comfortable—it's like a tomb.*

—DONALD TRUMP

Say what you will, Donald Trump and Steve Wynn do not love
each other. Trump visited Wynn's new casino in Biloxi, Mississippi, and was rewarded to find it troubled. Trump crowed
deliciously, "He's got huge problems!"

Trump at the time was between Marla and Melania. It was 1999,
and he had as yet no *Apprentice* reality television show. Trump did
have bad hair and a bad temper and some pretty bad troubles at his
own publicly traded casino company, Trump Hotels & Casino Resorts.

One of Trump's big anxieties was a complex series of lawsuits
and competitive skirmishes over Wynn's development plans in Atlantic City. Salt in his wounds: Wynn got great press and was the
"king of Vegas"—a place Trump himself wanted to break into.
Trump reveled in anything that resembled bad news for Steve
Wynn.

Wynn responded nastily to Trump's criticism. "He's an expert on
everyone's business but his own," Wynn snapped. "Donald Trump
doesn't know what he's talking about, and I refuse to have my business shaped by anything that imbecile says."

Strangely enough, though, Trump was right.

In November 1995, when Wynn left his lieutenant Barry Shier to oversee Biloxi, the casino was expected to cost $200 million—more than anyone in Mississippi could have imagined—and to open in 1997.

Barry Shier worshiped at the altar of Steve Wynn. He wore his hair with a Vegas mini-ducktail, like Wynn. He took his German shepherd to work. He was caught up in building himself a fabulous 14,000-square-foot home in Las Vegas. While others called Wynn Steve, Shier began to call him Stephen. Once, when Wynn was being fitted for a suit in his office, Shier clucked around him familiarly, repeating the words of the tailor—"Oh, that's a great fit, Stephen"— while others in the room rolled their eyes.

While Wynn devoted his attentions to Bellagio, Shier created the Biloxi project in its likeness.

Biloxi is a former fishing village, where Barq's root beer was first bottled in 1898. Beyond its historic center, dripping with live oaks and antebellum mansions, Biloxi become a daytripper's casino market in the 1990s. Gamblers drove to feed $40 into the slot machines there before splurging on a steak and heading home. They liked bingo, country music, and a generous Southern buffet with hush puppies and greens.

Wynn aimed to do with Beau Rivage what the Mirage had done in Las Vegas in 1989. "We thought it was going to compete with the Ritz-Carlton in Naples, Florida," says Alan Feldman.

To those working on the project, it wasn't clear that there were any budgetary constraints at all. "The finest casino that could be built. That was the goal," said Bill Yates, chairman of the resort's builder, W. G. Yates & Sons Construction in Philadelphia, Mississippi.

Concrete ceilings were sanded to a perfect smoothness, rather than sprayed with a cheaper and more common rough "popcorn" to cover flaws. Shier hired a boat captain to advise him as they traveled all over inspecting the finest marinas so he could build a top-notch one. Eventually, Shier spent $10 million building a thirty-one-slip marina of Brazilian *ipe* wood. It was touted as the most expensive marina in the world on a per-slip basis. According to people at the company, Shier bought expensive speedboats for high-rollers without consulting Wynn, who was a speedboat aficionado.

Shier had absorbed his boss's penchant for luxury. While living in a Best Western Hotel across the street during Beau Rivage's construction, Shier personally taught the maids how to triple-sheet his bed—a luxury practice where a third sheet is laid atop the blanket.

Wynn's well-established abhorrence of riverboats was troublesome. Most riverboat casinos are boats parked at water's edge with ramps connecting the land-based hotel to the floating casino, in accordance with state laws. But mooring ramps rise and fall with the tides on the Gulf of Mexico. Wynn didn't want his customers walking up or down a steep ramp to the casino.

Wynn's refusal to use the standard technology "drove the naval architects crazy," said Mac Johnson, Yates's project manager. Adapting technology used to stabilize offshore oil platforms, they floated the casino on five barges that were anchored by nine million pounds of structural steel. It was like holding a float just underwater by anchoring it from below. It was so strong that years later, when Hurricane Katrina chased other Biloxi riverboats onto land and across the road, Beau Rivage's held steadily.

Like Bellagio, Beau Rivage was to have an elaborate conservatory. It was planted with fully grown magnolia trees that had been dug up from surrounding homes and farms. Unfortunately, no one advised Shier or Wynn that magnolias fare poorly indoors. As the magnificent trees defoliated in the ensuing months, crews wired fake leaves and blossoms onto the trees to make them look alive.

Shier may even have out-Wynned Wynn in his attention to detail. He released seven mating pairs of finches into the conservatory to provide authentic birdsong. The recorded variety—used to great advantage around the Mirage's volcano—just wouldn't do. "It felt right," Shier explained. "When you're sitting in a park and a bird lands on your table, you say, 'This bird's friendly and I'm friendly.'"

Early plans had Beau Rivage fronted by dancing water fountains like Bellagio's. To cut expense, the water show was changed to something more Southern, said Mac Johnson. Gracing Beau Rivage's drive were fifteen seventy-five-year-old live oak trees—transplanted from a local farm at a cost of $67,000 each.

Spa treatment rooms were lined with 250 yards of fine silk. The sushi bar was made from Rosso Verona marble. In hotel rooms, a tiny museum light was attached to each picture that hung from the wall.

Wynn didn't pay much attention to Beau Rivage until after Bellagio had opened. "By the time Bellagio opened, they were in so deep with Beau Rivage," says one former Mirage executive.

Beau Rivage ultimately cost $680 million—quadruple its original rough estimates. It swelled to 1,780 rooms from 1,200. Four restaurants had grown to a baker's dozen. "Every time you'd turn around, it'd be another ten million," says a former senior executive. "They kept raising the operating assumptions to make it look like they were going to earn what they needed to earn."

Wall Street remained obliviously sanguine as the costs rose, predicting returns of as much as 20 percent—well over the returns being earned in Las Vegas at the time. Shier was now suggesting that Beau Rivage would become a competitor to big casinos in Las Vegas and Atlantic City.

Internal reports from Mirage Resorts suggested the casino needed to draw customers from a six-hundred-mile radius across the Southeast. That required regular, cheap jet service into the Biloxi area. Shier tried but failed to entice rival casinos to subsidize flight service. Three months before Beau Rivage opened, he settled a deal with fledgling AirTran Airways Inc., formerly known as ValuJet, which was trying to recover from a devastating 1996 crash into the Florida Everglades. Beau Rivage subsidized flights from Dallas and Atlanta and paid to open a gate in Nashville, which research showed was an important feeder market.

Wynn came up with his own idea to advertise Beau Rivage on television. He asked Elizabeth Taylor to do the voiceover for a television commercial, says John Schadler. She wouldn't take money—"I don't do that anymore, Steve"—but instead asked Wynn to make a donation to an AIDS charity.

They did the recording at Elizabeth Taylor's Bel-Air home in Los Angeles. The crew waited more than two hours in her living room while the aging legend got prepared. They were led to her boudoir, where Taylor worked from her bed in a purple muumuu and a wig, her poodles in her lap.

She spoke in a lilting Southern accent, her voice soft and dreamy, melting like ice cream on a summer day. Later, her voice was laid over filtered film of Gulf life—a lady picking flowers, shrimp boats, a girl on a tree swing among live oaks.

> *People said it was bound tah happen. Kinda half-wishin', half-knowin', thinkin' if they said it enough that would make it so. Then everybody'd go back to just smellin' the wet Gulf air. The shrimp boats would sail. The magnohhlias would bloom. But nothin' would change.*
>
> *And then. One day. It happened!*
>
> *We looked up and there it was, jest like a stohhry book written lahrrge across the sky. And they gave it suuch a pretty name!* [sweeping aerial shot of the new casino tower and its sign.]
>
> *And after that, nothin' was evah the same.*
>
> *Course. We still lahk smellin' the magnohhlias.*

"Steve loved it," former spokesman Alan Feldman recalls.

But it landed in Biloxi with an ugly thud. Taylor's put-on Southern accent insulted Mississippians. "We fucked up," says Feldman. "The number-one question we heard was, 'Is that actually how they think we talk?' The whole tone and tenor of the commercial was, 'There ain't shit going on in this community until Beau Rivage came along.'"

Beau Rivage opened on March 16—a Tuesday—with plenty of proud state politicians in attendance. The New York Stock Exchange remained blissfully unaware of any troubles brewing in Biloxi. The excitement surrounding the opening drove Mirage Resorts' shares up a dollar to a heady $22 a share. In May, two things happened to boost them even further.

Wynn was already planning his next new casino—this one in Atlantic City, where he would go toe to toe with Donald Trump. Mirage Resorts announced an equity offering with Goldman Sachs to raise money for this casino. Snaring Goldman, one of the last anti-casino stalwarts on Wall Street, attested to Mirage Resorts' new panache. In fact, Goldman competed aggressively for the assignment, agreeing to buy 16.6 million shares at $25 apiece that it planned to resell. It was an all-time high for Mirage Resorts shares.

Mirage Resorts announced its first-quarter earnings that same week, touting the success of its new resorts. The earnings release, crafted by Dan Lee, carefully avoided discussing net income, which had plummeted to $1.5 million from $38.1 million in the same quarter the previous year due to the huge costs of opening Beau Rivage.

Instead, the release noted that Bellagio had generated $282 million in net revenues (defined as revenues minus the value of room, food, beverage and other comps provided to gamblers). "Mirage Resorts believes this to be the highest quarterly revenues of any casino in Nevada history," the release announced.

Given all the special charges and restated pre-opening expenses, it was hard to tell how things were actually going at Mirage Resorts casinos. But then, no one was pressing for details. Wynn surely knew, however, when he sold the stock to Goldman, that the first heavily subsidized flight to Biloxi from Nashville had carried a single passenger in its 105 seats.

"Nashville was a flop, and we got out," Wynn said later. Airtran officials complained that Mirage Resorts hadn't advertised early enough or heavily enough in target markets. The airline deal cost Beau Rivage $5 million that March alone.

And what about all those wealthy vacationers who were expected to fly in from Houston, Atlanta, and New Orleans?

"If you were in Houston and you consider yourself a stylish person who would go to the Ritz-Carlton, do you know what it is to say, in 1998, 'I'm going to Biloxi for the weekend'?" Feldman asks. "What a jackass I was. In all the conversations I had with people down there, they knew I was a fool the moment I opened my mouth. But no, it would be rude to tell a person. They felt insulted. And by the way, I think they had every reason to."

Beau Rivage's spa therapists struggled to sell standard massages while seaweed body scrubs and ayurvedic therapies from India languished. The ayurvedic Shirodhara treatment, which involves dripping warm, scented oil on the center of the forehead—an area known as the "third eye"—scared some customers.

"You talk about the third eye, and they think you're talking about some kind of devilment," said a therapist named Karen.

Many customers didn't appreciate Beau Rivage's highfalutin' idea of food. Lobster crepes generated complaints from diners who expected a lobster tail. Some servers couldn't pronounce "foie gras."

In Biloxi, Mirage Resorts officials were overwhelmed with workforce problems. Unlike in 1993, when the project was born, unemployment was now at record lows and job-hopping workers streamed from Beau Rivage "like a faucet," said one manager. Workers in Mississippi hadn't learned the ropes working at other casinos on the Strip on their way up to Steve Wynn's place. They were less productive than their Nevada counterparts, and they weren't as loyal to Mirage Resorts.

"If we had known more about Mississippi, if this had been our second hotel instead of our first, we would have staffed even more, because there's less productivity," Wynn told investors in a fall conference call. Such comments insulted Beau Rivage's employees. Shier was forced to apologize in a series of employee meetings.

The situation at Beau Rivage was, in Wynn's own words, "chaos." The first guests waited in ninety-minute valet-parking queues only to arrive at hour-long lines at the front desk.

Shier and Wynn had failed to comprehend local idiosyncrasies. In Las Vegas, gamblers like to park their own cars, so Beau Rivage planned valet service only for hotel guests. But Biloxi customers, spiffed up for an evening on the town, place a high value on handing their car keys to the valets, who were overwhelmed from day one.

The guys at Harrah's would never have overlooked the following point: Mississippi gamblers hate a stingy joint. Avid gamblers like "loose" slots that make frequent payouts in small doses. This feeds people's need for rewards and helps their $40 budget last through the evening. These casino customers also want "comps" like free buffets or show tickets. Beau Rivage's slots weren't as loose as its competitors, and the casino didn't comp as generously.

The Mirage executives even overlooked Southern weather. Shampooing the carpets regularly, something Wynn insisted on in arid Las Vegas, caused them to mildew in humid Biloxi. The carpets had to be replaced. "It was like concentric circles," says Alan Feldman. "We didn't get the South. We didn't get the Gulf. We didn't get Biloxi."

Wynn again visited Beau Rivage a month after its opening, in April 1999. That first morning, the mogul called room service for his routine breakfast: two boxes of Special K cereal, skim milk, one sliced banana, and coffee with Sweet'N Low. He was delivered a bowl of oranges, one box of cereal, and a quart of milk.

"You can imagine the panic that sets in," Wynn said. "If they screw Steve Wynn, what's happening to everyone else? Disaster."

On the second day, Wynn made the order-taker read his exact order back to him. Nevertheless he received two bananas, one box of Special K, cream for coffee, and regular milk. "Now I feel like an idiot," Wynn recalled a few months later. "What am I going to do—have an argument with one of my employees?"

He picked up the phone and asked to speak with the room-service supervisor. But the telephone operator was unable to put him through. "Two separate screwups for the chairman of the board," Wynn said. "It was miserable. My perception was that we've got chaos."

On the third day, room service got the order wrong again. "This time, I called Barry [Shier]," Wynn said. "This is the kind of breakdown that tends to reverberate with your best players."

Maurice Wooden, a veteran of Sheraton Hotels who was running operations at the Golden Nugget, got a call from Shier and Wynn the third week of April. Beau Rivage had troubles, they told him. They flew him in two days later to look the place over. He returned home to Las Vegas, packed his bags, and moved into Beau Rivage, where he expected to live for the next eight months or so, except for the occasional trip home to visit his wife and three-and-a-half-year-old daughter.

Wooden canceled the triple-sheeting in all but the suites—enough to keep a high rating from the American Automobile Association. He ended nightly turn-down service in standard rooms, saving $6 per room per day. He armed parking valets with scripts so they would greet arrivals with a friendly "Welcome to Beau Rivage." He fed restaurant employees the dishes they were serving and taught them how to pronounce "foie gras."

By May, they had replaced every manager in every restaurant, nearly every department head, the assistant front-office manager, the bell captain, and four telephone operators. "I needed to cleanse the place," Barry Shier said. They made the crabcakes bigger and blander, eliminated the lobster crepes and added an 11.5-ounce T-bone steak. To draw local gamblers, they began offering monthly themed dinners and weekly food specials: prime rib on Mondays and all-you-can-eat ribs on Tuesdays.

Soft rock replaced opera in the elevators. The annual flower bill was sliced to $250,000 from $1.1 million. The horticulture department was cut to 28 from 60 employees. Staffing dwindled 20 percent to 3,680 jobs.

Desperate to fill rooms, Beau Rivage advertised special low prices from Florida to Texas—$69 a night and for another $10, tickets to see the resort's struggling Cirque du Soleil show, *Allegria*. (Tickets to *O* at Bellagio were selling for more than $100.)

One honeymooning couple from Tampa paid $238 for airfare and two nights in the hotel for both of them. They were shocked to find how nice it was, given the Motel 6 price. Yet locals still complained of "Las Vegas–style prices."

These prices attracted a different clientele from the kind Wynn was aiming for. Several thousand bathrobes were stolen from hotel rooms in the first month, according to Wooden. The hotel discontinued offering bathrobes in its standard rooms.

To save the hemorrhaging cash that fall, Mirage Resorts began laying off employees in Las Vegas as well. Mirage's corporate offices cut back nightly cleaning to twice-weekly.

Beau Rivage was unintentionally boosting business for its rivals on the Gulf Coast. People gawked at the resort before heading to the smoky, cheap-eats casinos down the road that were reporting record numbers of visitors. Casino revenues on the Gulf Coast rose 43 percent in April 1999 over the previous year, according to the Mississippi State Tax Commission.

Wynn ordered Shier to go live in Biloxi. By September, instead of improving, the hotel's occupancy plummeted perplexingly. One weekend, shortly after the college students had returned to their leafy campuses, nearly three hundred of the resort's 1,780 rooms sat empty. Casinos give away rooms for free to big gamblers. This makes it hard to excuse having more than 5 percent or 10 percent of hotel rooms empty. (The MGM Grand in Las Vegas once reported an occupancy rate of more than 100 percent.)

Shier sat in his office staring at the results: 85 percent occupancy on a Friday night when the casino should have been bursting. He called Bill Yates, the Mississippi construction contractor who built Beau Rivage.

"Bill, what are you doing this weekend?" Shier asked.

"I'm going to the Ole Miss game," Yates replied. "Everybody will be there."

Next, Shier called an old friend, former star quarterback Archie Manning, a Southerner and an Ole Miss graduate.

"Archie, how big is this?" Shier asked, referring to the game.

Manning replied, "It's life."

So Shier became a student of Southern football. He kept college and professional team schedules in his top-right desk drawer and promoted the resort in cities where there wasn't a big game. "I'm feeling my way every month," Shier said that November. "What does Halloween weekend do to you in any other market? Nothing. Here, it's significant. Maybe it's the voodoo. Maybe it's the goblins."

All that fall, Shier and Wynn continued to believe that Beau Rivage would gain its footing as the South's premier gambling resort. "We'll have the triple-sheet back," Shier pledged. "It's personal."

♣ ♦ ♥ ♠

Kirk Kerkorian and his chief casino lieutenants sat around the conference table at the MGM Grand that spring of 1999, discussing their casinos' growth strategy.

The table included MGM Grand's chairman and chief executive,

Terry Lanni, Kerkorian's protégé, Alex Yemenidjian, and the company's new young chief financial officer, Jim Murren.

Murren had left his $2.5-million-a-year job as a Deutsche Bank analyst to join MGM Grand in January 1998. He had left a home in Connecticut and an apartment on Central Park and had accepted a substantial pay cut ($375,000 in salary, plus a bonus and options) to take up a challenge from Yemenidjian, delivered over dinner at Cipriani: "You're a young man, you've done very well. You can be on the sidelines all of your life, or you can get in the game."

Murren and his wife, Heather Hay Murren, then a leading consumer-goods analyst with Merrill Lynch, had recently been planning to check out of the game entirely. They had bought some raw acreage in Costa Rica and planned to move there to raise their young family, barefoot and carefree. But Heather pushed Jim to accept the offer, despite warnings from friends on Wall Street that he would be cleaning up the company's balance sheet in preparation for a sale.

A short time later, Kerkorian related the fable of the hungry alligator. Murren took it as his marching orders to find a way to buy Mirage. "Kirk said very early on that Mirage would be the company we should try to get," Murren recalls.

Murren pushed instead to acquire Harrah's or Station Casinos Inc. Talks with Harrah's went as far as a secretive meeting at MGM Grand's Mansion high-roller complex, which was attended by Lanni, Yemenidjian, and Murren as well as Phil Satre and Colin Reed from Harrah's. The talks did elicit one surprise. Satre pulled Lanni and Murren aside and told them, "The guy you've really got to focus on is Gary [Loveman]. He's a star."

Yemenidjian wasn't interested in buying Harrah's. Stay prepared, he argued, and one day Mirage would come available.

"You're crazy," Murren told him. "Steve Wynn will never let it go."

♣ ♦ ♥ ♠

Beau Rivage faced yet another problem that fall of 1999. Harrah's was opening a casino in the lush nearby city of New Orleans, right next to the French Quarter.

Unlike Wynn, who thought he could bend Biloxi to his will, Harrah's brought in executives who could weave themselves into the city's complex fabric, figuring out the society and politics. Harrah's executives charted New Orleans family trees, studied social clubs, and wined and dined on a nightly basis.

When restaurant and hotel owners complained that the casino would sponge off their businesses, Harrah's was forced to agree not to open restaurants or hotels that would compete with the locals. Imagine a major casino with no flashy limousines, no sumptuous restaurants, and no hotel rooms. In New Orleans, gamblers would have to pay cash at Harrah's 250-seat buffet, or eat at restaurants outside the property. They would have to sleep off the premises at nearby hotels like the stately Windsor Court or at the Hilton or Westin. Even the limos had to be leased from private local companies.

In addition, Harrah's had to guarantee at least $100 million a year in tax payments to the state of Louisiana. Thus strapped, the casino was expected to report losses for at least its first two years of operations, according to an analysis at the time by Bank of America Securities.

Harrah's New Orleans wasn't even allowed to decorate its own facade. That was handled by an eager committee of local residents. To Satre's consternation, they picked works by two local artists, including a neoclassical figure who appeared to be grimacing over an entrance to the casino.

All this was something of a relief to Wynn. "New Orleans Harrah's is going to lack in the resort experience," Shier guessed correctly that fall.

But Phil Satre and Harrah's executives were better poker players than they seemed. The local ownership entity, called JCC Holdings, had made all the concessions and was barred from the hotel, restaurant, and limousine business. But technically, Harrah's Entertainment Inc. was not beholden to JCC's agreements—a detail the Louisiana attorneys hadn't caught. Harrah's top executives were secretly planning to expand onto two adjacent land parcels that the company had purchased. Two hotels were planned, at three hundred to four hundred rooms each. They had even built a large space for a restaurant on the second floor of the casino.

In fact, Harrah's had quickly caught on to the New Orleans style of doing business, then bested the natives at their own game. Harrah's stocked a French Quarter humidor with Cuban cigars to hand around and set up an apartment for entertaining civic leaders late into the night. Company officials went duck hunting and redfish fishing with the city's elite. They hired well-connected New Orleans natives for key jobs and asked them to cut deals with the local gentry. These connections got them discount agreements with nearby hotels, advertising in tourist kiosks, and a turn to host an influential awards event for hotel concierges.

Fred Burford, the president and chief executive of JCC Holdings, at the time said he gained twenty-five pounds and a double chin as he negotiated his way through the city.

Steve Wynn could have used a fellow like him.

chapter fourteen

IMPLOSION

Steve is a real entrepreneur. His ego has gotten to be bigger than this airport.

—Mark Greenberg, investment portfolio manager

ynn conceded he had erred with Beau Rivage.

"God lives in the details," he said one morning with a sigh.

For the first time with any of his casinos, Wynn hadn't even conducted the standard pre-opening pep rally for employees at Beau Rivage. He had left that honor to Shier, whom he now blamed. "Barry Shier dreamt up Beau Rivage," Wynn said.

Having placed Beau Rivage's shortcomings at Shier's feet, Wynn took the long view. "Sometimes you just misfire," Wynn said that fall. "There's plenty of time. It's going to be there forever. The place has never not made money. The question was, how much money would it make?"

This outlook was both correct and fatally wrong. The summer after the Mississippi casino opened, Wynn told investors, "We spent too goddamned much on Beau Rivage." His surprising candor might have been better received had he promised to be more careful in the future. Instead Wynn seemed to imply that overspending was a key to Mirage Resorts' success.

He also seemed wholly unsympathetic to the suffering people who had bought his stock at $20 a share. He wanted investors who could weather a few bumps and hold on for the long run. It didn't seem to occur to Wynn that many were counting on him to help maintain their meager retirement savings or to help finance their own dreams. He may as well have said "Let them eat cake."

On July 1, 1999, just a few weeks after shareholders bid the company's stock up to an all-time high, and after Goldman had bought those 16.6 million shares at $25 each, Wynn warned that Mirage Resorts earnings that quarter would be between 7 and 10 cents per share—roughly a third of what Wall Street analysts had been predicting.

The following day, Mirage shares closed at $15.25—a decline of 25 percent in one month. Finally, Wall Street zeroed in on problems at Bellagio and the Mirage. Wynn's main rivals, MGM Grand and Donald Trump, were happy to help. "Bellagio is soft, but Mirage is dead," Trump crowed on July 2. "First of all, the guy builds funeral parlors. The guy can't see."

MGM Grand's Jim Murren pointed out that MGM Grand casino hosts were seeing mid-level players heading for the Mirage instead of Treasure Island, implying that Mirage was becoming a low-roller joint.

The following week, Wynn addressed a room full of analysts and investors at a Goldman Sachs investor conference. They asked about earnings. Wynn wanted to talk about his next resorts. He was infuriated at their short-term focus on the next ninety days.

"I was really surprised at the extremely low level of intelligence," he said on July 12. "They were dumber than I thought. . . . It was very transparent. Everybody just had angst that the short term wasn't going to be what they thought it would be. . . . Ninety days? What does that tell you about these guys? Excuse the expression, but fuck the market. They're hysterical. I got better things to do with my time. I mean it."

So Wynn went hiking in Sun Valley.

Wynn's hubris was met with sadness by people who knew him well. "I sensed a transformation in Steve. Prior to Bellagio opening, he had his feet on the ground," says Alan Feldman, his spokesman. "He was so stable. He knew that this was the show; we were the guys behind the stage pulling the ropes. When Bellagio opened, he was catapulted into stardom."

Suddenly, Bellagio was the "it girl" in style-conscious magazines like *Vanity Fair* and *Town & Country*. The strategy was working. Check-in lines at Bellagio were full of well-heeled guests in business suits and demure dresses. They had come to see Las Vegas' first real luxury hotel. Wynn began asking Feldman to negotiate for magazine covers or big stories, rather than simply agreeing to be interviewed. "It went way beyond 'Steve Wynn, developer of this hotel.' It was 'Steve Wynn, fine art collector. . . . Steve Wynn, purveyor of fine foods.' It was heady stuff," Feldman says. "He became the public persona. . . . After Bellagio, he became bored with all the mundane stuff."

Wynn wasn't interested in operations problems. He wanted to design his next resort in Atlantic City. In July, as Mirage Resorts stock plummeted, Wynn huddled in his design office at Atlandia.

One afternoon, he was followed through the offices by Bora, one of his German Shepherds, into a vividly lit room fitted with a double-long drafting table and two tall stools. The table was covered with those plans that are called blueprints, despite being printed on large sheets of white paper. Wynn reached for a rack with a couple dozen colored markers. He grabbed a marker, spilling the rest, and impatiently swiped them aside with his forearm. He aimed his struggling eyes at the designs for a new casino resort.

The Atlantic City casino was to be called Le Jardin. Wynn had completed the design five months earlier for a "souped-up Mirage—a tropical hotel with lots of gardens," Wynn said. It would have 1,500 rooms and an estimated cost of $1.35 billion.

"We had renderings. We had models. We were finished," Wynn said.

But Wynn had been unhappy. "I had this thing— I was around the house. I was, uh, uh, uh . . . I didn't know what to do. So Elaine says, why don't you call John Jerde?"

Jerde, an architect who worked in Southern California, had designed the Wynns' home at Shadow Creek as well as Bellagio's low-rise lakefront and other projects. Wynn trusted him. "I think I sent out one of the jets for him," Wynn said.

"What's bothering you is you've got a really nice hotel in a field," Jerde told Wynn. "You've got no sense of place."

So Wynn tore up the "finished" plans and started anew, just as he had after deciding to turn the French Beau Rivage project in Las Vegas into the Italian Bellagio. Le Jardin would become the Trilogy. Aiming for intimacy, Wynn wanted fabulous gardens and three smallish high-rise hotels—one with 230 suites, and two seven-story hotels with 461 rooms each, leaving room on the land for two more hotels later. It would be "very petite, very lovely. It's one hotel masquerading as three hotels," Wynn said happily, seated at his drawing board with the colored pens strewn about.

The age of huge casino resorts was over, Wynn said. He wanted to be in the forefront of a revolution—a return to small and intimate establishments. "If we're right about this, there'll never be another megaresort," he said, looking pleased and excited. "They're too awful. Too big."

♣ ♦ ♥ ♠

So naïve.

A midlevel financial manager at Mirage Resorts—a Mormon fellow, Wynn made a point of saying—notified Wynn one afternoon that Mirage Resorts had been providing financial estimates to Wall Street analysts before the company's earnings were made public.

This practice was common on Wall Street at the time. It enabled the analysts to publish extraordinarily accurate "forecasts" of earnings and to tip off their clients. This helped explain why stocks often traded up with uncanny accuracy shortly before a company released strong earnings—or down shortly before disappointing earnings.

Wynn must have been the last chief executive in America not to know of this wink-wink game, known euphemistically as "giving guidance." It had a great deal to do with how well analysts were paid. Their accurate intelligence, provided ahead of the markets, was worth millions of dollars in salaries and bonuses. Analysts lived in fear of being cut off from the information flow that so richly fed them.

The Mormon fellow correctly pointed out to Steve Wynn that

leaking estimates of earnings per share to analysts technically amounted to illegally trading on insider information. Then, Wynn said, the fellow announced he could no longer work under those circumstances. "I left my office and went down two doors and took a left," Wynn recalled later. That led Wynn directly into Dan Lee's office. Wynn ordered Lee to stop giving "guidance."

Here is the way Wynn describes the scene:

"So I say to Danny Lee, 'You can't do that, man. He's right.' And Dan Lee says to me, 'Hey, uh, you're tipping over the apple cart. You don't want to be doing that. I'm going to object to this.'"

"I'm telling ya, in a public company, an employee brought it to my attention, and he's right. Stop doin' it. And if any of those so-and-so and so-and-so and so-and-sos bitch at ya, send them to me," Wynn countered. "How can they get angry at you if you're obeying the law?"

While he was at it, now that he'd gotten interested in financial reporting, Wynn decided to further cloud the analysts' crystal balls by no longer providing financial results for individual casinos. This made it easier for him to hide the suffering of the Mirage and Beau Rivage.

Wynn was right—ethically and legally. But analysts on Wall Street received this as a giant F-you. Cut off from the golden flow of information, they did what came naturally: They downgraded Mirage Resorts stock. Wynn realized later what he'd brought on himself. "Well, did I get it!" he said. "It was punishment time: 'We'll teach that son of a bitch.'"

Wynn might have predicted the fallout if Dan Lee's access to him hadn't been curtailed since the move into the new offices at Bellagio. "He can be intimidating," Lee said in 2005. "And at the Mirage, the offices were simpler. You'd run into Steve at the copy machine. At Bellagio, getting to Steve was like the opening sequence of *Get Smart*. You had to go through two sets of double doors, even after you were in the luxurious executive area. It was like going to see the Great Oz."

Lee was becoming increasingly distraught over Wynn's spending, and not just on art. He told Wynn that the Walt Disney Company had two planes, compared to Mirage Resorts' four. The company turned down an offer of $28 million for the MD-87, the plane that

Elaine Wynn preferred to use when flying the family to Sun Valley, according to people familiar with the planes and their operations.

"For months, I'd been telling him we needed to do something," Lee said in a 2005 interview. "He had to cut costs. The art was out of hand."

Mirage's board was made up of the Wynns—Steve, Elaine, and Kenny—Mirage insiders, and several of the Wynns' friends, including Ron Popeil, the Veg-O-Matic mogul, and Melvin Wolzinger, a Las Vegas casino operator who had joined the board in 1973 along with Wynn. There was also George Mason—Kirk Kerkorian's good friend and stockbroker.

According to the company's own proxy statement filed annually with the SEC, this friendly board allowed Wynn to decide his own salary, bonus, and stock options, as well as those of his top executives. "[Wynn's] recommendations in each case were based on his subjective evaluation of each officer's [including his own] contribution to the Company and the level of compensation necessary to adequately motivate and reward the officer," the proxy said.

Little wonder that Wynn was one of the highest-paid chief executives in America, even as his company suffered from overspending and Wall Street bumbling. Yet so much heat was being generated by Wynn's art-buying that even this board of directors began to worry.

"The board members didn't want to say anything to Steve and get in trouble," says one senior Mirage executive at the time. "Some of the board members went to Dan, and he kind of got caught as the fall guy. . . . Dan was under a lot of pressure. Beau Rivage was flailing in the wind, the stock price was down."

Wynn's sales of his art to Bellagio raised questions about whether he was profiting at the company's expense. Before a September board meeting, a member of the board's audit committee asked Dan Lee about the people who were appraising Bellagio's art. Lee's response, distributed to the entire board, came in the form of a photocopy of a two-year-old article in the *New York Times*. It raised questions about the values being paid for paintings by art dealers in general.

Later that Thursday, September 2, Lee was in his office, meeting with Robin Farley, an analyst from Deutsche Bank, when his phone rang. It was Wynn, screaming so loudly that Farley could hear. Wynn was furious that he hadn't been warned. Wynn later stomped into Lee's office. "You don't have to work here anymore if you don't want to," he announced, according to Lee. Then he stomped back out.

Bobby Baldwin heard this stomping back and forth from his office—a plush sanctum much like Wynn's, only smaller. "Dan Lee is a wonderful character. He's kind of an exotic bird," Baldwin says. "You didn't always like what he said, and you didn't always know what he was talking about."

Wynn called Baldwin that day for "a last-minute gut check," Baldwin says. "Have you seen this?" Wynn asked, brandishing Lee's statement.

"No," Baldwin responded.

Wynn shot the article across his desk. "Take a look at this," he said.

Baldwin probably could have saved Lee's job at that point, but he chose not to.

"Do what you need to do," Baldwin says he advised Wynn. In two hours, Lee was gone. "Steve does not equivocate," Baldwin says. "When he's done with you, he's done."

It took a few days to negotiate Lee's stock options. He wisely wanted to keep them.

Time would tell, ultimately, that Wynn was his own victim that day, not Baldwin or Lee, whose careers would benefit from Lee's firing.

Wynn immediately entrusted Bobby Baldwin with the CFO job in the interim until he could hire someone better qualified. Baldwin was virtually unknown on Wall Street and lacked credentials and contacts to raise money there. "If they don't know Bobby, they're not worth knowing," Wynn blustered.

Investors responded to Lee's departure from Mirage Resorts with abject shock and grief. Lee had been responsible for Mirage's major land transactions, and he had restructured the company financially. "This is sad to see," said Ken Londoner, chief executive of the hedge fund Red Coat Capital, the day the news got out. "This is an industry leader going through some tough times. Dan Lee will be missed."

"He was as big an asset to Mirage from the financial end as Steve Wynn was to the creative side," said Jason Ader, still with Bear Stearns at the time. "It's a huge loss overall."

Curiously, despite the strong sentiment among investors that Lee's departure was bad news, the company's stock didn't spin into a free fall that day. On September 8, the first chance investors had to trade on the news, 11.4 million Mirage shares were traded—at least six times the normal volume, at around $12 a share. Someone was out there buying Mirage shares as fast as frightened investors could sell them. There can be little doubt that this person was Kirk Kerkorian, the hungry alligator.

Kerkorian later divulged that he had bought about ten million shares of Mirage at an average of $12 per share. Kerkorian has never revealed exactly when he bought the shares. But given the narrow window of time that Mirage shares traded at that price, it's clear that Kerkorian was buying like mad on the news of Lee's departure.

At about that same time, Kerkorian asked Terry Lanni, MGM Grand's chairman and chief executive, a seemingly casual question: "What do you think of Mirage?"

"Well, I don't think Wynn would ever let it go," Lanni replied.

Wynn soon heard that Kerkorian had taken a stake in Mirage. His conclusion was that Kerkorian was preparing for a takeover—much the same way he had done a few years earlier at Chrysler. Wynn attended a political fund-raiser at the MGM Grand's Mansion the following Wednesday. Kerkorian was there too, and Wynn marched over for a chat. According to Wynn and two witnesses, their exchange went like this:

"I have no interest in having you take over my company," Wynn told Kerkorian.

"How can you not buy the stock at that price?" Kerkorian asked Wynn.

"Are we going to do something unfriendly here?" Wynn asked.

"Absolutely not," Kerkorian responded.

Kerkorian stepped away, walking over to Terry Lanni, who had overheard the conversation from about three feet away.

"Steve isn't interested," Kerkorian said. "I'm just going to sell my stock."

"It was very clear to him that he was not a welcome investor," says a person close to Kerkorian. "He was surprised at how strong the reaction was."

Hours after his conversation with Kerkorian, Wynn wanted this information broadcast to the world. "I asked him about it today," Wynn said, recalling their long-ago games of tennis when Wynn had first come to Las Vegas. "He's not putting the stock in play. We used to be tennis partners."

Still, this is the moment when Wynn's and Kerkorian's relationship turns from rivalry into a deadly race to the finish. Wynn was ever more on the defensive, with Kerkorian more in control of his stock price—and Wynn's personal wealth—than Wynn himself.

When Kerkorian's stock purchases were revealed in a tiny news brief in *The Wall Street Journal* the following day, September 16, Mirage Resorts' stock price spun upward to $15 a share. Bear Stearns' Jason Ader upgraded the company's stock. He said something was bound to happen now, if an investor of Kerkorian's caliber was involved. He didn't know that Kerkorian had decided to sell his Mirage shares.

♣ ♦ ♥ ♠

Among Kerkorian's devotees, there is no one who has been more faithful than Alex Yemenidjian. His loyalty to Kerkorian was akin to a Doberman pinscher.

If Yemenidjian were a movie star—and he has the jaw and cheekbones for it—he could play the fastidious dictator with the flinty eyes. When Kerkorian found him, Yemenidjian was a Los Angeles tax accountant, married to his eighth-grade sweetheart. Yemenidjian and Kerkorian bonded through their Armenian heritage. Yemenidjian's Armenian parents had come to California by way of Argentina.

Yemenidjian's bachelor's degree in business administration and accounting was awarded by California State University, Northridge. He then earned a master's degree in business taxation from the University of Southern California. He was a partner in an accounting firm when Kerkorian invited Yemenidjian to be his accountant in 1989.

Thereafter, his capable but unspectacular career took on aspects of a fairy tale. Despite not making a success of Kerkorian's bid for control of Chrysler Corp., Yemenidjian landed at the MGM Grand. There, he obsessed on renovating the place. He worked all hours and rode an exercise bike for several more hours every day, dieting on cooked egg whites until his body appeared skeletal under the drapery of his custom haberdashery. He designed his own starched white shirt collars—a peculiar pairing of overlapping arcs that hide the knot of his ties.

Yemenidjian, part of Kerkorian's coveted Saturday tennis circle, considered himself the son the billionaire never had.

In April 1999, Kerkorian moved Yemenidjian to Los Angeles, making him chairman of the Metro-Goldwyn-Mayer film studios. Yemenidjian remained employed as MGM Grand's president. This put Kerkorian's former accountant knee to knee with Sharon Stone to arrange the details of her appearance in *Basic Instinct 2*. (Yemenidjian was captivated by her legs during one meeting in his office—could not stop thinking about *that scene* in the original movie.)

Kerkorian might prefer a sandwich at his desk, but Yemenidjian was soon being seated at his very own table in the well-known courtyard at Spago's. Wolfgang Puck, the celebrity chef, would stop by Yemenidjian's table to say hello. One of Yemenidjian's peculiar habits, for a time, was to carry in his jacket pocket a jar of Lawry's seasoned salt, which he sprinkled on almost everything. Puck, on one occasion, picked up the small jar and turned it over, reading the label with an expression of puzzled amusement. The chef handed the jar back to Yemenidjian and offered to procure some Lawry's seasoned salt and to provide it in the future "in a nice shaker" for Yemenidjian.

Kerkorian and Yemenidjian appreciated the same things about the film and casino industries, the protégé said. As investments, they were more fun than raising corn. Las Vegas and Hollywood for Kerkorian were "the sizzle on the steak," Yemenidjian said. "And the women. Oh, the women," he added.

Yemenidjian's polar opposite was Terry Lanni, who had interviewed for a job with Kerkorian by telling him that the MGM Grand was poorly designed. Lanni is a conservative sort of fellow, both politically and socially. He says, quite seriously, that he considers Southern California to be practically a socialist state. He once told a Volvo-driving friend that he considers Volvo automobiles to be Communist vehicles.

Lanni's sense of humor is self-consciously self-deprecating. He raises thoroughbred horses as a pastime, for instance, and says, "Unfortunately, I run faster than my horses." (That is actually not true. At the moment he made this joke, Lanni was part owner of Sinister Minister, a bay colt who broke from the starting gate and easily won the Blue Grass Stakes at the blueblood Keeneland Race Course in Kentucky, collected $450,000, and went on to run in the Kentucky Derby in 2006.)

Early in his career, Lanni worked for Gerald Ford's campaign. He forged close ties with Ronald and Nancy Reagan—a happenstance that would put him at Reagan's funeral many years later during a crucial Vegas moment. Lanni also once worked for the conglomerate Republic Corporation. One of his responsibilities as Republic's chief financial officer was to attend the annual Canton (China) trade show, buying home-improvement products to sell in the United States. After joining Caesars in 1977, Lanni found that his social mobility was limited. He was no longer eligible for membership at certain clubs, such as the Los Angeles Country Club, where the casino business was considered less *nice* than Hollywood.

But Lanni did find that his contacts from the Canton trade show were an invaluable source of custom for Caesars. The Chinese, for reasons no one is able to fully explain, have a cultural penchant for gambling—and they are, as a whole, the world's most avid gamblers. Lanni began bringing his Chinese contacts to Las Vegas. These powerful customers, along with his organizational and financial acumen, made Lanni a very valuable casino asset.

In October 1999—in the midst of Wynn's turmoil—Lanni announced he was resigning as MGM Grand's chairman and chief executive to spend more time with his family in Pasadena. He said he also wanted to get involved with the Internet revolution, perhaps head an online gambling company. People close to the executives said that Lanni was sick of both the weekly commute from Los Angeles and his ongoing rivalry with Yemenidjian.

Two months later, Lanni changed his mind and agreed to stay on as chairman. His decision coincided with Yemenidjian's resignation as president of MGM Grand. Yemenidjian said he needed to focus full-time on the movie studio.

♣ ◆ ♥ ♠

As Lanni was resigning, Wynn was managing to further humiliate Goldman Sachs, which had been unable to unload many of the 16.6 million shares they had bought that spring. Wynn agreed to buy back at $15 about a third of the shares he'd sold to Goldman for $25.

Goldman lost more than $24 million that day—and possibly another $25 million on the other ten million shares the bank had bought, says one of Goldman's bankers who had worked on the deal. "The goal was we'd sell it to the marketplace at a higher price," the banker says. "We lost a pretty good deal of money on that shortly after we bought it."

With Dan Lee gone, the former poker player Bobby Baldwin displayed an almost comical lack of understanding of Wall Street—or even in fulfilling the role of CFO. During an interview on October 21, Baldwin confided "being a CFO takes about one and a half hours" out of his day. The rest, he said, he spent running Bellagio.

So Wynn was left to handle Mirage's banking business himself. When he called on bankers, the reception was frigid. One senior banker, the Goldman Sachs deal still in his mind, said, "He wanted me to jump. And I thought, you know, the last time I *didn't* jump for him, it saved me a hundred and forty-two million. Morgan [Stanley] won't talk to him. Goldman won't talk to him."

About a month after Lee's departure, Wynn appeared to realize he needed to cater to analysts. He agreed to again provide financial information on the company's individual casinos. Then he banned small investors from participating in the quarterly earnings conference call. This move would a few years later become illegal under the federal Regulation Full Disclosure law, because it gave large investors and analysts a considerable advantage in trading on any news revealed during the call.

The secrecy, piled on top of the other credibility issues, further convinced Wall Street that Mirage Resorts was spinning out of control. Wynn cemented this belief by participating in the company's earnings conference call one day. He was grumpy, short-tempered. In no mood to be questioned, he misbehaved. When Deutsche Bank analyst Robin Farley asked for an explanation in the "shortfall" in earnings compared with expectations, Wynn responded testily, "What shortfall are you talking about, honey?"

Then Baldwin iced the whole cake when an analyst pressed for an indication of Mirage Resorts' business strength in the fourth quarter. "I would ignore the fourth quarter," Baldwin blithely suggested. "Too difficult to forecast." It was tantamount to telling a blackjack player to ignore the dealer's hand.

Mirage shares traded down 8 percent in a steep slide after that day's call.

Wynn complained to the analysts' bosses about the barrage of tormenting criticism. One of these bosses was Ace Greenberg, the legendary chief executive of Bear Stearns, where analyst Jason Ader had been harshly critical of Wynn's management and behavior. Greenberg didn't tell Ader to shut up, but he cautioned him, according to Ader.

"Hope you're right, kiddo," Greenberg said.

chapter fifteen

MISS SPECTACULAR

*Here's a guy who is an artist. It's like Mozart [sic] composing, who
can't hear. Everything he does is visual—and he can't see! . . . How
can he relate to these guys who care about whether he earns a penny
or two?*

—RON BARON, MIRAGE INVESTOR

"I had a wonderful day yesterday," Steve Wynn said, sounding
pleased and a little giddy—the way he behaves when he's feeling
creatively satisfied. "Elaine and Sandy and Eydie Gormé and I
were dancing around."

He burst into a snippet of song.

"Sandy" was Sandy Gallin, a Los Angeles talent manager often
mentioned in the press as a member of the so-called Velvet Mafia.
This was a group of friends, some gay (but not all), who hold sway in
Hollywood. Other supposed members of the Velvet Mafia are David
Geffen, the music producer, and Barry Diller, the media mogul.

"That whole gang of the gay guys—they always stick together,
really, really, really," Wynn said. "And they're all wonderful."

Barry Diller, who is married to the designer Diane von Fursten-
berg, put Wynn together with Gallin after Wynn insisted he wanted
to "redefine the entertainment industry" in Las Vegas. "There's nothing they do in New York that we can't do just as well here," Wynn
said.

Wynn was aware that he had changed the quality of entertainment in Las Vegas, with Cirque du Soleil.

Wynn was bent on bringing something even newer to the entertainment scene, and of course, he looked to his own interests for inspiration. He wanted to produce live theater. He would create a stable of his own Broadway-style productions for Mirage casinos in Las Vegas, Mississippi, and, soon, Atlantic City—maybe even take his shows on the road. He talked about establishing a movie and television company. He formed a new subsidiary, Mirage Entertainment & Sports Inc.

In June, he hired Sandy Gallin to run this new subsidiary. Gallin was once Dolly Parton's manager, and he helped put the Beatles on *The Ed Sullivan Show* in the 1960s. He has had an encyclopedia of famous clients, many of them aging. Among them were Richard Pryor, Michael Jackson, Neil Diamond, Cher, Barbra Streisand, and Mariah Carey. He has produced television shows, including *Buffy the Vampire Slayer,* and a couple dozen movies. He has won an Academy Award, two Grammys, and four Cable ACE Awards. The *Hollywood Reporter* called him one of Tinsel Town's top powerbrokers.

Gallin looks weirdly like Steve Wynn. It's something about the dyed-black hair, the strange cosmetic tautness, the visible hunger for attention. Wynn was so enthusiastic about Gallin that he agreed to pay his new entertainment guru more than he paid his right hand, Bobby Baldwin. Gallin ditched everything he'd built in Hollywood for a seven-year contract at Mirage Resorts worth $2.5 million a year in salary and bonus. Gallin promised to relocate to Las Vegas from Los Angeles; he turned his embattled talent agency, Gallin-Morey Associates, over to his partner Jim Morey; and he folded the production company, Sandollar Productions, that he ran with Dolly Parton.

Las Vegas entertainment in the late 1990s was like a New Orleans funeral—diverting, but sad nonetheless. The place was a pasture for has-been entertainers. Tony Orlando, Three Dog Night, and scores of former stars eked out the last days of their careers in the city's theaters and lounges. David Cassidy had a long run at the MGM Grand—a job that would later be taken by Rick Springfield, another former teen wonder. Andrew Lloyd Webber's musical *Starlight Express* had just died an ugly death at the Las Vegas Hilton.

There were entertainers, such as the impressionist Danny Gans and the magician Lance Burton, who made excellent livings performing full-time in Las Vegas, and there were a multitude of salty comedy troupes and celebrity imitators. There were even a few long-lived remains from Las Vegas's glory years, like the *Folies Bergere* floor show at the Tropicana. Mirage Resorts had the best shows in town: Cirque du Soleil at Treasure Island and *Siegfried & Roy* at the Mirage.

Gallin did not make himself popular among his new colleagues. He was widely thought to be "an absolute idiot" who said little during key meetings and neglected important details, says Dan Lee, who sat through many of them.

For a part of Bellagio's opening festivities, at Gallin's direction, Mirage Resorts hired a philharmonic orchestra and arrayed them behind the fountains to accompany the dancing waters. It turned out that the sound wouldn't carry over the noise of the splashing. The musicians were told to do the orchestral equivalent of a lip-synch, Lee says.

So perhaps it shouldn't have been surprising that a year later, Mirage Resorts didn't have a lot to show for Gallin's costly presence. He still hadn't made the move to Las Vegas, and there was no stable of theatrical shows or television and movie deals in the works. There was one musical, and Wynn had cut a deal to bring the impersonator Danny Gans to the Mirage from the Rio.

One evening in late September 1999 Gallin joined the Wynns for dinner in Las Vegas. There, Wynn accepted Gallin's resignation—just three weeks after he had fired Dan Lee. "I'll just say you didn't want to spend that much time in Las Vegas and you'll stay with Mirage Resorts in a consulting, advisory capacity and you're still part of the Mirage Resorts family. And that's all true, isn't it?" Wynn said, according to Gallin.

It's a sign that Wynn was trying to clean up his company, but it looked like another failure at the time, exaggerated by Lee's disappearance and that of another Mirage Resorts stalwart—advertising head John Schadler, whose sudden departure was startlingly similar to Lee's.

At first, Gallin and Wynn kept up the pretense that it was a friendly parting from a successful relationship. "It really was a reevaluation of my life," Gallin said a day later. "All my friends and family are in New York and L.A. Steve wanted me to be by his side to do all the entertainment and to help him with the advertising and the public relations, and I just couldn't make that commitment. I thought, 'I don't need the money. And I should really be in a place where I'm really happy.'"

"I lost Sandy Gallin. It's murder," Wynn said the day of Gallin's departure. "Elaine and I are so depressed."

But Wynn seemed to recover from his depression with alacrity. "I need somebody different than him, actually," Wynn continued cheerily. "I need a really serious production manager. A schedules guy. A shopping guy. Or a girl, for that matter. I don't need a deal maker. I've met everybody in show business now."

He wanted to pay "much less money" and find someone willing to live in Las Vegas. "We gotta find a guy," he continued. "Or a girl. It might be a woman. You never know—they're just as good."

The most important thing to come of Gallin's short tenure was Wynn's introduction to Jerry Herman, the composer of the musical that Mirage Resorts had in the works.

When you think of Herman, you think "Hellooo, Dolly." He composed the music and lyrics for *Hello, Dolly!; Mame;* and *La Cage aux Folles*. He has won Grammy and Tony Awards.

Wynn hired him to create an original Broadway-style production for the Mirage: *Miss Spectacular.* They hoped it would open in 2001, around the same time that Siegfried & Roy's long contract was due to run out. "Steve called me," Herman said. "He said, 'I have the most beautiful hotel in Las Vegas. I have the best restaurants. I have my own art collection, and I have Cirque du Soleil. But the only thing I don't have is a Jerry Herman musical.' And I said, well, anyone who talks to me like that can have anything they want."

Miss Spectacular is an old-fashioned musical. It is a love story about a simple girl named Sarah Jane Hotchkiss from South Bend, Indiana, who wants to be a star. Her family and friends tell her to forget it, but she enters a contest to be a spokeswoman for the Hotel Spectacular in Las Vegas. Her daydreams become the show's musical numbers, two of which are cued by the sound of wins on slot machines.

In the finale, Sarah Jane chooses her boyfriend, Charlie, over Las Vegas, and they head for the hotel's wedding chapel. She pulls the lever of a slot machine and coins jingle, turning her wedding into a glitzy spectacle. It was big, it was optimistic, and it was a fairy tale. Steve Wynn fell in love with it.

Herman believed the role of Sarah Jane was grand enough for a superstar. But in the same way that Wynn liked to own all his restaurants and shops, Wynn wanted to create his own superstar by hiring an ingénue.

Before casting it, they decided to record a concept album with the music Herman had composed, performed by a collection of stars. They included Steve Lawrence, Christine Baranski, Michael Feinstein, and Faith Prince.

On the first Friday of October, the Wynns and their daughter Kevyn met Jerry Herman at the vine-covered O'Henry Sound Studios in Burbank, California. A full orchestra was working on the score in the big room, conducted by Don Pippin, another Tony Award winner. Larry Blank, another big name on Broadway, was responsible for the orchestrations and arrangements.

Herman sparkled with joy. He is a tiny, slightly built, gentle man. He looks frail and a bit bent—as though the upper half of his body is perpetually seated at a piano. Born in 1933, he is a man of his generation. "My boy makes me cookies," he said of a valet. Herman's reddish hair was carefully groomed and that day, he wore a black shirt with a gray belt.

Herman's somber presentation contrasted with that of Wynn, who wore a yellow silk shirt with short sleeves and a Chinese collar over black pants and a pair of black suede shoes.

Wynn pointed to Baranski, who was recording in a small studio room. "She sings in that room alone," Wynn stage-whispered. "And then later we can add twenty people singing. Is this fun or what?"

As Baranski belted out Herman's lyrics to "I Wanna Live Each Night," Wynn and Herman told the story of Miss Spectacular. They were giggly. "There's a little wink-wink irony," Wynn said. "It's meant to let people escape for the ninety minutes they're in the theater. We want people to laugh. We want people to get a little catch in their throats. And we want them to walk out humming."

"I have never had so much fun in my life," Herman said adoringly. "I love this man. Because we have the same sensibilities. We never grew up."

Wynn interrupted his composer. Baranski hadn't nailed it, in his opinion. "Jerry, Jerry," Wynn said, "when she sang that line about the crisis, she sang it, but she didn't interpret it. It's about *sex.* She's gotta chew on it."

Wynn almost did *West Side Story* at the Mirage. Then he decided he needed an original show that he could own and use as he deemed fit. Wynn and Herman were slipping marketing messages into the lyrics of *Miss Spectacular.*

"Here comes a little pitch," Wynn whispered as Baranski continued and one pitch for his casinos followed another:

"Come see a fabulous art collection. . . . "

In another song, Baranski sang a line of Herman's that referred to the jeweler Cartier.

"They tell me I look smashing. My Cartier necklace is free."

Wynn pointed out that Bellagio had a Tiffany store, but no Cartier. Herman asked the singer to come back and sing "Tiffany" into the mike, so they could mix it in later.

" 'Cartier' sings better to me," Herman interjected. They discussed it and agreed that if Herman didn't like "Tiffany," he could restore "Cartier."

"It was a cute thing," Wynn said with a shrug. "The payoff for all of this, besides the fun, is its entertainment."

He then turned to singer-actress Faith Prince, who was also there to record a song. "This is the most fun I've had in twenty-six and a half years on the job," Wynn said with a grin.

"Honey," replied Prince, tapping her chest. "You and me both."

"This is like spittin' and hittin' the floor," Wynn continued. "That's how easy this show's gonna be in Las Vegas."

Prince, a handsome actress in her early forties, confided that she was dying to play the lead in *Miss Spectacular,* even though it would mean living in Las Vegas. "I'm a New York girl," she said wistfully. "I should have been born thirty years earlier. No one is creating this stuff."

Later, Wynn whispered out of her earshot. Prince had no chance, he said. "Too old."

Wynn and Herman went into the studio with Pippin and the fifty-four-piece orchestra and Wynn donned a headset and sat on a tall stool. Outside in the control room, a crew of sixteen munched on bagels, cheese, and fruit and drank coffee.

The orchestra worked through *Miss Spectacular*'s overture. Herman got tears in his eyes. When the orchestra launched into a love song, Herman and Wynn sat side-by-side holding hands. Herman's eyes were closed. "This song is perfect," Wynn said, and Herman echoed, "It's perfect."

Wynn said he wanted to understand the music, so he got a lesson from the master. Pippin explained, "There are thirty-four lines, one bar for each line. . . ."

In the middle of recording the finale, Wynn's cell phone rang discordantly. The orchestra waited while Wynn chatted, showing no sign of embarrassment. When the call was over, Pippin raised his arms and called out, "One more time, without the cell phone."

"Stevie finally has his own musical," Elaine Wynn said, giving her husband a hug. "I think this is worth half a cent on the share."

Mirage had 190 million shares outstanding. That put the show's price tag at $95 million.

Wynn confided that he was two-timing *Miss Spectacular.* He and Elaine had been to London to see *Mamma Mia!,* a musical set to the music of the Swedish pop group ABBA. He was considering adapting *Mamma Mia!* for Las Vegas. That meant reducing the show to the shortened attention span of a gambler or conventioneer who had a lot of partying, eating, shopping, and wagering to fit into a few days in Vegas.

As they headed out of the Burbank recording studio, Elaine wondered if *Miss Spectacular* could win a Tony Award. It couldn't, since Las Vegas isn't Broadway.

"We'll make our own awards," Wynn said with a grin. "The Carmine Award. No, the Bugsy Awards." He pretended to give an acceptance speech by an actress who had won many theatrical awards: "But my Bugsy means the most!"

"What's next?" Elaine Wynn asked her husband.

"Schmilken," he replied. "Schmilken. Schmilken."

And they headed off to a late lunch with their friend Michael Milken.

♣ ♦ ♥ ♠

As if he didn't have enough troubles already, Wynn took *Miss Spectacular* on the road long before she was ready.

He invited Joe Coccimiglio, the analyst who had compared the Bellagio to *Titanic* and *Waterworld*, to fly from New York to Las Vegas on the sleek Mirage Gulfstream jet.

This was heady stuff. Before Dan Lee had left, analysts rarely had access to "Mr. Wynn." On the plane, Coccimiglio asked if they might become more familiar. "I asked him if I could call him Steve, and he said it was fine," he said a few weeks later. "That was the highlight of my career," Coccimiglio gushed. "For five hours you just feel completely at ease with him."

Wynn spent an hour of the flight giving the analyst the full pitch on *Miss Spectacular*. He played the music and sang along with the songs. "It was a little corny, but I kinda like that stuff," said Coccimiglio. "I think it has enormous potential to be a crowd draw."

Coccimiglio was planning to come out as gay—an unheard-of move on Wall Street, where social attitudes haven't moved forward much since 1960. He introduced Wynn to Ken, his partner since 1986. Wynn admired the courage involved in being forthright. Wynn wanted to offer Coccimiglio a job as his chief financial officer. But Coccimiglio was finished with Wall Street and its environs.

"It was hard to be gay on Wall Street," he said several years later.

"At Bellagio's opening, I went down to the party and Ken stayed up in the room. I couldn't take him to the party with Dan Lee and Steve Wynn and all those guys."

Coccimiglio stunned his colleagues and clients the following June by broadcasting a letter announcing that he was gay. "I knew I was leaving, so it wasn't brave," he said later. He resigned his job shortly thereafter.

Coccimiglio came away from that flight with the sense that Wynn had "got the message about Bellagio and Beau Rivage going over budget." The new Atlantic City project would come in on budget at about $1 billion, he felt sure.

Given this extraordinary level of access, Coccimiglio tentatively suggested that Wynn demonstrate his faith in Mirage Resorts after his sales of stock. He suggested that Wynn consider selling his art and using the proceeds to buy back stock in Mirage Resorts. "He really bit my head off on that one," Coccimiglio said. "He thinks he has the right to spend money on a personal basis, and he gets a great deal of personal satisfaction out of it."

♣ ♦ ♥ ♠

Out of the frying pan and into the fire.

Wynn agreed to be keynote speaker for a Deutsche Bank Alex Brown conference about a month after the recording session for *Miss Spectacular.* This was one of those duties that Dan Lee used to handle.

These conferences amount to cattle calls for corporate chief financial officers to market their stocks before a room full of an investment bank's clients. Typically, each company gets thirty minutes to present in a day that's broken up with lunch and a keynote speaker.

Jim Murren, president and chief financial officer of Kerkorian's MGM Grand, was in New York to present at the same conference. Murren took advantage of his trip to the city to do some secretive due-diligence fact finding on Mirage Resorts.

Murren stopped in at the company's marketing office and went by the Wynns' Upper East Side apartment building, where he spoke with the doorman. "Is this where Steve Wynn lives?" Murren asked.

"He said, 'Yeah'—and of course it wasn't true," Murren says. "Mirage Resorts owned that apartment." Typically, a company-owned apartment would be available for corporate use—and not be the home of a single executive.

Steve Wynn strode into the New York Palace Hotel around noon on Tuesday, November 9, 1999. At twelve thirty, the mogul began a riveting half-hour history of his role in Las Vegas's renaissance. Then he told the audience of analysts and investors about his plans for entertainment and about *Miss Spectacular* and the 1,800-seat theater he planned to build for his very own "Broadway" show.

"I know all of you measure things in charts and graphs, but that's not how I look at this industry," he told the room full of three hundred investors, according to one attendee. He didn't acknowledge the company's recent troubles. He didn't discuss the cost cuts or other efforts he was making to fix them.

Instead, Wynn went visionary. He brought out a sound system.

And, just as he had been doing for months, he played several songs from *Miss Spectacular*. Steve Wynn being Steve Wynn, he didn't just stand dumbly while the music played. He hammed it up. He sang along. He closed his eyes and swayed.

Unfortunately, this was a room full of conformist Wall Street types who didn't know Steve Wynn. Given his vision problems, one person there says Wynn's swaying with eyes closed looked "like Stevie Wonder."

"People were looking around the room like, 'This guy has completely lost his marbles,'" said one of the corporate presenters.

Someone called the *New York Post*.

The next day's headline on the *Post*'s Page Six gossip column read:

WARBLING WYNN SHOCKS WALL ST.

Page Six is an institution. (It doesn't always appear on page six—on that day, it actually appeared on page eight of the paper.) It's the kind of column that gets read early by a broad array of people, its reach extending far beyond New Yorkers who buy the *Post* each day.

What readers of Page Six learned on November 10, 1999, was that witnesses to Wynn's lip-synching raced from the room to call in their sell orders on Mirage Resorts stock.

Yet, as at the time that Dan Lee was fired, somebody thought Mirage shares were worth buying that day. The *Post* item ended by noting that "If Wynn's performance yesterday did trigger some sell orders, the stock didn't suffer in the long run. It dipped after he stopped singing, but it recovered to finish 12 cents up on the day at $13.625."

People back at Mirage Resorts in Las Vegas didn't perceive a threat. The stock was fine and besides, Wynn's performance didn't strike anyone in Las Vegas as particularly noteworthy.

"My thought was that he did nothing at that conference that he had not done at countless meetings in the past," says Alan Feldman, then Mirage's head of communications. "The first time I heard about it, it appeared on Page Six in the *New York Post*. I almost never take something seriously in the *New York Post*. I didn't realize it had legs for several weeks. Plus, it sounded to us just like more of the same old Steve—no big deal."

But Wynn's performance did have legs.

Dan Lee by that time had moved to Seattle for a job as chief financial officer of HomeGrocer.com, a start-up Internet grocer. "I was at my office in Seattle, trying to get HomeGrocer off the ground," Lee later recalled. "Suddenly, my phone was ringing off the hook. People were saying, 'You're not going to believe it—Steve was singing!'

"I was like, 'So?'" Lee said.

Wynn had also sung along with *Miss Spectacular* for forty-five minutes at a commercial bank meeting at the end of October, according to someone involved. But that one hadn't gotten back to the guys at MGM Grand.

What Feldman and Wynn didn't realize was that Kerkorian's team recognized an Achilles heel when they saw one. They let it slip that day that Kerkorian had sold his 4.9 percent stake in Mirage Resorts—though he had actually sold the ten million shares weeks earlier.

On the day that the *Post* item appeared, Jason Ader, the casino industry's leading analyst, downgraded Mirage Resorts' shares to "neutral." It was a bugle call to investors to sell their shares.

"We had viewed [Kerkorian's] investment as a potential catalyst for the stock, as Mr. Kerkorian is a brilliant investor who does not sit idly while a stock price languishes," Ader wrote to Bear Stearns clients.

"Separately, we are concerned about reports of erratic behavior by Mirage chairman Steve Wynn at an investment conference in New York on Tuesday, November 9, and little evidence that the company is focused on creating shareholder value."

Mirage shares fell to $12.50 that day.

The Mirage Resorts team was blindsided. "There was an enormous overreaction to whatever happened at that meeting," Feldman says. "[Steve] was not losing it. . . . I still feel guilty that I didn't react more aggressively [to counter the adverse publicity]. I feel as though I failed him."

Thereafter, Wynn's troubles multiplied like Job's.

Wynn hopped onto the company's fourth-quarter conference call the following January, thrilled that his company had met Wall Street's expectations for the quarter. He expected a warm reception, given the solid performance. Within moments, he boasted that his cost of capital, the effective interest rate his company was paying, was "six point five percent, give or take, depending on what Mr. Volcker's been doing lately."

As anyone on Wall Street knew, Paul Volcker's run as chairman of the Federal Reserve had ended more than a decade earlier in 1987. Wynn clearly meant to refer to Alan Greenspan. His slip of the tongue wasn't as weird as it sounded: He sat on a think-tank board with Mr. Volcker and saw him regularly.

But the erroneous reference to Volcker raised questions among some investors about his competence. Wynn's eye disease doesn't affect mental capacity, but not everyone understood that. One major Boston-area investment-fund manager ranted, "Did you hear that conference call? Paul Volcker? Hello? I've decided I want to live in his world. It must be a beautiful place. I mean, whooaaa. . . . He clearly doesn't possess all the skills necessary to run the thing by himself. . . . The fear is that he doesn't allocate the capital in a blood-less way instead of worrying about where the flower beds go."

Wynn, without anyone to protect him from Wall Street, recoiled.

"The market is hopelessly short-term," he complained in a sad in-terview. "They don't get it. I wish I could do it without them."

chapter sixteen

CHOMP

It's the deals. It's the chase—when it's a woman or a deal.

—ALEX YEMENIDJIAN

Kirk Kerkorian was watching the big bait float by.

As Mirage's share price tumbled to less than the company's assets were worth, Kerkorian asked his forces to consider a takeover. His attorneys at Christensen, Miller, Fink, Jacobs, Glaser, Weil & Shapiro worked out a plan that would enable him to take control of the company without alerting Wynn, according to several people familiar with the plan.

The attorneys proposed acquiring a controlling stake in Mirage Resorts stock through an investment bank that would hold title to the shares. There would be an agreement that MGM or Kerkorian could buy the shares from the blind holder in the future. The method was dicey and complicated, and Kerkorian rejected it. "Kirk doesn't like things that are complicated, and he didn't like this," says Jim Murren.

By February, Mirage Resorts stock was being further buffeted by Wynn's announcement a month earlier that he would spend $250 million expanding Bellagio. Then Wynn was astoundingly honest in discussing his difficulties at Beau Rivage. He went over his mistakes in gory detail in a high-profile article in *The Wall Street Journal*. Wall Street does not reward refreshing honesty. What's more, Wynn was nasty to analysts who criticized Mirage Resorts.

Mirage stock hit an amazing new low: $10.625.

On Valentine's Day, Kerkorian opened *The Wall Street Journal* to see a startling column on the cover of the newspaper's Money and Investing section. The article began like this:

> *When Steve Wynn, chairman and chief executive officer of Mirage Resorts, held his first investor conference call in July, it went badly. "I was surprised," Mr. Wynn says of the analysts who follow Mirage. "They were dumber than I thought."*

Smelling blood, Kerkorian pulled in his circle of advisers that day. He located Gary Jacobs, his longtime lawyer, at dinner in Aurangabad, India, where he was visiting the Ajanta caves with his family. Jacobs worked from the hotel restaurant that night while his vacationing family dined for two hours. He used a telephone that the hotel brought to their table.

One person involved says the MGM group came to the conclusion "that the stars were aligned perfectly." For the rest of the week, Jacobs vacationed by day in India and worked on the Mirage deal at night. Jim Murren canceled a family vacation to Hawaii and got to work on the finances. Alex Yemenidjian worked from his office at the Los Angeles film studio.

They code-named the effort to buy Mirage "Project Platinum"—a play on Mirage Resorts' original name, Golden Nugget.

It was Gary Jacobs's idea to send Wynn a bear-hug letter—so-called because its grip is suffocating. Wynn would receive a polite letter offering to buy Mirage Resorts. The letter would name a price significantly higher than the company's current stock price, and it would set an expiration date on the offer.

Donald Trump once ignored a verbal offer for his troubled casino company from Tom Barrack, chairman of Colony Capital LLC. Barrack, a friend and a fan of Trump's, chose not to force the issue, so he never publicized his offer or put it in writing. That was friendly.

Releasing a letter publicly wouldn't be so friendly. It would force Wynn's hand, because he had a legal obligation to get the most value for investors. Mirage's board would have to come up with a plan to create as much value for shareholders as Kerkorian's offer, or face years of lawsuits.

The letter was drawn up, reviewed by the group—including Kerkorian—and signed by Terry Lanni as chairman of MGM Grand.

A week after the effort had begun, Kerkorian picked up the telephone and called Steve Wynn at Shadow Creek. It was a Tuesday evening, and Wynn was out to dinner. He was surprised to return home that evening to find two messages from Kerkorian. He guessed the calls had something to do with the land Wynn owned in Atlantic City. He called Kerkorian back around ten p.m.

This is the way that Wynn describes the conversation that ensued.

KERKORIAN: "I got a new idea. How about if I buy Mirage—the whole thing—for stock, cash, anything?"
WYNN: "Are you kidding?"
KERKORIAN: "If you don't want to do it, I'll forget about it. I wanna send you a letter."
WYNN: "If you send me a letter, I have to respond through the board."
KERKORIAN: "Oh. Well, Terry sent a letter. I didn't want to, but he did it."

Then Kerkorian mentioned his price: $17 per share.
Wynn laughed.
Wynn says Kerkorian agreed that the price was low.

♣ ♦ ♥ ♠

After concluding the call with Kerkorian, Wynn told Elaine. She recounted their conversation six years later. "What do you want to do?" she had asked her husband. She says he responded, "I want to sell."

Wynn immediately got Michael Milken out of bed, according to another person involved. Milken called Kerkorian.

At midnight, Wynn called another adviser, Bobby Baldwin. "Are you sitting down?" Wynn asked. He explained the terms.

"What do you think?" Wynn asked.

"It's not enough money," Baldwin remembers telling him.

The letter arrived the next day, as simple as a handshake, signed by Terry Lanni. The combination of Mirage Resorts and MGM Grand "would be the undisputed leader in our industry by any measure," Lanni noted. There was a sweetener for Mirage's board members, allowing them to join the board of the combined entity and thereby keep all the goodies associated with a casino—theater seats, hotel rooms, and party invitations.

Lanni insisted the offer was "friendly"—meaning they wouldn't take the bid directly to shareholders and try to buy the shares without Wynn's agreement. Those were somewhat hollow words, given that both companies were incorporated in Nevada, which virtually outlaws hostile takeovers.

Kerkorian's team put the letter out over the newswires and notified the SEC. This move had one aim—to force Wynn's hand, Jacobs says.

When a Goldman Sachs banker named Dino Fusco saw the letter on the newswires, he and a colleague called Wynn's home around five thirty a.m., Las Vegas time. A house servant answered and said Mr. Wynn was sleeping. "Wake him up, he'll want to hear this," replied the excited bankers, who had no idea that Wynn even knew about the offer.

When Wynn got on the phone, he didn't let on. "Oh, that's interesting," Wynn said coolly.

Mirage investors weren't sure what to think. Ken Londoner, chief executive of the hedge fund Red Coat Capital Management LLC, said excitedly that the deal would form a behemoth casino company. "It creates a dominant leader—nobody could compete with this thing. Lights out," Londoner said.

Later, Londoner wondered if Wynn would let go. "It'll be interesting to see if Steve Wynn champions his shareholders, of which I'm one of them."

In fact, doubters were all over Wall Street. Normally, when a publicly traded company receives a significant unsolicited offer, the arbitrageurs of Wall Street immediately bid the stock price up close to whatever price they believe will close the deal—which is often at a higher price than the initial offer. In Mirage Resorts' case, Wall Street was so skeptical that Wynn would let go that they wouldn't even pay Kerkorian's opening bid of $17 a share. The stock ran up only to $14.50. It was inconceivable that anybody could take Steve Wynn's company.

Still, it lit a fire under the entire Strip. Phil Satre, Harrah's chairman and chief executive, was visiting his daughter at Stanford that weekend. From his room at the Crowne Plaza Hotel there, he sent his financial troops to investigate the possibilities of a rival bid. Arthur Goldberg, chairman and chief executive of Park Place Entertainment, had just bought Caesars from Starwood Hotels. He opted to stay out. Park Place had just paid dearly for Caesars Palace, Paris, the Flamingo, and the Las Vegas Hilton. "I think I'd have real antitrust problems in Vegas," he said. "For once it's nice to be on the sidelines calmly watching, not having my gut wrenched."

Smelling a high-profile takeover battle, the Goldman bankers flew to Las Vegas that same day. They informed Bobby Baldwin of their fee: $25 million. When Baldwin relayed this news, Wynn asked that the bankers be ushered into his office.

"Let me get this straight," Wynn shouted, his face reddening. "Just so I understand. So I get a letter from Kirk Kerkorian. So far, he's spent thirty-three cents. And you want to charge me twenty-five million to respond?"

Wynn's ranting excited his dogs. Perceiving a threat to their master, the German Shepherds commenced to case the room for danger. One dog shoved his nose into Dino Fusco's crotch in an attack position. The dog stayed that way, staring at the investment banker, for the full length of Wynn's tirade. "I was petrified," Fusco recalls. "I'm thinking, 'This job isn't worth this.' I didn't have children at the time and I was worried I wouldn't have any."

Wynn's tantrum proved to be worth $10 million. Goldman reduced the fee to $15 million.

In those first days after the letter, Wynn seemed nonplussed. "How about that guy," Wynn remarked to one old friend, referring to

Kerkorian. He called on advisers—many of them, like Michael Milken and George Mason, were friends with both hunter and quarry.

Several days passed, and as each side studied and worked on its strategy, Wynn made comments that suggested he was thinking about getting the price higher, rather than escaping Kerkorian's clutches. He met privately with Gary Loveman and Phil Satre from Harrah's, but they couldn't match Kerkorian's cash price. "I need some competition," Wynn said a number of times, as though he hoped another bidder might drive the price up.

Mirage scheduled a board meeting for February 29. Just prior to the meeting, Lanni sent a second letter. If Mirage's board rejected Kerkorian's $17-a-share offer, Lanni nudged, Mirage's stock price would need to rise significantly higher in the future to provide the same return on a present-value basis. Naturally, Lanni put that out in a press release too.

As the Mirage board meeting opened, the Goldman bankers passed out the "book." The book is a standard strategy manual used in mergers and acquisitions. In a time-honored tradition, companies are given code names. Fusco explained that one of the junior bankers, a basketball fan, had used the names of Dallas and San Francisco teams. Mirage would be code-named Maverick. MGM would be Golden State.

Elaine Wynn raised her hand: "Can we be Golden State?"

"If we did that," Fusco responded, noting that the books had already been printed, "you would be buying them."

Among the things the board accomplished that day was to give Wynn and his top executives lucrative new employment terms. These contracts seemed to obsess Wynn, according to several people at MGM Grand, in particular their effect on the New York apartment, Shadow Creek, the art that Wynn had collected, and the company's Gulfstream III jet. "More time was spent on that than some of the substantive corporate issues," Murren says.

Later, Wynn called Kerkorian. "Me and my board have just met," Wynn told him. "We've all decided that seventeen dollars is inadequate."

Wynn and Kerkorian agreed to meet privately at Bellagio to discuss a higher price. To prepare, Wynn says he called Michael Milken.

"Milken had said when I spoke to him—'cause I had talked to him before the meeting—to listen for Kirk to say he'd put his own money in." If Kerkorian was investing his own cash, Milken advised, it was a sign that he'd bitten.

♣ ◆ ♥ ♠

Kerkorian arrived at Bellagio through Wynn's private backdoor. Wynn admired the way Kerkorian looked, in powder-blue slacks and a cream-and-blue checked sportcoat. "He looked like a model," Wynn says.

The two moguls sat on chairs in an alcove of Wynn's office. Knowing his rival was deaf in one ear, Wynn took care to sit on the side of Kerkorian's good ear. He ordered them each a cup of coconut sorbet from a shop in the casino. "I only want a little bit, Stevie," Kerkorian said.

Jim Murren had told Kerkorian that Mirage Resorts was worth as much as $22 or $23 a share to MGM Grand. But Kerkorian didn't let on. He told Wynn he could go as high as $19. Wynn said he wanted $21. Kerkorian grimaced.

Wynn says he also informed Kerkorian of two nonnegotiable provisions. He wouldn't sign a noncompete agreement, because he intended to start work on a new casino almost immediately. And Wynn wanted to put out the press release announcing the deal—an honor that is normally left to the acquirer. Nevertheless, Kerkorian reached his hand across to Wynn. They shook on it.

On a white notepad personalized with STEVE across the top (a Christmas gift from Mirage's former entertainment chief, Sandy Gallin), Kerkorian took notes about Mirage Resorts' financial status. Wynn dictated. Bank debt, bonds, revenues, and cash flows—all was scribbled down, sometimes with Wynn speaking so quickly that Kerkorian asked him to slow down.

The more Wynn spoke, the more excited Kerkorian got. Much of the debt would have to be refinanced, Wynn warned. Kerkorian asked how much. He could handle that himself, he told Wynn. Like Milken had predicted, Kerkorian was in.

"He was like eighteen years old again," Wynn says. "He started eating his sorbet real fast."

When they were done, Kerkorian returned to the MGM Grand executive offices, which looked dowdy in comparison with Bellagio's. He told his executive team that he had been entranced by the attention to detail at Bellagio—even in the back of the house, in areas the public would never see.

"I don't think his feet were on the ground," says Murren. "You could imagine him with a pair of boxing shorts on."

Kerkorian was electric. He stood up. He slammed his hand on the table. "This is the opportunity of a lifetime, gentlemen!" the octogenarian announced.

♣ ♦ ♥ ♠

Alex Yemenidjian was busy trying to cut a deal with the Showtime network to show Metro-Goldwyn-Mayer's films and attempting to lure Francis Ford Coppola into a ten-film deal. Kerkorian didn't want him interrupted. So Wynn's and Kerkorian's representatives met at Metro-Goldwyn-Mayer's offices in Santa Monica to work out the details.

Wynn sent Bobby Baldwin and Stanley Zax, chairman of Zenith National Insurance Company. Zax's presence as he sat beside Baldwin flummoxed Lanni.

"I don't know Mr. Zax, because he's not on the board," Terry Lanni said, more as a question than a statement, from the head of the table. Zax replied that he was the personal representative of Mr. Wynn. "And that's the last thing he said in the meeting," Lanni says.

Zax had once introduced Wynn to Michael Milken. He advised Wynn throughout the dealings with Kerkorian and received a $3-million fee for his efforts, according to people involved—an expenditure that irked Lanni for years afterward.

Baldwin opened with his cool poker player's mien: "Gentlemen, I want to make this very clear. Under no circumstances will this company be sold for a penny less than twenty-one."

The MGM Grand team left the room and called Kerkorian. They had hoped to pay $20 a share.

"Well, do you want it or not?" Kerkorian asked. "Do you want to lose it for the extra dollar?"

♣ ♦ ♥ ♠

Wynn flew to Sun Valley with Stan Zax for the weekend, leaving Elaine Wynn behind in Las Vegas. Elaine was still arguing against a sale. Wynn was highly strung and seemed to be suffering some separation anxiety, according to people who spoke with him that weekend. He was particularly emotional about the fate of some of the art and the New York apartment. And of course, they still hadn't yet signed the deal.

Meanwhile, Kerkorian's team was drawing up legal papers and financing for the $6.4-billion deal—the biggest ever in gambling at that point. An MGM attorney suggested inserting a standard noncompete clause that would bar Wynn from opening another casino for a period of time. "Absolutely not," Kerkorian responded, according to a person who was there. "The best thing that could happen to us is that Steve comes back and builds a place across the street."

A flurry of phone calls between Zax, Wynn, Yemenidjian, and Lanni led to more hard feelings. (Wynn says he chastised Yemenidjian for returning a call that Wynn had made to Kerkorian, saying "First of all, when I call Kirk, it's not your place to call me back.")

Zax suggested Kerkorian might come back with a lower counteroffer.

"There's not going to be a counter," Wynn responded. "Kirk wouldn't do it. We shook on it."

When analysts from *Standard & Poor's* rating service told Terry Lanni he needed $1 billion in equity to maintain MGM Grand's credit rating—or face higher borrowing rates and angering existing bondholders—Lanni stepped out of the room to call Kerkorian.

"How much do you think you can raise?" Kerkorian asked.

"Maybe half of it," Lanni replied.

"I'll give half of it," Kerkorian replied without hesitation.

The MGM executives were pinching themselves as they went public with the news that they had just taken out Steve Wynn.

In the following days, headlines from Japan's *Yomiuri Shimbum* to *The Washington Post* heralded the end of an era. The London *Independent* famously announced: THE KING IS DEAD.

It was poker to The *New York Daily News:* KERKORIAN SWEETENS THE POT BY 1B, STEVE WYNN DEALT OUT OF GAME. In Zurich, the *Sonntagszeitung* saw it in battle terms: *DER KOENIG VON LAS VEGAS STRECKT DIE WAFFEN* (translation: "The King of Las Vegas Lays Down His Weapons").

The following day, Alex Yemenidjian smiled in triumph, perhaps carried away by the elation: "It's all mine!" Yemenidjian said. "I can do what I want with it."

♣ ♦ ♥ ♠

Mirage held a lame-duck annual meeting a few weeks later in a meeting room at Bellagio. Coffee and cookies were provided on silver service. Elaine wore a cheerful peach-colored suit, but her face looked ashen. "It felt like we were divorcing the employees," she says. Days later, she burst into tears at a meeting of the University of Nevada Las Vegas board, on which she sat.

Steve had moved on almost immediately, she says. "I can't be taking care of those people for the rest of my life," he told her. "I have other things I want to do."

To his 27th annual meeting at Mirage Resorts, Wynn wore a deep-blue suit and royal-blue tie. He donned a pair of glasses to read his letter from the company's annual report—a letter that recounted the company's accomplishments. Wynn peered around the dark room—certainly seeing very little—and asked, "Is there anyone here who's been a stockholder since 1974?" Several hands rose, and Wynn asked if he could have a photo taken later with one of them.

Dan Lee, his former chief financial officer whose demise with Mirage probably led to Wynn's own fall, was also in the audience that morning. "It's the end of an era—I had to be here," he said. Seated beside Lee was his friend Bruce Leslie, a local attorney who said that Lee had talked him out of buying Mirage shares three days before the merger was announced: Lee had so firmly believed that Wynn would wriggle out of Kerkorian's snare.

A shareholder asked Wynn if there had been an alternative to selling.

"As much as I'd have loved to buy back the company myself or buy a bigger share of it, it's not that easy to do," Wynn answered. "So I found myself a bit trapped."

"I'm very upbeat about what comes next," the former casino mogul told them, "and thanks to Kirk Kerkorian, I'm going to be able to do that. But I don't think I'm going to be a public-markets man. I find the stock market an unreliable measure of value. I'm going to opt out of the stock-market measurement of value."

Wynn said he doubted he could be agile enough for Wall Street. "How can we ever cater to a sixty-day time frame for investors when we're building resorts for the ages?"

He summed it up that day by saying, "I never thought that we would have this choice. I thought we were too big to be bought, frankly. It's come upon me with speed and deliciousness. I think what's going to happen to me is what I love—I like building stuff."

♣ ♦ ♥ ♠

Alex Yemenidjian did not get to do with the Mirage casino what he wanted. Presented with the MGM-Mirage juggernaut, Terry Lanni decided to take back his old job as chief executive, in addition to chairman. This was a setback to the aspirations of several gentlemen with ambitions.

♣ ♦ ♥ ♠

When the Wynns moved out of their offices, Elaine Wynn grimly embraced Bobby Baldwin, who was staying behind. "Take good care of my people," she told him.

The closing dinner for Mirage—an event at which corporate executives and bankers congratulate themselves on a deal—was festive. Several Goldman bankers joked that "of course" they did the deal at $21 a share—*it's Las Vegas*. Blackjack.

Elaine, Steve, and Kenny Wynn laughed and high-fived.

MGM Grand got stuck with the $15-million Goldman Sachs bill. Murren, who had done Kerkorian's banking work himself, called the fee highway robbery for a deal that took twelve days to consummate.

Vengefully, he taunted Goldman's Dino Fusco that they should have negotiated harder.

"We would have paid twenty-two," Murren shot wickedly.

The blast ricocheted. Fusco replied, "We would have taken twenty."

♣ ◆ ♥ ♠

So, was it friendly or unfriendly?

This is a question of great importance to Steve Wynn. He says he wanted to sell Mirage Resorts. That's how he wants to be remembered.

"People thought it was a hostile because of that letter," Wynn says, six years later, during a full-out rant in his office. The bear-hug letter was a "mistake" on Kerkorian's part, he says. It was a move of naïveté, not cunning.

"I don't think that Kirk understood what that letter meant," says Wynn. "'Cause when I said I'd have to take it to my board, he said, 'Oh.' And it was a *real* 'Oh!'"

"So Kirk supposedly didn't understand what he was doing?" says Jim Murren. "That's such a crock."

"The discussion was not so much over whether or not to send it, but whether to make it public," says Gary Jacobs, Kerkorian's lawyer, "and you didn't have to be a genius to recognize that the way to bring pressure was to go public with the initiative."

Kerkorian could have canceled the crafty letter, or sent it to Wynn without filing it to newswires and the SEC. Lanni, Murren, Jacobs, and others involved all say the company wasn't for sale until they'd publicized their bid and Wynn realized he had no escape route.

Hostile. Friendly. Call it what you like. Wynn's eggs were moved to Kerkorian's nest.

chapter seventeen

WALKING ON AIR

When Kerkorian comes, he says, "Do I need a tie? Do you have a seat for me?" When Stephen Wynn comes, it's a production: He has his advance people come two hours early.

—Restaurateur Sirio Maccione

Terry Lanni moved into Wynn's creamy office at Bellagio. For some time he kept a memento of the former occupant hanging on the wall across from his desk.

It was the severed head of John the Baptist, the popular orator, still bleeding as it was presented on a silver platter to the biblical Kerkori—er, Salome.

This gory seventeenth-century masterpiece by Peter Paul Rubens was one of Wynn's purchases. Lanni eventually sold it for about $4 million to a New Jersey dot-com millionaire. Lanni replaced it with another memento of Wynn—a Rembrandt.

The executive suites at the new MGM Mirage bubbled with rumors about the Wynn heyday. Lanni was told that the burled-elm millwork in the office had cost $1.4 million. Two naked holes in the elm are all that remains of the two baseball bats, Babe Ruth's and another. Lanni says he was told that Mirage Resorts had purchased the bats at a charity auction, but there was no record of them in the company's inventory.

To Dale Chihuly's great joy, Lanni quickly requested removal of the orange filters from *Fiori de Como,* the glass ceiling sculpture in Bellagio's lobby.

157

Pets and zoo animals no longer roamed the executive halls. Lanni wryly keeps a photograph of his two golden retrievers on a coffee table. He says, "I told people, 'We can have *pictures* of dogs now, but no dogs.'"

At Bellagio, Kerkorian "walks on air," according to Jim Murren.

Kerkorian celebrated his rise to the top of the Las Vegas heap by jetting to the south of France on his Boeing 737. He spent much of the summer on a yacht there, according to court documents in an unrelated lawsuit.

To the victor go the spoils. The credit awarded previously to Bellagio's creator began to disappear from print. Wet Design, the designers of Bellagio's fountains, published a book about them in 2004—*The Fountains of Bellagio.* Wynn was barely mentioned. The concept album and compact disc notes for *Miss Spectacular*—produced by Jerry Herman, Don Pippin, and Larry Blank—don't mention Wynn at all.

Lee says he eventually apologized to Wynn for letting the mogul spin out of control. "I should have been in your face, screaming. Instead, I mumbled and I grumbled and I wrote little memos," Lee says he told Wynn.

Bobby Baldwin's decision to stay on with MGM Mirage, based in part on advice from Michael Milken, stung the Wynns. But Baldwin, like many others at Mirage Resorts, welcomed the calmer seas at the new MGM Mirage.

"It was a nice change for me to come work for Kirk," Baldwin says. "I never really socialized with Steve. He and Don Trump—they're all alike. The only time they pay attention to you is if they need you. That's when they close the door and say, 'How do we get out of this mess?' But at dinner with six other people, you'd get more attention if you were the waiter.

"Kirk is the most humble person you'll ever meet," Baldwin says. "He's not going to grab the wheel just because of a little bump in the road."

Wynn's dolphin getaway suite at the Mirage was taken over by the staff. "Once he was gone, everybody just squatted on the real estate to make it useful for them," says one employee there. Tanks of exotic fish were removed from the back room. The photographs of Wynn swimming with the dolphins were taken down. One keepsake remained, dusty and leaning against a cabinet on the floor: the original three-dimensional model used to build the dolphin habitat, entitled "Steve Wynn's Mirage Hotel dolphin habitat."

Wynn continued to visit the dolphins. He raced over to be present when a baby dolphin was born. And when Bandit died at the age of forty, Wynn called one of the dolphin handlers and asked what had happened. "Are they getting what they need?" he asked.

Lanni opened the Shadow Creek Golf Course to the public, removing the screen of mystery that had surrounded the place and turning it into a cash generator. About a year after the takeover, *Golf Digest*'s golf course architectural critic, Ron Whitten, wrote a column saying it was worth $500 to play the course, which he called "one of a kind, and arguably Tom Fazio's finest work ever."

Whitten took time to sympathize with what he imagined to be Wynn's feelings about losing Shadow Creek. "When his Mirage Hotel empire was swallowed up by a hostile takeover by MGM Grand last year, Steve Wynn also lost Shadow Creek. I can't imagine his frustration. He had created a vision (one that's achieved critical acclaim: Shadow Creek ranks 20th on *Golf Digest*'s ranking of America's 100 Greatest) and then had it taken away from him. . . . We're entitled to just one dream course per lifetime, I guess."

Wynn despised the sympathy.

He began hinting that he had encouraged Kerkorian to make a bid for the company—something dismissed by Jim Murren and others involved.

"I was bored," Wynn would say. He struggled with being viewed as the *former* King of Vegas. "The King of Vegas, I never liked. It was like saying, 'You're done,'" he said. "I like being the youngest guy. Everybody said, 'You can't make it.' It was fun like that."

It was Elaine Wynn who voiced the emotions of the forced sale. She called it "character-building" and said, "Steve was sad. It's made me realize that nothing is forever. You have to know that every day, something can happen to change your life. It's like 9/11."

She conceded though, that she and her husband had fallen into a rut at Mirage Resorts. "There were days that I would just go home and read, because I didn't want to entertain people one more time or show people the art gallery one more time. If we were still at Bellagio, I'd still be planning parties. We're starting over—from a higher plateau, of course. . . . Complacency is the biggest threat when you're running something that successful."

Wynn managed to bury a few surprises in his deal with Kerkorian. The agreement gave Wynn the right to buy back the Gulfstream III aircraft and the New York City apartment on Fifth Avenue. MGM executives universally thought the $7-million price for the lavish Manhattan apartment vastly undervalued it, despite an official appraisal.

MGM, meanwhile, was required to buy in cash, payable in a lump sum within thirty days following the date of Wynn's request, the Wynns' house at Shadow Creek, including the furnishings, artwork, and personal effects at the Wynns' cost.

This appeared to have slipped past the attorneys in their haste to close the deal quickly. In effect, the Wynns had been licensed to spend anything they wanted, including hundreds of millions on art, and to be reimbursed. "I could buy the Getty Museum and make MGM buy it," Wynn said later with a grin. After a personal plea from Terry Lanni, Wynn agreed to drop "art" from the agreement.

The MGM team learned that Mirage Resorts had a spectacular medical plan for several top executives that required the company to pay for "surgical procedures of an elective nature for the purpose of altering body design."

Since the plan continued for several years after the sale of Mirage Resorts, MGM was responsible for the Wynns' and other Mirage executives' health care, including cosmetic surgery, liposuction, and hair plugs, even if Wynn was running another company. Also covered were travel expenses and hotel stays before and after the treatments, as well as private-duty nurses.

Terry Lanni soon discovered Steve Wynn's charitable pledge of $10 million to the University of Pennsylvania to build "Wynn Commons."

Mirage Resorts had already paid out $6 million on the pledge. Gary Jacobs, Kerkorian's lawyer and MGM Mirage's new general counsel, feared the university might sue the company for breaching the promise in the middle of its budget year. So Jacobs approved the payment of another $600,000 to round out the year's contribution. Jacobs received an acknowledgment that rankled him: The school thanked the company for its donation "on behalf" of Steve Wynn.

In July of 2000, Jacobs sent the university a letter saying they weren't going to pay any more money to the University of Pennsylvania.

"You can get sued for refusing to fulfill a charitable commitment, but I felt very comfortable about canceling that one," Lanni says.

Lanni and Murren had promised Kerkorian at least $75 million in cost savings in Mirage. As they drilled into the company over the coming year, they found a bit more: $175 million, on an annualized basis, Murren says. The deal was a sleeper. They went to work selling off Steve Wynn's toys and artifacts of the Mirage era: artwork, airplanes, homes, and land around Shadow Creek. They saved $18 million a year in interest expenses on the art debt alone. "It was the deal of a lifetime," says Yemenidjian.

Life at Shadow Creek became difficult for the Wynns.

"It was a little awkward," Elaine Wynn said in late 2005. "It was more awkward for Steve than it was for me. Going to the club, it was *their* customers. The employees were kind, gracious."

Instead of sparking high-end development, as Wynn had been betting, Shadow Creek was being surrounded by tract homes selling for only $99,000 to $300,000.

The Wynns and MGM Mirage continued a debate about acquiring the Shadow Creek house for several years. The Wynns didn't consider selling it on the open market. "No one was going to give up the price that we put into it, in North Las Vegas," Elaine Wynn said.

It rankled Lanni, Murren, and Jacobs to have to pay the full cost rather than the depreciated value for the Wynns' used household goods. They even ended up buying the old kitchen garbage disposal for its original cost, according to Atlandia's detailed purchasing records: $287.04.

Among the more than $3 million in furnishings and equipment that MGM bought at the Wynns' cost were:

Custom-dried floral arrangement in the kitchen	$395.84
Rectangular soap dish caddy	$18.56
Wall-mount hand shower—her bath	$975.40
Showerhead—her bath	$1,481.70
Whirlpool tub—her bath	$11,506.51
Three sets of valences—her suite	$4,125.30
Two whirlpool tubs—guest baths	$5,581.32 each
Eyeglass holders—master suite	$40.44
King-size bedspread—master suite	$1,961.67
Throw pillow—library sofa	$339.85
Assorted antique books—library	$2,407.23
Fifty-eight imitation library books—library	$1,340.10
One set faux books—library	$205.84
Two decorative frogs—library	$766.09

Jacobs asked for clarification on the $10,000 cost listed for an early and outmoded plasma screen television. The television had been a gift of no cost to the Wynns, and the price of such televisions had fallen dramatically.

Wynn argued for every penny. In a letter dated June 6, 2003, Wynn said, "While the Employment Agreement speaks to the 'cost' of the furnishings, the intent was for the purchaser to pay the value of what was invested in the home, measured on a cost, as opposed to fair market value basis. That the television set in question happened to have been a gift should not change the analysis, as it would result in me having to choose to either take the television with me or unjustly enrich the purchaser."

Calling Wynn's insistence "tacky," MGM Mirage executives agreed to buy the overpriced TV.

The dialogue continued until the following May, when the MGM Mirage group decided to draw the line at buying the Wynns' "Great Books" library—a gift of Stewart and Lynda Resnick, chairman and vice-chairwoman of the privately held Franklin Mint. Jacobs claimed the books fell into the excluded category of art.

Jacobs wrote a May 4, 2004 letter that dripped with sarcasm:

Dear Steve,

We discussed internally whether or not we would have an interest in acquiring your "great books" library, which were given to you by the Resnicks.

I am sure they function beautifully in the house as works of art (I collect rare books myself, with a focus on Dickens and Twain, so I know how satisfying this can be). However, we will pass on them—I am sure they will find a beautiful place in your new home.

Best regards.

Finally, in a letter dated Dec. 8, 2004, Wynn notified Jacobs that he and Elaine were ready to move. The price, Wynn wrote, "should be $17,329,248.12, plus any items that were inadvertently omitted on the last schedule that was sent to you, such as the patio cover that was custom made for entertaining outdoors on the grounds of the home. I will send you an updated schedule of costs shortly."

chapter eighteen

DUPED

It's all over money. All over money when it's got to be a meaning-less commodity because he has so much of it.

—LAWYER FOR LISA BONDER KERKORIAN

Kira Rose Kerkorian was born on March 9, 1998, a few months before Bellagio opened. It is difficult to say what is most re-markable about this wide-eyed child's origins. Her mother was thirty-three years old; her father eighty-two.

Kira's parents were married the year following her birth on the inauspicious wedding date of Friday the 13th of August. They were divorced twenty-eight days later, per mutual agreement beforehand. Kerkorian hadn't wanted to get married, but old-fashioned morals broke his resolve, friends say. He wanted to legitimize Kira, whom he loved.

The girl's mother, the leggy former tennis pro named Lisa Bonder, who was at Kerkorian's side when he opened the MGM Grand, asked for joint custody and thereafter kept his name. She continued living for a time in Kirk Kerkorian's Beverly Hills mansion on a twenty-three-acre estate overlooking Benedict Canyon, where he occupied the guesthouse.

For quite some time, the baby's mere existence was enough for gossips and newshounds. It was just another sign of Kerkorian's re-markable genes, several of his friends said.

Kirk Kerkorian's first marriage had lasted for ten years and his second had lasted twenty-nine. He met Lisa Bonder Kreiss in 1986—

two years before she quit the pro tennis tour, while she was still married to Los Angeles businessman Thomas Kreiss. Kerkorian began seeing Bonder Kreiss romantically in 1991, according to legal documents, after the failure of her first marriage, which produced a son, Taylor. Bonder and Kerkorian eventually lived together, and she was his companion for several years until they split in 1995. They had a week-long reconciliation in 1997, according to legal papers filed by Kirk Kerkorian. Three months later, Lisa told him she was pregnant.

Kira's first birthday party was held at the leafy Hotel Bel-Air, which has swans in its pond and suites named for stars who frequent them, such as Oprah and Russell Crowe. The party cost $70,000.

In August 2000, a year after their divorce, Lisa Kerkorian walked into a Los Angeles restaurant and discovered her ex with another woman. She split for New York, and their relationship became acrimonious.

When Kira was three, Lisa Kerkorian told a Los Angeles court she needed $320,000 a month to raise her daughter properly. It was the largest child-support request in history, according to lawyers at the time. Kerkorian had begun paying $50,000 a month, and later temporarily raised that to $75,000 a month. In addition, he had bought Lisa a house and given her $3.15 million to refurbish it.

A few days after her court filing, Kerkorian put the MGM movie studio up for sale. Even this could not compete with the headlines about Kira's child support. Kerkorian became the butt of late-night humor and bad jokes. "Never before have the side effects of Viagra been more frightfully clear," joked Steve Lopez, a *Los Angeles Times* columnist, in a searing piece in which he noted that he had no idea whether Kerkorian had used the impotence drug.

In court papers, Lisa Bonder Kerkorian titillated the world with details of her and Kerkorian's life. She said that he walked around with $10,000 in cash in his pocket, that he would drop $45,000 a couple of times a year for custom Brioni clothes, and that he preferred cash to credit cards because it doesn't leave a paper trail. She claimed they lived together off and on until August 2000. He claimed they hadn't lived together since 1995.

Nothing about the case was more breathtaking than the budget Lisa filed with the court for her three-year-old daughter. Three nannies, security guards, a houseman, housekeeper, household manager, and cook. There was $3,388 a month for tutors in French, ballet, tennis, piano, and riding; $5,920 a month for eating out and another $4,300 a month for eating in. Kira's monthly phone bill was $945, and she needed $1,339 for laundry and dry cleaning as well as $2,500 a month for clothing.

Kira needed $1,000 a month for toys, books, and videos; $473 for subscriptions, $436 for pet care for her bunny; $7,083 for charitable contributions; and $5,000 for cash on hand.

Kira's extraordinary travels were detailed as well.

When she was two Kira spent April 2000 in the Kerkorian suite at The Breakers in Palm Beach, having traveled there by chartered Gulfstream V on a vacation costing $150,290.

In June, she traveled to the Four Seasons Hotel in Maui, by Kerkorian's Boeing 737. The estimated cost was $158,550.

She spent July and August in a Malibu rental house costing $211,000.

After the run-in in the restaurant that August, Lisa hightailed it to New York, holing up at the Regency Hotel until December. The cost to stay at the Regency was $41,000 a month.

A three-day trip back to Beverly Hills in November 2000 cost $298,000, including flights in Kerkorian's Boeing 737 and a bungalow at the Beverly Hills Hotel.

In April 2001, Kira again made her annual trip to Maui, where they stayed this time in a suite at the Grand Wailea—a trip whose estimated cost was $138,900.

A vacation at Cap D'Antibes in July 2001 cost $527,328— including a chartered Gulfstream jet, car, and villa.

The intensely private Kerkorian and his longtime lawyer Terry Christensen responded with a lawsuit accusing Bonder Kerkorian of breaking six confidentiality agreements. Documents said she'd tossed a toy Mickey Mouse phone, his gift to Kira that day, over his gate, and threatened to toss over the pet rabbit he'd given Kira as well. She wanted a $25-million trust in return for living in Los Angeles, where he could easily see Kira, rather than New York, documents said.

Things really got exciting in January 2002 when the billionaire insisted that he was sterile and therefore wasn't Kira's biological father. For a time, Lisa Bonder Kerkorian claimed he was lying, but in the sordid end, it turned out to be true. She'd had a fling with a Hollywood producer playboy named Steve Bing, who coincidentally was facing other paternity claims by a former girlfriend—actress Elizabeth Hurley.

Faced with DNA evidence, Bonder Kerkorian admitted faking an earlier paternity test by convincing Kerkorian's adult daughter Tracy to give her son a swab of saliva for an alleged school experiment and then submitted the swab as Kira's.

Kerkorian claimed he discovered that Kira is a biological Bing after hearing rumors of the fling. His attorneys sent private detectives to root through Steve Bing's trash, where they discovered a strand of dental floss. The DNA from the floss, when compared with a strand of Kira's hair, turned up a 99.993% certainty that Bing was the papa, according to Kerkorian's court documents.

It's worth noting that Kerkorian knew he wasn't Kira's father long before this information became public, and yet he continued to spend time with her and pay her mother $50,000 a month in child support.

For her trouble, a judge ultimately awarded Lisa Bonder Kerkorian an extra $316 a month, calling her demands "grossly excessive." The former Mrs. Kerkorian, her blond hair dyed brunette, raced from the courtroom crying, "I can't afford this," according to news accounts.

That might have been the last the public heard from her if it hadn't been for Anthony Pellicano, a Los Angeles private detective who was later accused of illegally tapping the phones of a variety of Hollywood types, including Sylvestor Stallone and Keith Carradine.

Terry Christensen was indicted by a federal grand jury in February 2006, accused of hiring Pellicano to tap Lisa Bonder Kerkorian's phone. Christensen said he was innocent of the wiretapping and conspiracy charges. Kerkorian issued a statement calling him a "paragon of integrity."

Christensen, at the age of sixty-five, subsequently left both his law firm and the board of MGM Mirage to focus on his legal battles, making it unclear who was the biggest victim of the whole affair: Christensen or Kira.

chapter nineteen

PROPELLER HEADS

I won $119.05!

—Delores, gambler at Harrah's East Chicago casino,
who spent $200 gambling but considered herself
a winner that day

G ambling mogul? Kathy Welsh had married a scholar. By the time Gary Loveman was teaching at Harvard, he and Welsh had three school-age kids settled in a comfortable home near Cambridge, Massachusetts.

Welsh, who kept her maiden name, had never set foot in an American casino when her husband took the job with Harrah's. Like many wives who are offered the opportunity to move to Las Vegas— a place where professional poker player Annie Duke once complained that people don't own books—Kathy Welsh declined. So Harrah's new chief operating officer commuted from Boston to Las Vegas.

His rumpled shirttail flying out of his pants and his overgrown hair poofing over his ears, the thirty-eight-year-old Loveman dived into Harrah's with all the joy of a child at Christmas. He had the cherubic face and unruly clothes of filmmaker Michael Moore, and he also shared Moore's critical curiosity.

Because he didn't accept many of gambling's well-worn maxims, Harrah's general managers shuddered when Loveman arrived. Their phones would ring at midnight with reports of him nosing around back-of-the-house asking questions and suggesting changes.

Loveman devoured books related to his new job. Sitting on his desk one day in 1999 were: *Why We Buy: The Science of Shopping*, by

169

Paco Underhill; *Casino: Love and Honor in Las Vegas*, by Nicholas Pileggi; and *Discovering the Soul of Service: The Nine Drivers of Sustainable Business Success,* by Leonard L. Berry.

The professor's arrival stirred the pot at Harrah's among people like Colin Reed, Harrah's cagey, acerbic chief financial officer, who was heir apparent to Phil Satre.

Loveman disdained the casino industry's predisposition toward hiring its own. He began recruiting talent from far afield—people like Richard Mirman, a thirty-three-year-old former University of Chicago math whiz, and David Norton, who came to Harrah's from American Express. Neck chains and pinky rings to them were a bad joke. These special forces of Loveman's were highly educated, middle-class talents. They were as surprised as anyone to find themselves in Las Vegas. "I never thought about the casino business," said Mirman early in his tenure. His father and brother are college professors. "My parents are still crying."

Like the early Clinton White House, these wonks felt they had a higher purpose. Mirman often dashed home for dinner with his wife and two sons before heading back to the office to huddle with Loveman. "We decided we would rebuild the company around marketing and we'd study best practices of other industries to do it," Mirman says. "Within the first six months, we knew what we were going to do."

They didn't bother to familiarize themselves with the casino business's close-knit social structure. Rather than look to MGM Grand or Mirage Resorts, they studied Rite Aid and Victoria's Secret. A year after coming to Las Vegas, Mirman still didn't know who Terry Lanni was—the chairman and chief executive of one of the industry's leading companies. Instead, Mirman's idol was Richard Fairbank, the chairman and chief executive of an innovative credit card company, Capital One Financial Corp. ("What's in *your* wallet?")

Having operated for so many years as industry outsiders, this crew at Harrah's watched Wynn's melodrama from afar, the way one might view a fire at a house down the street—feeling curious and hoping the firemen won't trample the begonias.

When they did stumble into evidence of it, they were shocked at the insular nature of their new industry and the long, intertwining relationships between rivals. "It's like a Kentucky wedding—the Smiths and the Joneses," said Loveman, who also had no love for beautiful casinos. The billions of dollars lavished on malls and marble bathrooms had cut investment returns in half over the previous decade. "The casino industry loves hardware," Loveman said. His voice turned mocking: "'We used to have a chair over here, and after considerable deliberation, we moved it over there. Isn't that better?' I was like, I haven't the slightest freaking idea. What I want to know is what *drives* consumer preferences."

Loveman slashed and burned, insulting casino industry stalwarts and his own bosses. "The casino industry is an embarrassment in marketing," the wunderkind told Wall Street analysts and the company's biggest investors during a meeting in New Orleans. "We give better care to chips than customers. We let customers sit idly on the floor all the time. We'd never leave a chip on the floor."

Loveman disagreed with the habit of catering to high-rollers while small-time gamblers were left to fend for themselves. "As an industry, we have taken very good care of our VIPs. Better than banking and any other industry," Mirman said, parroting Loveman. "But below that level, there's no intimacy."

Loveman noted that Harrah's gamblers spent only thirty-six cents of every wagering dollar at Harrah's. Loveman viewed gamblers as "promiscuous." If he could get them to spend just one more penny of every wagered dollar at Harrah's, Harrah's annual earnings would jump by more than $1 a share.

"I'm in the business of fostering customer monogamy," Loveman said, evangelical. "I'm like the Ladies' Temperance Movement."

In the late twentieth century, the casino industry was still run by the early "gods" and the people who had trained under them, said Colin Reed. Many casino managers were superstitious. They might send a blackjack dealer home for the night, believing she was experiencing an "unlucky" streak. The homegrown talent at Harrah's sometimes clashed with the new fancy-pants management and their fresh ideas. In the year or two after Loveman joined Harrah's, a stream of longtime Harrah's managers marched for the door, including the head of Nevada operations who had worked for the company for twenty-three years.

Those who welcomed Loveman's newfangled insights found their careers rising. Tom Jenkins, a gravel-voiced casino veteran, rose from running Harrah's Las Vegas casino to overseeing the entire Western region in just a few years. Jenkins leaped at the new technologies for tracking how much individual customers were gambling. In a sea of gamblers it's easy to identify the high-rollers, he said, but without the aid of technology, it was impossible to identify those steady grazers in the middle. "Everybody's great at [catering to] the high-level customer. But not against the four-hundred-dollars-a-day customer," Jenkins said. "They didn't have stamps on their foreheads, so we couldn't identify them."

The wry Jenkins called Loveman's new brain trust "propeller heads," in reference to the proverbial nerd with a beanie cap, saying they were smart and naïve at the same time.

"I get to worrying when these propeller heads spend too much time talking to each other," Jenkins said with a chuckle. "They need a dose of reality." He took Rich Mirman to a country music concert, then teased him for wearing Tommy Hilfiger jeans with his cowboy hat.

♣ ◆ ♥ ♠

It is impossible to win over the long haul at gambling. This is why professional poker players regard gamblers—those who play slot machines or roulette or baccarat—with disdain. Poker is a game of skill, which is why casinos don't bank poker games; they charge a fee for the use of their tables.

Casinos do not gamble—the odds are always fixed on their side. Whether it's the programming inside a slot machine or the payout table for blackjack, a casino sets the percentages that result in its profits. The more you gamble in a casino, the more you lose.

This is why casinos try to keep customers around longer, especially if they've been winning. Because they know. Over time, a gambler has to lose.

A casino calls whatever it keeps of a player's wagers the "hold." In

Las Vegas the hold for slot machines generally runs from 2 percent to 4 percent. Over time, they will hold on to anywhere from 2 percent to 4 percent of the money that is wagered on them—though one person might win big and another might lose big on any given day. (At tribal casinos, where there is less competition, the hold can run as high as 20 percent, according to some estimates.)

Las Vegas casino operators generally believe that their customers will notice if they raise the percentage of the hold, which is exactly the same thing as raising the price of gambling. Which invites a question. Is it just a superstition that gamblers notice? "I believe there's a lot of money to be made for the person who has the answer to that question," Loveman says.

The real question was: could casinos raise prices without anyone noticing? This is a titillating question for an economist. It is Economics 101, a problem of demand elasticity. The less elastic the demand, the more a producer can raise the price without losing customers. Gary Loveman is an economist.

"I have met virtually no CEOs who would rather talk about numbers and algorithms," says Tom DeLong, a Harvard organizational psychologist who consults for Harrah's and found that Loveman was one of those CEOs.

Gambling is betting on the probability of various outcomes, so it lends itself to mathematical models like the ones economists use. Loveman's mathematical model predicts how profitable gamblers might be to Harrah's. In the early days, Mirman liked to call it Harrah's "secret recipe"—as powerful as the famous unrevealed formula of Kentucky Fried Chicken.

The gambling business was a trove of treasure to these fellows. What other industry could provide such detail about the buying habits of its consumers? By signing up for the Total Rewards, and dutifully sticking that card in the machine, Harrah's customers were volunteering to be guinea pigs. Loveman and his propeller heads began conducting thousands of clinical-style trials to determine what gets people to gamble.

The sixteen million gamblers in Harrah's database were grouped according to characteristics such as zip code, how long they'd been a Harrah's customer, how much money they were likely to lose, how frequently they gambled, and the types of games they played. Harrah's tested hypotheses against control groups in a series of "conjoint analyses." That's just an academic term for measuring which bundles of goodies people prefer.

In one case, Harrah's chose two groups of slot players from Jackson, Mississippi. The control group was offered a typical casino marketing package known as RF&B, or "room, food, and beverage," worth $125. They were offered a free room, two steak meals, and $30 of free chips at the Tunica casino, for a grand-total value of $155.

The test group was offered just $60 in chips for gambling.

Tradition has it that gamblers prefer the fancier RF&B offer—it has been around for decades. But in the tests, the more modest chips-only offer generated far more gambling.

Once again, the casino industry's traditional wisdom had failed. The propeller heads concluded that certain avid gamblers aren't motivated by hotel rooms and meals. They just wanna gamble. So Harrah's had been wasting money giving away free rooms and meals to people who didn't care much about the goodies. After revamping the promotion, profits from it nearly doubled from $33 to $60 per person per trip.

Harrah's sent all sorts of offers in the mail each month, personalizing them and adding expiration dates, which encouraged people to come to the casino before they expired. Response rates rose from 3 percent to 8 percent.

The propeller heads found they could discover a lot from how fast people hit the buttons on slot machines. They called this the "velocity" of gambling. It turned out to be a powerful indicator of people who could be easily convinced to gamble more.

Harrah's focused on a group of once-monthly gamblers who hit the buttons fast and lived near the casino. To entice them to make two visits that month, Harrah's sent cash and food offers that expired in consecutive two-week periods. The gamblers responded like maze-running rats: The group's average number of trips per month rose from 1.1 to 1.4.

Harrah's new direct-mail programs were so successful that, in its

Las Vegas casino alone, the rate at which people responded to mail offers more than doubled. In Tunica, Mississippi, Harrah's revenue rose at twice the rate of nearby casinos.

The propeller heads' technique was Pavlovian. Unbeknownst to the gamblers, Harrah's statistical model set calendars and budgets that predicted when they would gamble and how much. It calculated how much each gambler was likely to lose to Harrah's over his or her lifetime: their "predicted lifetime value" to Harrah's.

Harrah's computers spit out "behavior modification reports" so personalized that they could suggest that one gambler would respond best to a cash offer while another would be more motivated by a free hotel room.

A lady who showed up every two weeks would be labeled "past due" if she didn't show up for a month, but a guy who showed up twice a year wouldn't be past due for fourteen months.

A gambler who was overdue for a visit to the casino would receive an "invitation" by mail or e-mail. If they didn't respond, they got a phone call from a Harrah's telemarketer. "We get him motivated, back in an observed frequency pattern," Loveman said.

This is the kind of thing that casino hosts have traditionally done for high-rollers. Harrah's database and a staff of telemarketers made it possible to do the same for the low-rolling masses.

Working off their computer-generated call lists, Harrah's telemarketers were trained to listen for a set of trigger words, such as "hotel." If they called a past-due customer and the person mentioned that they loved the hotel, the telemarketer was trained to respond by offering a free or discounted stay in a hotel.

Later, Harrah's used this for its VIPs, too, assigning lists of five hundred customers to a "host" who was required to call each gambler once a month. Harrah's monitored the hosts' outbound e-mails, how many phone calls they made, and how many letters they mailed to the people on their list. Their phone calls were scripted to ensure they hit just the right note.

Many hosts left Harrah's when faced with their new telemarketing-type jobs. The old hosts "were spending all their time on the loyal customers," says David Norton, describing the traditional job of a host. "We wanted them to stimulate sales."

Loveman was enthusiastic about applying technology in every way possible. In a 2005 pilot program, Harrah's put radio-frequency tracking tags on cocktail waitresses at the Rio to study how long it took them to serve their customers.

Taking a cue from banks and airlines, Harrah's launched tiered frequent-gambler cards with gold, platinum, diamond and, eventually, Seven Stars thresholds. Like carrots on sticks, the rewards escalated as customers gambled more with Harrah's. Diamond echelon players were expected to lose at least $5,000 a year. Seven Stars players were expected to lose about $50,000.

Loveman's new systems were effective. Sales growth at its existing casinos went from 9.1 percent in the fourth quarter of 1998 to 11.4 percent the following quarter and to 14.6 percent the quarter after that. Customers were also becoming more loyal, traveling from one Harrah's casino to another: Cross-market revenue rose 36 percent in the first quarter of 1999 compared to the year before.

The accolades were pouring in by 2000. *Forbes* named Harrah's to its "Platinum List" of 400 best performing companies—the only casino company on the list, in such company as Time Warner, Marriott International, and *The New York Times*. *InformationWeek* magazine named Harrah's to its list of the 500 most innovative companies.

By the time Wynn was selling Mirage Resorts to Kerkorian—two years after Loveman's arrival in Vegas—Harrah's was garnering more respect on Wall Street. Its earnings more than doubled that year. Rivals were beginning to talk about data management.

♣ ◆ ♥ ♠

Loveman was also discovering an unhappy truth about the casino business: Casino customers are often miserable.

"You ask someone how they're doing," Loveman said, "and in a casino, they say, 'Shitty.' I didn't know how to have that conversation—I didn't know how to respond." Loveman was astonished at the magnitude of losers' distress. "I was surprised at how big it was," he said.

There was a fundamental disconnect between Loveman and his customers. The professor believed that people were gambling for recreation, so he didn't expect them to feel so upset about losing their money. He believed gambling was games.

Loveman isn't a gambler and has never been a gambler. Unlike Kerkorian and Wynn, he is not an entrepreneur. He can analyze customers' behavior, but he doesn't *get* them deep in his belly.

One fall afternoon in Las Vegas, Loveman walked through the Rio, looking professorial in a black turtleneck and tan corduroy jacket. He passed one of the Rio's "bevertainers"—waitresses who set down their trays, climb on platforms, and dance to energetic songs. The bevertainer shimmied in her black bikini, running her hands up and down her body and smiling brightly.

"Now, here's an example of something that I thought was just not going to work," Loveman said. "The local management here had the idea. I thought it was going to be just *awkward*. But it's been a hit. The customers love it."

Wynn and Kerkorian were selling products they loved to consume themselves. Loveman was selling something foreign to him, based solely on his wits.

When Loveman realized that losers are miserable, he figured he could keep them gambling longer if he could reduce their *perception* of losing. "We have to be more diligent about identifying people who are losing disproportionately and doing something about it," he said.

Harrah's began tracking gamblers' losing streaks in real time—while they were still sitting at the slot machine. As soon as a gambler stuck their Total Rewards frequent gambler card in the machine, the computer started comparing their actual losses and winnings against the predicted odds. Big losers were flagged in the system. A "luck ambassador" was then dispatched to perk them up with friendliness and a token gift.

Casino employees were put through a three-day training program on how to deflect gamblers' misery with empathy. Using scripts and role-playing, trainers instructed them to ask if the customer had had fun—to keep the focus on the game rather than the loss. Comp them a free meal or a small cash voucher. Sustain the conversation. A little sympathy, it turned out with mathematical precision, kept people gambling longer.

The propeller heads were closing in on that other big question: whether gamblers recognize lower odds on slot machines. They studied how speed and amounts of payouts on slots create a perception of winning, gleaning valuable information on how to set a slot machine's price.

"Everybody else, like Wal-Mart, knows how to price their product," Mirman said. "We should be the Wal-Mart of [gambling]."

♣ ♦ ♥ ♠

Phil Satre moved Harrah's headquarters from Memphis to Las Vegas, linking the company more closely with its counterparts. Satre was also preparing for his retirement on a ranch in Reno. He set up a horse race between Loveman and Colin Reed to succeed him.

Satre created an "Office of the President"—an awkward triumvirate of himself, Loveman, and Reed. Reed, and then Loveman a few months later, was appointed to the board of directors.

Loveman had been the manager of little more than a research assistant at Harvard. He struggled with the breadth of his new management responsibilities for thousands of employees. With the board, he sometimes stepped into his old professorial habits.

"He's gotta watch himself," Satre said once. "I had a board member come up to me and say, 'Would you please tell Gary that we're not his students?' I had to take him aside and say very carefully, 'Gary, please remember when you're talking about our marketing, these aren't students, they're our board members.'"

With the move to Las Vegas, Harrah's dowdy casino there became all the more obvious. It was neither large enough nor nice enough to house the headquarters, so the executives set up shop in a suburban office park.

Satre and Colin Reed thought they'd found a solution in the Rio, where Tony Marnell had introduced high-calibre restaurants; one of Las Vegas's most popular impressionists, Danny Ganz; and all-suite hotel rooms. In August 1998, Harrah's agreed to buy the Rio for $518 million in stock and the assumption of $370 million in debt.

Then Bellagio opened, and then Mandalay Bay—a new resort from Circus Circus, which promptly changed its name to Mandalay Resort Group. One new combatant was fancy, the other hip, and both competed for the Rio's sophisticated-traveler business. Without the savvy Tony Marnell to help guide it, the Rio got trounced.

Loveman and his managers became obsessed with the Rio's unnerving baccarat business. Rating customers, extending credit, reviewing surveillance tapes, negotiating for business—Loveman found it all "about as romantic as a ball-bearings contract." And it paid off with disappointing and huge swings in earnings.

Kerry Packer, the swashbuckling Australian media giant, lost an eight-figure sum at the Rio in 1999, only to win it back again the following year, swinging Harrah's earnings each year. Something was going terribly wrong, and no one could figure out what it was. The Rio's earnings before interest, taxes, depreciation, and amortization fell from $98.7 million in 1999 to $29.2 million in 2000.

People have since speculated that the Rio was hit by a sophisticated card-counting syndicate. Bruised and frustrated, Loveman shut down the high-roller operation, laid off the personal chefs, and started offering the Rio's high-roller suites to conventioneers. "You don't know who's swimming naked until the tide goes out," he said. "It turned out that we had naked people all over the place."

It took four years to bring the Rio's cash flow back up to its 1999 level. Meanwhile, the Rio's food quality deteriorated, the famous Napa Restaurant was shut down, the jolly sommelier Barrie Larvin left for greener pastures, and the air got smokier. Soon, the place that Tim and Nina Zagat had heard was the best hotel in town was much like any Harrah's—in need of a good vacuuming.

Loveman argued that there was little that could have been done to compete with Bellagio and Mandalay. "The Rio was my responsibility, and I take the blame for the things that didn't go well with that," he said. "It's fair to say we paid too much."

But the rest of the world looked at the Rio and concluded that the folks at Harrah's couldn't handle a classy place like Bellagio or even Caesars Palace.

♣ ♦ ♥ ♠

When he offered the job to Loveman, Phil Satre had warned the professor that he would have to be licensed as a gambling executive by every state the company operated in.

Thanks to the industry's underworld history, casino executives undergo repeated background checks so thorough that their childhood neighbors and their own children may be interviewed. They routinely turn over checkbooks, credit card and bank statements, even medical records. The idea is—and this goes back to Bobby Kennedy's attempts to clear the Mob out of Las Vegas—that running a casino is a privilege earned only by upright citizens.

Loveman wasn't emotionally prepared for the invasion. "When you sit in a room like this and have an Indiana state cop ask you what kind of medication you're taking—I find that outrageous," Loveman says. "Who would you rather license than me? I'm thirty-eight years old, married to the same woman my whole life, an academic of modest means."

Loveman publicly compared casino regulation to McCarthyism, the Crusades, and the Inquisition. Personally, he found the argument academically enticing. The nation's gambling regulators, most of them former cops and FBI agents, did not share his enthusiasm. They turned up the heat on him. Loveman expected that other casino executives would join him in pushing to rewrite the casino licensing laws. They wisely didn't.

"When I did that, exactly no one came out and supported me. Because they all knew," Loveman says. "I was so naïve when I took this job."

New propeller heads continued to come on board. A woman in Internet marketing had a PhD in physics from Cornell. A new guy in casino operations held a law degree from Harvard. Loveman recruited talent from Columbia University, MIT, Duke, and Northwestern University.

"I'm glad I got hired when I did," joked one old-time gambling manager, Michael St. Pierre, who had run several casinos for Harrah's. "I'm not sure I'm smart enough to get a job here now."

Every once in a while, one of Loveman's old students would show up. One of them, named Damian Mogavero, pitched him on a technology that would analyze restaurant performance. Loveman took a quick look and called two of his lieutenants. "Can we do this?" he demanded, wanting to know if they could develop it themselves. They couldn't. Loveman called for a car to drive them to the Rio. Twenty minutes later, Mogavero was making a presentation to the property's operations people.

The product, called Slingshot, collects every form of data imaginable in a restaurant, including who ordered what dishes at every seat at a table, and which waiters got the highest tips. Waiters and waitresses are a restaurant's "sales force," Mogavero says. They need to be taught how to sell the "Perfect Check": a patron who orders an appetizer, entrée, dessert, and drink.

The propeller heads had taken over.

Six years after Loveman had joined Harrah's, the propeller heads' work culminated in an "alpha site" for testing the innovations in East Chicago, Indiana. East Chicago is a blue-collar town scrunched between the big city of Chicago and the more roughneck Gary, Indiana. A four-deck riverboat docked on the shore of Lake Michigan, the Harrah's casino there was attached, via a wide plank hidden under carpeting, to a Harrah's hotel tower that sat on land. Next door sat one of the picturesque steel mills for which the region is famous.

The propeller heads laid out the casino floor based on lessons from drugstore retailers like Walgreens and CVS. The concept was to place high-demand products, such as Wheel of Fortune slot machines, in hard-to-reach places where customers would seek them out, just like they have to seek out the sinus medication.

A "party pit" was built in a hard-to-miss, attention-getting central area, stocked with blackjack and roulette table games. Dealers in the party pit were extroverts, trained to periodically break into song. This was the casino's high-energy core.

Around the edge of this core, Harrah's replaced nickel slots with $5 Double Diamond and Hot Pepper games that had previously been cloistered on an upper deck for high-rollers. Now low-rollers could turn from the party-pit tables and take a flier on their way out. "This is the candy bars by the cash register," said David Patent, vice president of casino operations.

The average bet on these machines soared to $10, compared with $2 in the casino overall. Overall, East Chicago's profit margins rose to 15 percent in the third quarter that year, compared with 12 percent in the busy first quarter, when that casino usually expects to earn its highest margins.

Harrah's tested its luck ambassadors at East Chicago.

To demonstrate one afternoon, Brenda Freeman Winfield peered into her computer and discovered Richard Pearlman, an eighty-one-year-old from Buffalo Grove, Illinois. Pearlman had lost about $100 at video poker. This was not, normally, enough to qualify for an "intervention," as Harrah's called it. But for the purposes of demonstration, Pearlman really was lucky that day.

His face showed signs of disgust as Winfield approached his Deuces Wild machine with a cheery greeting. How was he doing?

"Terrible," Pearlman growled.

"This will change your luck," Winfield told him perkily, and she handed the old man a $5 cash voucher. Pearlman's craggy face brightened as he signed for the voucher, and he seemed to regain some zip. He winked and asked Winfield to throw in "a blonde and two redheads."

Then he turned back to his Deuces Wild machine, tucking his voucher into a rear pocket.

chapter twenty

AVID

I don't think of myself as a predator.

—TERRY LANNI

Most casino titans don't see themselves or their business the way many others do.

When a new journalist approached Gary Loveman for an interview in 2005, Loveman asked what the fellow's beat was. "Alcohol, tobacco, pornography, and gaming," the reporter replied.

"Now, I don't want to be in *that* group," Loveman later griped, horrified.

Yet a great part of the world views gambling as a vice. Perhaps it's the early Mafia days or the remnants of America's Puritan origins, but it is never far from anyone's mind that gambling has the power to ruin.

Few people agree on how big the population of addicted gamblers is. Estimates on the low side are in the range of 3 percent of all gamblers. According to some researchers, another 4 percent or so are headed toward addiction, and the rest are simply playing for fun. Anti-gambling advocates insist the number of pathological gamblers is several times higher and that impressionable teenagers are at an increasing risk, given the growth in legalized gambling available and advertised in the United States.

The industry's lobbying group, the American Gaming Association, estimates that revenues of casinos, racetracks, lotteries, and other places where bets are taken legally amounted to $78.6 billion in 2004.

Roughly $50 billion of that was wagered in commercial or tribal casinos—an increase of 10 percent in one year.

Harrah's took in $7.1 billion in revenues in 2005. By comparison, the entire U.S. box-office receipts for movies in 2005 were a mere $9 billion, according to the Motion Picture Association of America. And while movie attendance continues to drop, gambling revenues have doubled in the past ten years.

As a result of its riverboat focus, Harrah's has derived much more of its revenue from gambling than many of its competitors—85 percent in 2005, compared with 46 percent for MGM Mirage, which is busier selling food and hotel rooms than gambling. So while one might compare a Steve Wynn casino resort to a Disney resort—for the variety of available activities—a Harrah's casino has nothing to hide behind.

If we take the gambling industry's figures for granted, it would be easy to assume that only a small percentage of that $78.6 billion came from gambling addicts. That would be a poor assumption. Harrah's propeller heads discovered that 90 percent of Harrah's profits come from about 10 percent of its most avid customers.

Harrah's data suggests that addicted gamblers are providing a disproportionate share of all casinos' profits. Which raises an uncomfortable, if moot, question: What would happen to casino profits if the addicts were eliminated? (The same could be asked of the lottery—a state-run system of gambling with far worse odds than a slot machine and where a number of heavy players also provide a disproportionate share of profits.)

Even casino operators are uncomfortable with gambling when it comes right down to it. They prefer to use the euphemism "gaming," which sounds like more fun. Most of them don't even advertise gaming: They focus their ads on food, shows, and shopping.

Loveman says "gambling" with regularity. "I don't think it needs a euphemism," he says. He doesn't accept the premise that gambling is any more harmful than, for instance, alcohol manufacturing. "It really pisses me off," Loveman says. "It's the constant presumption that you're a criminal. I'm proud of the company. I'm proud of the entertainment we provide.

"Nobody goes to a Best Buy and asks why poor people are pushed to buy warranties that are of no use to them," he says. Loveman points to tobacco as an example of a truly problematic business: "You're talking about a product that is addictive to its customers en masse. The vast majority of cigarette customers cannot quit without heroic efforts."

Casinos argue that they can't tell which of their customers are pathological. Loveman argues with near-religious fervor—and the evidence bears him out—that the vast majority of people are responsible about their finances. Gambling, he says, should be a matter of freewill.

How much freewill is involved though when a retired receptionist and her truck-driver husband are pitted against a team of MIT-educated mathematicians armed with meticulous studies of Pavlovian response? At least as much as is involved when those same scientists are working for credit-card issuers or Best Buy. Consumers are bombarded by highly researched and heavily disguised marketing strategies everywhere, whether they realize it or not.

So the question is—is gambling moral and ethical?

It wasn't long ago that pathological gambling was viewed as a moral problem. Researchers generally agree these days that some people are prone to addictive behaviors because of the way their bodies respond to certain kinds of stimulation.

There are physical similarities in the brains of pathological gamblers and alcoholics and drug addicts. For instance, as with drug addicts, studies have found that a high number of heavy gamblers have abnormal dopamine receptor sites, leading them to get too little or too much dopamine, a chemical messenger in the brain. Drug addicts may use illegal substances to stimulate their brains. Gamblers are also stimulus seekers. "Gamblers, if they're addicted to anything, it's the action and excitement," said Henry Lesieur, a sociologist and president of the Institute for Problem Gambling, in 1997.

Arnie Wexler, a former pathological gambler who now consults on responsible gambling programs, describes it this way: "Somebody puts a card in the video poker machine and a guy comes out and says, 'Jack, Happy Birthday!' The compulsive gambler gets juiced up and the endorphins [start] flying when somebody recognizes them. It fuels the fantasy of a gambler. They get high off it. . . . A noncompulsive person would just say, 'That's nice.'"

Casinos figured that out intuitively long before Harrah's made a mathematical science of it. But the old-time casino operators were more prone to concede the dark side of their business. "The only part that's fun about gambling is when you win," Frank "Lefty" Rosenthal told PBS *Frontline* in 1997. "I don't agree with the premise or the concept that it's entertainment."

Rosenthal once ran the Stardust, Hacienda, and other Las Vegas casinos before being run out of town for alleged Mob connections. Once a gambler himself, his biggest innovation was introducing horserace and sports betting to casinos. He gained real fame when he was played by the actor Robert De Niro in the movie *Casino,* alongside Sharon Stone, who played Rosenthal's wife, Geri.

"The public, being so uneducated, doesn't realize how vulnerable they really are to what we call 'the heat'—the heat being you start out very lightly, very small, very conservatively, and then you lose your control," Rosenthal said to PBS. "And when you work in the industry and you work behind the counter and you watch their eyes and you watch their habits and you see someone with an extremely high I.Q. go down the tubes, you recognize that we all have an Achilles heel. And I've witnessed that on thousands of occasions.

"It's the only industry that I'm aware of in the world," Rosenthal said, "where the player really has virtually no chance."

Someone who would agree with Rosenthal, but works on the other side of the line, is Tom Grey, a former Green Beret and an ordained Baptist minister. Grey is an evangelist, but he doesn't preach about God these days. He preaches about gambling. Slot machines are a mindless plague spreading across the world, in Grey's opinion.

Gary Loveman is Tom Grey's dream come true. Grey has spent the past fifteen years looking for a smoking gun that will do for the casino industry what internal memos did for the tobacco lawsuits. "Their goal in marketing—all that data—they know exactly what's happening to those gamblers," Grey says. "[Slot machines] change the equation. . . . Now I can monitor how many drinks a guy had in my tavern—and I'm responsible. . . . I think the technology is going to be their downfall.

"[Steve Wynn] sees the problem with his pirate ships and understands that his resorts' success depends on being unique and in limited supply," Grey says. "But Loveman sees it just like golf courses or Wal-Marts—you ought to put them everyplace.

"He believes his own bullshit," says Grey in an unministerial turn of phrase. "He's the guy who's going to stand in front of Congress with his arm raised and answer yes when they ask him, 'Did you really mean to turn this lady who gambled once a week into an everyday gambler?'. . . Loveman is going to be key because he's a person who is going to talk freely and with pride about addicting the nation."

Loveman's biggest problems in trying to "normalize" gambling in the minds of Americans are some of his own steady customers.

Consider Shirley Cotton.

A resident of Hobart, Indiana, Cotton frequented the Harrah's riverboat near her home because of all the exciting drawings and promotions, which she viewed as chances to be lucky. One winter Tuesday afternoon in 2004, Cotton visited Harrah's East Chicago on a day that the casino was abuzz with a joint promotion between Harrah's and Hasbro, the maker of Monopoly.

Hundreds of gamblers stood in line, holding vouchers that had been mailed to their homes. They stopped at a desk in the lobby to pick up a Monopoly game and register for a Harrah's drawing to win prizes, including cash and trips to other Harrah's casinos. Gamblers love chances to win things.

Shirley Cotton spent the day by a $1 Sizzling Seven slot machine hoping to hear her name called. Her neck, below her short-cropped gray hair, was draped in green and gold "Total Rewards" Mardi Gras necklaces that Harrah's hands out by the caseload.

Cotton was grossly overweight and, she quickly disclosed, diabetic.

The disease explained her bare feet, encrusted with ulcers, which she had propped on the slot stool beside her. Her shoes lay on the casino's vibrant carpet. She sat with her arms crossed over her T-shirt, which was decorated with teddy bears and cherries, and across her round belly. "I'm waiting for the drawings. That's why I'm here," she said with a frank and friendly smile.

Cotton wasn't gambling. She had no money left. A sixty-three-year-old former U.S. Postal Service employee, she said she lived primarily on $967 a month in government disability payments. "Now, that sounds like a lot, but it's not," she said. "My house payment is three hundred dollars."

To save money to pay for eye treatments for her diabetic retinopathy—a progressive eye disease—she had canceled phone service to her home. "I only brought ten dollars with me today because I have to make the bank payment for my house," she said. "But I played yesterday: eighty-eight dollars."

Having lost ninety-eight dollars in two days, she was now hoping to win a car or one of the cash giveaways, whose results Harrah's announced periodically over a loudspeaker.

It was late afternoon, but Cotton planned to wait for the big ten-p.m. drawing. This meant making the twenty-mile drive home to Hobart in her 1978 Cadillac with no headlights. The car had headlights when she had purchased it for $1,500. Now that they were out, she said, "I don't know what I'm going to do about that."

Cotton said she received enough cash vouchers and other offers from Harrah's and other casinos that she had begun to figure out their system. "When you stop going, that's when they send you stuff," she said. Once she was even invited to spend the night at Harrah's. "They let me spend the night in the hotel one time. 'Oh!' I asked them, 'am I ever going to be able to stay in the hotel again?' They said I have to come [to the casino] more."

There was something odd about Shirley Cotton's mouth. Her lips folded in, wrinkling slightly, and when she spoke, she sucked on her words.

She had lost her dentures.

Admitted to the hospital a few weeks before, she said she had left her hospital room to undergo some medical tests. She had returned to find her room cleaned and her dentures missing.

They must have fallen in the trash, Cotton figured. She and the nurse had looked everywhere for those teeth.

This is a side to gambling that is less noticeable on the Las Vegas Strip, where the casinos make more of their money from show tickets, restaurants, and hotel rooms than from gambling. Steve Wynn and Kirk Kerkorian, with their disdain for riverboat gambling markets, serve a prettier clientele.

That's not to say they don't cater to addicts. But the Shirley Cottons of the world can't afford to fly to Vegas for the weekend. They're found by the masses at their local gambling joints, the ones that are spread all over the country, like Harrah's. With his cerebral focus on selling gambling to low-rollers, Loveman had opened himself wide to the anti-gambling crusaders.

chapter twenty-one

VICE

*Are those people suckers? Honey, I have to answer that like this:
You're talking to a sucker. Gambling is a vice. Drugs are a vice. Prostitution is a vice. You can't sell the poison unless you're willing to take
it yourself.*

—BOB STUPAK, GAMBLER AND CREATOR OF VEGAS WORLD,
NOW THE STRATOSPHERE CASINO, IN 1997

unica, Mississippi, was a quiet old cotton town, surrounded by
farm fields that ran down to the edge of the Mississippi
River—until the state legalized casino gambling there in 1990.
Thereafter, cotton fields began to be plowed under and tall hotel towers sprouted from the rich, black soil.

It was a good bet that the fine citizens of Tunica County wouldn't
be filling the new casinos with either patrons or employees. The
population of Tunica was only 8,164 in 1990, according to the U.S.
Census, and they were a downtrodden bunch. More than half the
county's residents lived below the federal poverty level, and their me-
dian household income was $10,965 a year. Three-quarters of the
county was black. Of the residents over twenty-five years old, 30 percent had no schooling beyond the eighth grade.

Yet it turned out that, from the middle of nowhere, Tunica became the middle of *everywhere.*

Across the river lay the state of Arkansas. Memphis was a half-hour's
drive to the north up U.S. Highway 61. People drove in from Jackson,
Mississippi; from Birmingham, Alabama; even Atlanta. It wasn't long

before Tunica had become one of the world's biggest gambling destinations. From $11 million in 1992, Tunica County's gambling revenues rose to $848 million in 1997 and to $1.2 billion in 2005 (the Las Vegas Strip's revenues, by comparison, were $6 billion).

Former tractor drivers were now driving stretch limousines for casinos. Farm employment dropped precipitously.

A decade after the first Splash Casino opened there, the two-lane road south from Memphis widened at the Tunica County border into a broad, $50-million superhighway "built to resort standards," according to a county brochure. More was spent on the new roads to bring gamblers in than was spent on school improvements for the poorly educated citizens—$35.9 million of the county's share of gambling taxes went to schools over the same period.

With its broad cross-section of Americans, Tunica represented a perfect test market. Soon, propeller heads like Rich Mirman and David Norton were studying gamblers there in their real-life laboratory.

"This is the most information-intensive business in the world," Mirman said after a year of information gathering. "We're trying to apply science to try to find out ways to run this business optimally."

Gary Loveman was stimulated by the intellectual challenge of applying his academic theories to an industry as backward as gambling. Some propeller heads, in carrying his vision out, came face-to-face with the customers more regularly than their leader. Loveman's strong belief that gambling is a personal choice—and a healthy one for most people—was sometimes harder to apply in practice than in theory. Propeller heads were faced with some tough decisions about their new chosen professions.

At first, Mirman loved the mathematics of it all. Over breakfast one morning at Harrah's Tunica, he grabbed a pencil and scribbled several Greek mathematical symbols—a sort of algebraic equation. "This is what my life boils down to on a granular level," Mirman said. He sought the variables that correlated to the number of trips people made to the casino and the number of hours that they played.

"This is a game-theoretic problem," he said another day. "You have all sorts of customers who have all sorts of information that they're giving to you. So you have to decide on a set of actions that are going to lead to a response that you want.

"I hate to use the word 'opponent,' but it's about what the other team is going to do. . . . This is game theory. . . . Right now, I'm just a punky kid having fun."

When Mirman left his management-consulting job at Booz Allen & Hamilton to join Harrah's in 1998, a senior partner from Booz Allen called him aside to talk about the gambling industry.

"Are you comfortable with the morals of this?" the partner asked Mirman.

"I've worked in subprime-lending marketing," Mirman shot back, referring to his work for lenders to the poor and bankrupt. "Casinos at least are open about what they do. I'm totally comfortable."

Yet Mirman didn't really see his move as joining the casino industry per se. He was attaching his star to Gary Loveman. Unlike most casino executives, who spend their careers in a succession of casino jobs, Mirman saw no future for himself at any other casino company. Privately, he worried that future A-level employers would look askance at his employment in gambling.

Later, other propeller heads would believe this was the case. David Norton noticed by 2005 that, after several years working at Harrah's, he had received a few outside offers, "But not as many as I expected," he said. Casinos were beginning to seek outside talent, but the flow to a great extent was one-way. Corporate America wasn't—isn't—seeking talent from casinos.

Harrah's, like any company that loans money to its patrons, had access to all sorts of banking and financial information on its customers. Phil Satre mandated that Harrah's not use this information for marketing. This avoided thorny issues. The company could claim it didn't know if a gambler couldn't afford to make that next bet.

Mirman was relieved to be barred from access to gamblers' financial condition. "If I had that information, I'm afraid I'd make the right decision and the wrong decision" to go after more of gamblers' disposable income, he said.

He loved to adjust the gears of his machine to send the right offers—coupons, discount meals—to the customers who were most motivated by them. Coupons were tracked with bar codes, gambling on slot cards.

Mirman rejoiced when roughly 75 percent of the "coin in"—a term that represented the total bets made on a Harrah's slot machine—came from loyalty-club members. That meant that Mirman could "watch" every move made by those gamblers: when they made their bets, how much, how fast, when they took breaks, when they moved from machine to machine . . .

"I am watching everything. I see it all," Mirman said.

Harrah's littered its print and television ads with subliminal gambling messages, such as a pair of dice hanging from a rearview mirror or showing a gambler in that tense split second prior to winning. Mirman compared this to Nike ads that show sweaty athletes in that explosive instant just as they push beyond their physical limits. "There is nothing more exciting than the moment the two sevens are lined up and the third reel is spinning—that is a great moment," Mirman said.

With the Internet revolution came e-mail—a cheaper and faster way to deliver offers to customers. Harrah's made its Total Rewards loyalty program completely national so that points earned at one casino finally equaled points at another and could be spent like cash on anything from a hotel room to a Coach handbag—especially a Coach bag, as Loveman served on Coach's board and was eagerly importing aspects of the handbag company's famous customer-service strategy.

To launch the new national Total Rewards card, Mirman and his crew of mathematicians created a "pot o' gold" promotion. Each property would have a prize, some sort of pot o' gold. "The more you play, the better your chances of winning," Mirman said, his voice rising in excitement.

"Now, you notice that not at one point have I told you what the prize is. We've tested this! People get more excited by the description of *how* they're going to win than about *what* they're going to win."

His desk was littered with Slinkys, dice, and travel cups imprinted with the Total Rewards logo.

By early 2000, Loveman and his crew had established, in great detail, that the players who hit the button the fastest were of far higher value than the slow-hitters. The average slot player hit it six times per minute. They delved deeper. Which denomination machine and what type of game produced the most valuable gamblers?

♣ ♦ ♥ ♠

One week in Tunica in November 1999, Rich Mirman sat down with me and several of the casino's best customers for a *Wall Street Journal* article. This was his first chance to talk freely—outside of a closely managed focus group—with high-value customers.

There was Linda Maranees, a cheerful Diamond card–holding retiree from Memphis, Tennessee, whose blouse was embroidered in gold-colored thread with the word JACKPOT.

Near her sat Tina Montgomery, a real-estate agent from ninety miles away in Oxford, Mississippi, who drove to Harrah's in Tunica about twice a month. She was often accompanied by her husband, who didn't care for gambling but stayed alone in the hotel room the casino provided while his wife gambled through the night down-stairs. It was nearly as easy for Montgomery to drive to the casinos in Shreveport, Louisiana, as Tunica, but she aspired to work her way up to diamond level from platinum at Harrah's. "They just keep sending me those little hellos," Montgomery said.

A diamond-card holder named Robbie Ratliffe said she particu-larly liked the Red White Blue $10 machines. "If you put a card in here, there's someone coming by saying, 'Hello Robbie, how are you, have you eaten yet?' You don't tell anybody who you are—they *know* who you are."

Maranees nodded. "Harrah's has a secret none of the other casi-nos know about." A technician would lock down a machine for her— not allowing anyone else to play at it—whenever nature called.

Ratliffe said she hadn't bothered gambling at all for the first year or so after casinos came to Mississippi. Then she started visiting some of the new places, and pretty soon, she was a regular at the Treasure Bay, the Horseshoe, and Harrah's. By the fifth year of her gambling, she had decided to concentrate most of her business with Harrah's. "At Harrah's, everybody knows my name," she said.

Ratliffe said she made the drive to Harrah's two to three times per week, often going after work, gambling all night, and then driving back to work in a sleep-deprived stupor the next morning. Harrah's employees would check in to see if they could bring anything to her, so that she wouldn't have to go off in search of food or drink. "There have been times when I have been at the machine and the phone has rang," she said, her voice full of awe. " 'Robbie, do you need anything?' It's the truth."

Maranees, a retired hotel manager, had needed to earn extra money, so Harrah's had hired her in its Memphis travel-services office. The company scheduled her hours around her gambling, she said, allowing her to work from 9:30 a.m. until 2:30 p.m.—in time to head to Tunica for the evening. Harrah's even allowed her to go on a two-week leave of absence so she could play a slot tournament as a non-employee, since Harrah's employees are barred from participating in the tournaments.

The group launched into a discussion about the way they liked to gamble—in marathon sessions, lasting nearly a day in some cases.

"I don't have a gambling habit," Maranees said in a later interview by telephone. "I was down there last weekend, but prior to that, it had been two weeks since I'd been." She sorted through the pile of the current week's offers from Harrah's alone:

SATURDAY, JAN. 22: Laughlin, Nevada—Airfare, hotel for two days.
MONDAY, JAN. 24: Lake Tahoe—Airfare, hotel, for three days for
    $299.
WEDNESDAY, JAN. 26: Tunica—Win a House on the House
WEDNESDAY, JAN. 26: Tunica—Valentine dinner, invitation to
    "Nothing Says We Love You Like a Free Harrah's Slot
    Tournament."

Mirman was quieter than usual during this meeting. His round eyes looked worried.

"I know that these people will gamble at other places. I'm trying to get them to gamble more at Harrah's," he said later, his brow furrowing. "I think that makes me a smart marketer. Not an exploitive marketer."

He conceded that he was walking a fine line in enlisting patrons to gamble more at Harrah's without encouraging them to wager more overall. "I think about it a lot," he said. "I am trying to beat my competitors. I'm not competing with customers. I'm competing with competitors."

What about retirees who gamble all night, then work part-time jobs to make ends meet?

"I don't know what I think," Mirman said. He gave a long, pensive pause. "I have a very strong pedigree. I don't want it to be tarnished by my association with the casino industry."

Several months later, Mirman attended an opening of an exhibit of Salvador Dalí's early work at the Las Vegas Art Museum. Located out on Sahara Boulevard in a suburban community called Summerlin, the museum had a grand, new modernist building but little in the way of collections. A few miles away on the Strip, Steve Wynn was buying up a world-renowned collection of masterpieces. Few of Las Vegas's wealthiest businesses—its casinos—supported the museum, so the collection of people at this opening included other business leaders and politicians, including the ruddy-faced, gin-drinking new mayor, Oscar Goodman.

Mirman seemed to have banished the doubts that had assailed him in Tunica. "I'm out there training thirty-five thousand people right now. That's way cool, man," he said. "That's way damn cool. I've been out of school for five years."

He said he was sure that his methods led people to consolidate their gambling with Harrah's, rather than gamble more overall. "I'm comfortable with that. I'm comfortable with that," he said. "I'm satisfied that I'm a consolidator. I don't know the people I market to. I don't see their faces. I'm the masses guy.

"I don't know how you tell if someone's addicted," Mirman added. "My job is to capture a larger share of their wallet and the way to do that is to give them a set of aspirations for them to aspire to."

Despite his self-assured words, Mirman was struggling with moral and ethical questions. Once, returning from a business trip, Mirman approached a colleague named Jan Jones about his growing uneasiness. "Are we doing the right thing? Is it right to incent people to gamble?" he asked her.

Jones is Harrah's chief political operative—a lobbyist, strategist, and communications head all in one. She had been Las Vegas's mayor for eight years in the 1990s, prior to a failed run for Nevada governor. It was the savvy Jones who thought of reaching out to Harrah's best source of gamblers—retirees—by sponsoring Meals on Wheels trucks in retirement communities. The delivery vehicles were emblazoned top-to-bottom with Harrah's purple-confetti-and-Mardi-Gras-mask logo.

Jones was becoming accustomed to helping propeller heads adjust to the wilds of Las Vegas. "My guys are the science club," she said, her shapely legs descending into the highest stiletto heels imaginable.

If they were the science club, Jones, with her big hair and expensive wardrobe, was the lead cheerleader and valedictorian wrapped up in one. Her corner office was a jarring mix of political clout and girlish clutter. Pink stuffed animals and assorted bric-a-brac surrounded photographs of herself in the Clinton White House. She had raised her children while working her way through four wealthy husbands.

"Gary and Rich are genuinely nice. And so naïve," Jones once said fondly, noting pointedly that most of Harrah's senior staff were still married to their first wives. "There's nothing Machiavellian about these guys."

For Mirman's moral concerns, Jones offered a simple-minded sound bite: "You can't make people do something they don't want to do," she told him.

This gave Mirman a peg to hang his hat on. He'd attached himself to the gambling industry and he was seeking absolution. "She talked me off a ledge," he said.

♣ ♦ ♥ ♠

Five years and two job promotions later, Mirman hadn't shaken off that meeting with Maranees, Montgomery, and Ratliffe. He conceded that he had started to feel queasy as he listened to three top customers describing their gambling habits. These were not the comments of the cheerful AEPs that he and his colleagues were basing their theories on. Mirman thought these people would be better off if they curbed their gambling habits.

The feeling had stuck with him as he spent more time on the floors of Harrah's casinos in places like Shreveport, Louisiana, and East Chicago, Indiana. "You start to see who's gambling," he said one day. "Especially our VIPs. . . . I think that problem gambling is more pervasive than the research commonly says. I think it's a lot more than two percent."

In his next jobs with Harrah's, Mirman stopped coming into contact with customers. Mirman worked instead with advertising partners—credit-card companies, *Maxim* magazine and, later, with governments around the world that were considering legalizing casinos. "I'm more comfortable being in this industry than the credit-card industry," Mirman said, eight years after joining Harrah's. "The credit-card industry just exploits people's desires to buy things that they can't pay for."

The Mirman family was established in Las Vegas, their two boys growing up. His wife home-schooled their autistic son. They were able to afford a second home in their hometown of Chicago to spend summers in. Harrah's had been good to them.

"I'm at peace with it," Mirman insisted flatly, his boyish bounce gone. "I'm at peace with it. I am. It's just like any other business."

chapter twenty-two

PICASSO'S PENIS

You know, Kirk, Steve wants to be you.
—ELAINE WYNN TO KIRK KERKORIAN AT A HAPPENSTANCE
MEETING AT THE RESTAURANT CIRCO

Wynn hung *Le Reve* on a deep-red wall in his dining room at Shadow Creek.

Pablo Picasso was a fifty-one-year-old lothario in 1932 when he painted the portrait of his ripe, twenty-one-year-old mistress, Marie-Thérèse Walter. In this painting, she has fallen asleep on a crimson chair, her eyes closed and her head resting on her shoulder, seductively unaware. Her dress has slipped down over her shoulders, exposing one pale breast. Her face is divided in shadows.

Wynn described *Le Reve* ("the Dream") to the television interviewer Charlie Rose in July of 2005:

> Now, this picture has half of Marie-Thérèse Walter's face in a shadow and half in the light. And if you look at it that way, it's two eyes and her nose and her profile. But if you realize that the part in the light is just the profile, then the part that's in the shade is a penis, and her tongue is on the penis.
>
> Now, Pablo Picasso did this deliberately, self-consciously, and it's called *The Dream*.

"Now, it's my picture," Wynn said, a sixty-two-year-old pit bull marking his territory. "And I have a take on this. And my take is, it's not about Marie-Thérèse Walter's dream—his girlfriend who was twenty-one when he was fifty-one. If you're fifty-one, you're old, with a twenty-one-year-old girlfriend. Your fantasy is that she's thinking of your body parts.

"The picture should have been called *Wishful Thinking.* Pablo— Pablo looked— Maybe he saw his girlfriend sleeping, you know, and hoping, 'Well, gee, I hope she's got the right idea about me.' You know. So I get humor from *Le Reve.*"

The painting garnered one of the highest prices ever for a Picasso when Wynn paid $48.4 million for it during his art-buying spree in 1997. "Now this is the most celebrated picture of the twentieth century still in private hands," Wynn the carnival barker told Rose with satisfaction. "It's a masterpiece. Has inestimable value. Everybody wants to own it." Wynn had no idea how notorious the painting would become within a few years when he agreed to sell it for $139 million to the hedge fund billionaire Steven Cohen. Before shipping it off in the fall of 2006, Wynn invited a few friends to see it in his office, including the writer Nora Ephron. One wild gesture—so typical for him—and Wynn had put his elbow through Marie-Thérèse's left forearm, leaving a six-inch rip. The sale was off, the now vastly less-valuable painting was repaired, and Wynn, ever the optimist, called the whole thing fate.

♣ ♦ ♥ ♠

Wynn had cut a deal to buy the old Desert Inn before Mirage's sale to Kerkorian had closed. It was April and Wynn made a little joke. He claimed that he had bought it as a birthday present for Elaine.

The Desert Inn was once the haunt of movie stars and glamour queens. It was where Howard Hughes holed up for several years near the end of his life, where Hughes stored jars of his own urine as he descended into madness. But by 2000, the casino had been for sale for several years. In his dotage, billionaire oil wildcatter Marvin Davis offered to buy it, then backed out. It eventually ended up with Starwood Hotels & Resorts Worldwide when that company bought ITT Corp.

Barry Sternlicht, then Starwood's chairman and chief executive, was no fan of Las Vegas. The town still had the aura of has-been about it, and unlike Kerkorian and Wynn, Sternlicht did not foresee its imminent comeback. Sternlicht came from a world of bargain-priced hotel deals that came from the Resolution Trust Corp. Until recently, he had been flying coach class on commercial airlines, and he had not yet become the luxury-obsessed mogul into which he would eventually transform himself.

Sternlicht visited Las Vegas shortly after Starwood had obtained the casinos. His lip curled with disdain as his stretch limo ferried him up the Strip. At Caesars Palace, he fussed about how much the casino's new ballroom had cost.

While Wynn was trying to right himself in 1999, Sternlicht unloaded the Caesars empire on Park Place Entertainment Corp. for the handsome price of $3 billion. Sternlicht says that selling Caesars was the weirdest deal of his life: "Wild! Wild! Wild!"

The way Sternlicht tells it, he called Wynn just before heading to Las Vegas for the fortieth birthday party of his former Harvard roommate, Jean-Marc Chapus, where he stayed at the Desert Inn.

Arthur Goldberg, Park Place's Machiavellian chief executive, had offered $2.5 billion for Caesars and wasn't budging. Sternlicht called Wynn to get an auction going. "Can you pay $3 billion?" Sternlicht says he asked after sharing some of Caesars' financial data. To which Wynn replied, "Yes."

"So I flew out there myself," Sternlicht says.

By the next day, Wynn had changed his terms slightly. "Two point eight five billion, but you keep the Indiana riverboat."

"He didn't wanna buy a boat," Sternlicht says. "But his offer was higher than Arthur's. . . . But somehow, Arthur had perfect information. We started getting frantic calls from Arthur: 'I'll pay anything.'"

Over the weekend, Wynn invited Sternlicht to play golf at Shadow Creek. "I get out there and he's got my name on a locker next to Michael Jordan and George Bush," Sternlicht says. "There's me. There's Michael Jordan!" Sternlicht breaks into a cackle of laughter.

When Arthur Goldberg ultimately won the gem, Wynn looked like a loser. It always seemed odd that he took it so well.

Wynn now says the bidding war was a ruse. "Sternlicht paid me twenty-five million to pretend to be interested in Caesars," Wynn said in an April 2006 interview. "[To be paid] I hadda walk through Caesars Palace and the Indiana boat [to look interested]," Wynn said. Goldberg had to agree to increase his initial bid by an established amount, which he did.

Goldberg died a year later of a chronic disease.

Financial records confirm that an unexplained $25 million wire transfer was made to Mirage from Starwood at that time. Mirage's Bobby Baldwin, who had argued against buying Caesars, calls it a "breakup fee"—as does Sternlicht. There is no record of a merger agreement or other contract calling for a breakup fee, however, which would be the standard way to handle such an agreement.

According to Mirage's records, the payment was made "in connection with a letter from Barry Sternlicht saying, 'We owe you $25 million' with no explanation," says Jim Murren, who looked into it in 2006. "It was very unclear as to why exactly that money was owed," Murren says. "So Steve's story is very likely to be true."

A year later, Wynn worked a quick deal with Barry Sternlicht to buy the Desert Inn for $270 million. "Barry owed me a favor," Wynn says. It would turn out to have been a crucial favor—the basis for his comeback.

Later, when Las Vegas was hip again and highly profitable, Sternlicht would seek to buy a casino or hotel there. It's impossible to imagine that he didn't regret having sold Caesars and the Desert Inn. In fact, selling it could be counted as one of Sternlicht's worst real-estate moves: Over the next five years or so, the value of land on the Strip rose 2,000 percent.

Others had quailed at the ailing Desert Inn's cash-flow statements, but Wynn was eyeing its acreage, which included a golf course. It was enough to create Wynn's Disney dream. He called his new company Valvino Lamore, after his grandfather's old vaudeville act.

From Mirage Resorts, he took along a handful of corporate loyalists and ninety architects and designers. He moved his office into a former high-roller suite at the Desert Inn. Nothing fancy, just a couple of Warhols on the walls and Elaine's girlish wedding photo. His assistants Joyce and Cindy were dispatched to an office-supply store for furniture.

To avoid taking his new company public, Wynn needed a wealthy partner and found one in Kazuo Okada, chairman and president of Aruze Corporation, Japan's largest maker of pinball-like *pachinko* gambling machines. Okada's fortune was estimated at $5 billion. The two men required an interpreter to communicate, but they came to a happy understanding. "It's a chance to be in on the ground floor of what promises to be the next generation of Las Vegas's growth," Okada said in a translated statement.

Okada went halvsies with Wynn, agreeing to put up $260 million for a 50-percent stake in October 2000. This pledge coincided with a flurry of investigations into Okada's tax problems in Japan, where he was accused of concealing income. Okada was later cleared of the charges, which could have threatened Okada's gambling licenses in Nevada. Wynn once again had bet right.

In August 2001, Wynn filed plans with Clark County, Nevada, planning authorities to build a 45-story, 2,455-room resort on the site of the Desert Inn. The plans sounded familiar: They called for a resort dominated by water themes, including a four-acre lake and fountain.

Wynn named it Le Reve and went about designing it undaunted by cost. He opted for a crescent-shaped skyscraper, more costly and less efficient than the Y-shaped and X-shaped towers he had built before.

He spent months considering the color of the building's glass shell. "Blue glass makes everything look blue on the inside—including women's skin—very bad thing," he said one day. He had six sliding-glass doors installed in the Desert Inn's old St. Andrews tower, which had been added in 1963, the year before the casino was sold to Moe Dalitz and friends. Each sliding door was in a different shade of warm bronze. Wynn stared at them until he had narrowed the choices to two, and then he had those doors installed on the Desert Inn garage so he could see them in the light.

The final choice—Wynn Bronze, he liked to call it—was a complex piece of glass with a reddish film electroplated to the back, then a clear sheet of glass attached for temperature control.

In a sign that Wynn had learned from losing Mirage Resorts, he went ballistic when the Associated Press reported erroneously that his new resort would cost $1.3 billion. "I'm going to look like an idiot," he fussed, knowing it would cost far more and fearing investors would believe his spending had gone out of control. "[With Bellagio] we announced a number with nothing but a lick and a guess," Wynn said later. "That was one of our mistakes."

In fact, Wynn never considered the ballooning costs of Bellagio and Beau Rivage to be overspending. "I never was over budget," he yowled as he complained about the mistaken wire story. "We had scope changes. In Mississippi, we went from four hundred rooms to eighteen hundred rooms."

Wynn fashioned a prototype Le Reve casino interior in a warehouse behind the Desert Inn. There, he squinted at the colors, inspected the lampshades, tried out various styles of seating. He settled on chocolate drapes, thickly padded stools, and rich, low lighting.

One never knew who might wander through. Steven Spielberg's appearances stirred up rumors that the Hollywood mogul was involved in the casino. "He's just a cheerleader," Elaine Wynn said. "He's a fan. Like we love his movies, he loves Steve's hotels. Steve loves to get his reaction because they're both so creative."

Former Nevada governor Robert Miller wandered in one day as Wynn chatted on a bar stool. "Bob, you see the sheared drapes here?" Wynn demanded, pointing to a wall. "We're going with that up there, by the ceiling."

"I love the lamps," the governor said admiringly.

With his German Shepherds, Palo and Bora, at his heels, Wynn settled onto the same scruffy drafting stool he had used for twenty years. He hung blueprints of his former casinos on the walls of his drafting room. "Thank you, Bellagio," he said with a chuckle one afternoon, referring to the lessons he'd learned. After discovering that he'd failed to put a restaurant overlooking the Mirage's volcano, he'd put restaurants by Bellagio's lake. But he put the choreographed music on the sidewalk. "I got it so screwed up that I put the people at my restaurants behind the fountains so they couldn't hear the music," Wynn said.

"It started with Mirage—a primitive place," Wynn said. "If I knew then what I know now, I would have put a Volcano restaurant and bar where you could enjoy the volcano. I put a tiger habitat, but I didn't put a restaurant there."

Wynn's eyesight continued to be the proverbial elephant in the room. The designer Vicente Wolf, hired to consult on restaurant design, says he felt unnerved after a design session where Wynn was presented with varied brown and bronze fabric swatches. Wynn rejected them all. "No—these are all the same color," Wynn said.

To make the huge building feel more intimate, Wynn wanted shorter-than-normal hallways, so he built a taller building, which required expensive heavily reinforced concrete.

"All my suites have their own entrance, their own lobby. It's a small hotel inside a big hotel," Wynn said in November 2002. "It's seventy-four feet through to the atrium to the VIP lobby. There is an atrium that is the single most luxurious thing we've ever built. It's designed to make everybody ooogle." There would be five elevators, 15 feet from the front desk. "The farthest you'll walk is fifty-eight feet. You're in a boutique hotel. It's so intimate."

Wynn used his hands to draw pictures in the air and he was passionate about explaining the painstaking detail. Once, when I was scribbling notes, he insisted I stop writing to get the full impact of the place. "Look up at me again," he guided. "On the left side of the restaurant . . .

"I want to resonate with thirty-to-thirty-five-year-olds," Wynn said. "Bellagio was designed for an audience that was"—he paused— "mature. Le Reve is a navy blue blazer with jeans. But it's cashmere and Armani."

Wynn was designing as he talked, off the top of his head. "You want to eat Japanese," Wynn said. "You gonna go to Mikado at the

Mirage—a little box? Or are you going to go to Kyoto—no, I won't call it Kyoto. If I call it anything, I'll call it Okada. Or Kazuo. Thank you, Kazuo!" (And he did call it Okada.)

Marc Schorr, who would be Le Reve's president, suggested that Wynn install a Maserati and Ferrari dealership. The idea worked on so many levels that Schorr giggled to think of it. High-rollers could spend their winnings there. The public could buy logo wear in the Ferrari gift shop. And Ferrari owners in Las Vegas, like Schorr and Tony Marnell, could finally get their cars repaired without shipping them to California.

Wynn's goal: "Could we make it so you could not stand to leave the building for three days running?" Wynn demanded. Chatting by telephone one morning while lying in bed—or so he said—in a Singapore hotel room, Wynn sounded infatuated with Le Reve. "It's lovely," he said. "It's the first building I'm proud of architecturally."

Unfortunately, the neighborhood left much to be desired. Across the street were a shopping mall and the no-frills Frontier Casino, which beckoned gamblers with a $13.95 fajita feast and ladies' mud wrestling.

One afternoon, architect DeRuyter Butler suggested using berms along the Strip to block the ugly view. That night, Elaine Wynn was sitting in the kitchen at Shadow Creek around eleven p.m. She thought, "Let's make that the backdrop of an amphitheater." She called her husband at work. "I knew I had to justify this to Steve," she says. "It's definitely a departure."

Wynn came straight home, where they stayed in the kitchen until morning, sketching a high-tech pile of concrete, steel, and hydraulics to rise between the Strip and the casino. The whole of Le Reve became a theater of waterfalls and fog, with casino customers gazing out at a stage built around them. From the street, there would be the back of a mountain. "That's where it parts with Bellagio and Mirage and Treasure Island," Wynn said. "They were built to play to the sidewalk.

"Mirage, Bellagio, and Treasure Island are the same idea with more or less budgets," Wynn explained. Bellagio was just "more of everything. Like Kirk—who loves size."

Wynn separated his shoulder that Christmas at Sun Valley. Elaine Wynn told Dan Lee—who was again living in Las Vegas, where everyone bumps into everyone—that it was the worst ski accident Steve had ever had. And that included the time, Lee said, that Wynn skied off a cliff at Mammoth Mountain and fell about fifty feet. "They came up to get him with a body bag and they found him sitting there, dazed," Lee said. "You gotta admire the guy—he's blind and he skis."

♣ ♦ ♥ ♠

Wynn's timing was uncanny. After he bought the Desert Inn, Las Vegas began to shake off its reputation as a nursing home for failed acting and singing careers, cheesy hotels, and bad food.

This was in great part because of Bellagio and several new casinos—including the Venetian and Mandalay Bay—that mimicked its focus on wealthier and more sophisticated travelers. New cuisine, bacchanalian wine lists, shopping, and new nightclubs were doing their bit to make Las Vegas hip. This new image was showing up in gossip pages as young celebrities partied there, putting out the word that the town was "cool."

Luxury hotel rooms, subsidized by casinos, were priced far below similar rooms in other cities. The Four Seasons Hotel in Las Vegas is usually one of the cheapest in that luxury chain. This plus inexpensive airfares made deluxe vacations in Las Vegas affordable to the upper middle class all over the world.

Cheap airfares also filled casinos on weekends with visitors from Los Angeles, San Francisco, Chicago, and New York who would fly in for a couple of days of debauchery—or just some good shopping and eating—before returning to reality. During the NCAA basketball series in the spring, Las Vegas casinos took on the aspect of Spring Break for young businessmen who went to relive their college years.

In 2002 and 2003, Celine Dion and Elton John would sign long-term contracts to perform at Caesars Palace. Barry Manilow signed on at the Las Vegas Hilton in 2004. These were huge stars with the pull to fill big theaters night after night. Cirque du Soleil continued to populate Las Vegas with its shows and opened a racy cabaret at New York-New York. With casino money to build brand-new high-tech stages, entertainers could do things they couldn't do anywhere else. *O*'s theater was a pool of water. At the MGM Grand, a Cirque show called *KÀ* defied gravity, taking place on a hydraulic moving stage that tipped at one point to right angles with the floor, dumping the cast off into a basement below.

Eventually, even the remaining Beatles and Yoko Ono would agree to a show in Las Vegas. Naturally, it was a Cirque du Soleil production, called *Love,* at the Mirage.

It helped that in the early part of the twenty-first century, the public's appetite for excess was running high despite, or perhaps because of, the war in Iraq and fears of global terrorism. To provide a thrill not readily available in Kansas, casinos sprayed jets of smoke and water on thinly clad patrons and hired performers at their new Dionysian nightclubs. Topless shows, which had become nearly extinct during Las Vegas's family years, made a comeback. Where there had once been feathers and rhinestones, strapless G-strings were, at the MGM Grand's *La Femme, Art of the Nude,* adhered with spirit gum.

The Rio's *eROCKtica—Sex, Sweat, and Rock n'Roll,* starred a gyrating and greased-up performer named Gabriella Versace. Treasure Island started calling itself the TI and replaced child-friendly pirate battles with the buxom and thinly clad Sirens of TI. For the ladies, there was a revue of taut male torsos in *Thunder from Down Under.* In a further stroke of genius, several casinos created topless swimming pools, thereby enlisting female patrons as part of the attraction. This adult action began to draw a twenty-something crowd that had previously shunned Las Vegas.

This, by design, attracted higher-spending baby boomers, who wanted to hang with the youngsters. To accommodate their fatter, middle-aged wallets, the hotels fancified their rooms and jacked up prices until the Las Vegas Strip was no longer the bargain it had once been—though it was still cheaper than most major cities.

A celebration of all things Vegas spread beyond the confines of the gambling city to the major centers of the globe and even into the world's financial markets. Jay Leno cracked jokes about the town's sin-happy slogan, "What happens in Las Vegas stays in Las Vegas," on late-night television. Queues of travelers threaded through Las Vegas's McCarran International Airport.

Four casinos starred in their own reality television series. They butted up against fictional competition in *Las Vegas, CSI,* and *Dr. Vegas.* Poker took off as a new national sport, complete with games televised on ESPN. Plastic replicas of the famous Welcome to Las Vegas sign sold for $39.98 apiece. The whole mood of the country was retro. Cards, sex, all-night partying, skin-baring pool scenes, and booze-swilling Paris Hilton. Sin was in.

As Las Vegas's renaissance ripened, it wasn't enough for some people to visit the Strip regularly—they wanted to *buy* a place there. Million-dollar condominiums replaced the MGM Grand's failed theme park, creating a race to build high-rise condominiums up and down the Strip.

Investors caught gambling fever and snatched up casino stocks and bonds, even going so far as to buy into Donald Trump's latest brush with corporate bankruptcy, which involved a worn handful of Atlantic City casinos and a Trumpish plan to do a casino someday in Las Vegas.

Most any entrepreneur with an interest in the gambling world came scouting for riches in Las Vegas, and the price of the little remaining land on the famous Strip ballooned. The Las Vegas bosses— not the ancient thugs, but the buttoned-down corporate chieftains who now occupied the big offices—wiped their brows and thanked the stars that they had gotten in when the going was cheap.

In the continual hunt for growth, Las Vegas began to look in earnest for new gambling jurisdictions outside of the United States. In February 2002, another of those serendipitous moments that have graced Steve Wynn's life offered up a new treasure. He and Sheldon Adelson—his nemesis and neighbor at the Venetian Casino—each won lucrative casino licenses in Macao.

Macao is a tiny island region of China, located in one of the richest gambling zones in the world. A former Portuguese protectorate that became part of China in 1999, it is located along the Pearl River Delta. It is just a fifty-minute hydrofoil ride from Hong Kong, which accounted at the time for more than half of Macao's nine million annual visitors. About a third of Macao's 440,000 inhabitants were employed in tourism there, where eleven dingy, smoky casinos produce about 35 percent of Macao's gross domestic product.

Macao casinos were emerging from forty years of monopoly control by business magnate Stanley Ho. The region's governor, Edmund Ho—a former banker—wanted to clean out troublesome organized crime syndicates and turn the island into a major tourism destination like Las Vegas.

Still, Wynn didn't initially envision building a palace. He told people he envisioned spending about $200 million on a Macao casino with no hotel or entertainment. That's riverboat stuff, he thought.

It turned out, though, that the Macao casino played a vital role in selling Wynn Resorts shares. Investors liked Las Vegas, but they *loved* the promise of the 1.3 billion people in China.

MGM Mirage failed to win one of the Macao licenses. Terry Lanni was rightly stricken by this costly loss. While many have speculated that Lanni somehow stumbled politically, it has never been clear why MGM Mirage, with all its well-placed Chinese relationships, lost out. Lanni regards it as the biggest error of his career. It's telling, though, that he says Kerkorian—to whom the magnitude of the loss was obvious—never bothered to chide him for it.

In the United States, though, investors remembered Wynn's behavior at Mirage Resorts. For two years, Wynn flew around the country trying to get investors to back his new casino. Aside from Kazuo Okada, he faced rejection after rejection. Despite his pledges never to borrow money from the stock market, he gave up in April 2002 and said he'd go public.

He needed a chief financial officer, and he called Ron Kramer, a New York banker, to ask for a reference. Kramer listened, then asked Wynn a pointed question: "Are you financing a project or are you building a company?"

"I want to build a company that's gonna outlive me," Wynn responded.

Kramer says he told Wynn he needed an unassailable balance sheet and absolutely no airplane-cosmetic-surgery-art-collecting hanky-panky. A day later, Wynn offered Kramer the job.

Kramer studied Kerkorian as he created the financial structure of Wynn's new company. He copied the way Kerkorian had financed the MGM Grand a decade earlier, using a public company to raise construction money. Kramer went so far as to point this out in his presentation to banks, riding on the coattails of Kerkorian's reputation for savvy and success. (In 2006, when Wynn wanted to take cash out of the public company, he would declare a huge $6-per-share cash dividend, something Kerkorian had done years before.)

Wynn filed paperwork for the initial public offering in June. Now he would need the aid of all the Wall Street analysts he had so callously insulted three years earlier.

The complexity of his corporate structure bothered the Securities & Exchange Commission. In its second round of review in September, the SEC came back with eighty-one questions—a surprising number of queries that one former SEC director called "ugly." Wynn refiled in three days. But lacking SEC approvals, he was forced to cancel a party where he had hoped to discuss his new company. "We're twiddling our thumbs waiting for the SEC," Wynn griped on September 26.

The SEC was particularly concerned with disclosures about Wynn's airplanes, which he had sold to the company, and the workings and value of the Macao casino. In its third round of review, the SEC came back with thirty more questions about Wynn's complex corporate structure. A former SEC official who investigated offerings on behalf of institutional investors summed up the benefits of the company: "You're making a total bet on Steve Wynn."

Wynn did the "teach-ins" with the brokerage sales forces himself, traveling around the country to do three grueling presentations per day and giving the people who would be peddling his stock the full force of his magnetism. One slide in his presentation showed the compounded growth of Mirage Resorts—24.7 percent over twenty-seven years.

Wynn had never paid much mind to Harrah's—a company so unlike his own. But one day, he made a comment that suggested he'd taken serious note of the revolution that was taking place over there.

"I never believed in any of that visionary shit," Wynn said one afternoon as he tried out his lines for the brokerage sales force. "What I did worked because of the people, not volcanoes. My programs were more like Harrah's than people know."

Wynn built in plenty of protections against another takeover. His 31 percent stake in the company gave him more control than the 12 percent he had held in Mirage Resorts. The company's bylaws barred shareholders from calling special meetings, but stated that they couldn't take action without a meeting. The company directors were empowered to issue "blank check" preferred shares, or additional shares, to thwart any takeover attempt.

By October, just as he was ready to sell shares in Wynn Resorts, the market for initial public offerings bottomed out. The seven-week deal drought that spanned August and September marked the longest period of time without IPOs in the United States since 1975, according to the market-data vendor Thomson Financial.

But Wynn had construction trailers lined up on the site in Las Vegas. He couldn't fire up the bulldozers until his offering "priced" and the stock started trading. "We'll price and break ground the same day," he said. He couldn't afford to pull out.

Wynn embarked on a grueling two-week road show that October to pitch Wynn Resorts Ltd. to big institutional investors. He requested one-and-a-half-hour meetings with fund managers who were accustomed to a one-hour time limit. He did every presentation himself, without the help of a B-team for smaller investors. He handed out his cell phone number to fund managers.

He was peppered, during these meetings, with questions about airplanes and art. Under pressure to prove he wouldn't take advantage of the company again, Wynn agreed to lease his art to Le Reve for virtually nothing, $1, and pledged to reimburse the company for his personal use of its jets.

Mario Gabelli, a famous fund manager, grilled Mr. Wynn over dinner at New York's Le Cirque Restaurant, according to both men.

"Why should I buy this stock now?" Gabelli asked.

"I have no answer for that," Wynn replied, "except nothing worth a damn is built in a week."

Gabelli eventually signed on, fascinated. "I just like Steve. I want to be in the areas that he's in," Gabelli said in 2002. "How does he do color when he can't see? I have no idea how he pulls it off."

Wynn called old friends for help. Stan Zax, Michael Milken's cousin and the chairman of Zenith National Insurance Corp., sat on the Wynn Resorts board. He directed Zenith National to buy one million Wynn shares. A number of his own shareholders complained, saying that Wynn Resorts made up too big a portion of the company's portfolio. Zax explained, "I thought the stock was too cheap [to pass up]."

Skeptical investors viewed the stock as a publicly traded construction loan. Few wanted to return to their bosses with shares in a company that wouldn't have returns for years. "The directors would have been all over us," says Larry Haverty, a managing director with State Street Research at the time. "You were buying a construction project and a dream." But it was Steve Wynn's dream—and they tend to come true.

The fact that Haverty was even included suggests that Wynn was exhausting every possible opportunity. Haverty's small-cap funds were unlikely to invest in such a large enterprise. So why did Haverty and dozens of other investors waste their time? Wynn was a celebrity doing his own legwork. "I was, to some extent, there under false pretenses," concedes Haverty. "If you have a chance to have a one-on-one with him, you take the chance."

Wynn hoped to price his shares at around $22 a share on Monday, October 21. Given the weak demand, he was soon forced to shear back the price to $18–$20 per share. To raise the $450 million he needed in the offering, he bumped up the number of shares being sold so that each share would buy a smaller stake in the company. Okada agreed, based on a single phone call, to join Wynn in buying more shares to make the deal work.

Things were then set to go live on October 23.

Wynn was again forced to knock the price down. Again, Okada agreed to kick in more money, leaving only $300 million to be sold publicly. Okada and Wynn would each own just under a third of Wynn Resorts.

Kirk Kerkorian, always a bargain hunter, even offered to buy a big stake in the IPO, Wynn said. "He told a friend of mine. We discussed it—and we said, no, that's really not a good idea."

Finally, on Thursday, October 24, Wynn Resorts started trading at $13 a share—not on the Big Board of the New York Stock Exchange, as Mirage had, but on the less glamorous NASDAQ exchange. The company was highly leveraged, with a $1-billion credit line in addition to $340 million in junk bonds.

"It was the toughest three days of my life," said Wynn that evening as he headed for his plane in New York, sounding bruised and exhausted. "I'm going to go home and celebrate in my bed at Shadow Creek.

"This company is going to be a case study in corporate governance," he added.

The next day, Wynn Resorts shares fell further, ending up for some time in the neighborhood of $12.

A week later, Wynn held the formal groundbreaking for Le Reve, where an all-star cast of politicians and Wynn's backers—and the first Wynn granddaughter—lined up on the dusty site for the shovel-in-hand photographs and speeches. "Steve, you're competing with yourself, which we all know will be very very difficult to do," said U.S. Senator John Ensign. He followed U.S. Senator Harry Reid at a Lucite podium before a black backdrop bearing the Le Reve logo.

"It took longer than we thought, but here we are," said Elaine Wynn, in a black suit over a white blouse whose Louis XIV ruffles enveloped her neck and hands. "Two and a half years ago, my husband bought me a very special birthday present," she said cutely. "The Desert Inn. It's kind of like getting a Black & Decker drill. You know it's a great thing to have, but you're not sure what to do with it. Steve really wanted to play with it. I had been taught by my parents to share my toys."

When it was his turn to address the crowd, Wynn took a moment to thank Kirk Kerkorian for the chance to buy the Desert Inn. "I'm a homeboy. Always gonna be a homeboy in Las Vegas—that's the way it is," said the man born in Connecticut and raised in Utica, New York. "Can you feel the ghosts of Moe Dalitz and Howard Hughes?" he asked with a grin.

Then he launched a round of fireworks.

Later, Elaine gave a sigh of relief that the new project was officially underway. "This is for keepies now," she said.

Wynn called Kerkorian the day after the groundbreaking and pretended to ask his advice. "What do I do? I never did an IPO," he says he teased.

Once again, Wynn set off an arms race in Las Vegas.

Call it the Wynn effect: Bigger suites, electric drapes, plasma televisions, and private high-roller gambling salons. Bellagio, Mandalay Bay, and the Venetian were suddenly erecting $825 million in super-luxury hotel towers and other improvements. MGM Mirage was goaded into locking up 603 management-level employees with long contracts—particularly its valuably connected casino hosts.

At Kerkorian's behest, Terry Lanni, Bobby Baldwin, and Jim Murren signed rich contracts, including raises of 50 percent or more, extending six years—well past Le Reve's opening. Lanni's annual salary was doubled to $2 million. He also received a generous $6.2 million in restricted stock that year, and a $2.5 million bonus.

Under the terms of the merger agreement, MGM Mirage continued to pay for the Wynns' medical care for several years, even after Wynn Resorts went public, according to people familiar with the situation. They claim Wynn made ample use of the plan, which covered cosmetic surgery as well as eye care and all medical care for himself, Elaine Wynn, Kenny Wynn, Marc Schorr, and at least one other former Mirage executive through 2003.

People who knew the Wynns well noticed that their appearances seemed to have been tweaked since the sale of Mirage Resorts. They sported tauter necks and foreheads. They looked smashing.

♣ ♦ ♥ ♠

As he departed Le Reve's groundbreaking ceremony, Wynn stumbled down a short flight of steps. It was a frightening-looking pitch-forward sort of fall that seemed, for a split-second, as though it might end disastrously.

Wynn stopped his plunge with a skip of his size 13-D feet, landing lightly like a dancer, arms extended at his sides. Then he continued walking, and talking, as though nothing had happened.

chapter twenty-three

SUNDAY NIGHT FEVER

Las Vegas may not be the most elegant place, but it sure is fun, isn't it?

—STEVE WYNN

Midnight. Sunday, June 13, 2004.

Deep in the executive suites at the Bellagio casino, Glenn Schaeffer hugged Jim Murren.

Schaeffer prefers to say he grasped Murren's shoulders. Schaeffer is a guys' guy. He is scrappy and macho, wearing in middle age the remnants of a tough upbringing in Pomona, California. He was once an amateur boxer. He was a beefy man at fifty, and he strode through casinos with a street-savvy jock's swagger.

A back-slapper, maybe, but Schaeffer is no hugger. "Do I strike you as warm and effusive?" he challenges, chin thrust out.

That Sunday night, though, half the Las Vegas Strip was riding on Schaeffer's embrace. Earlier, he had cut a handshake deal to sell Mandalay Resort Group to Kirk Kerkorian. The trade would include a raft of Las Vegas casinos: the famous Luxor pyramid, the golden towers of Mandalay Bay, the cartoonish Excalibur. Eight billion dollars on a handshake. Another "biggest" for Kerkorian. By evening, though, the biggest deal ever in gambling was unraveling.

Glenn Schaeffer and Jim Murren had forged an unusual Las Vegas friendship. Schaeffer had been in Las Vegas twenty years when Murren arrived in 1998, fresh-faced from Deutsche Bank. Unlike

Schaeffer, Murren is a hugger. He embraces office colleagues and pecks the cheeks of acquaintances. He wears a deceiving air of innocence and he is an expert flatterer. If he stabbed you, you wouldn't know it until later. He is a rising star with Kerkorian.

Murren isn't one of those old-style casino bosses. He is in bed by nine p.m. and rises before five a.m. to head straight to his office (Dan Lee's former office) at Bellagio. There, he exercises and eats breakfast from a cart that is wheeled into his office by the hotel's room service. On Mondays, Wednesdays, and Fridays, he would breakfast on an egg-white veggie omelet, stewed tomatoes, and carrot juice. On Tuesdays and Thursdays, the meal was oatmeal with soy milk, and orange juice or watermelon. Murren once hoped to play professional baseball, but now he practices yoga. "I just love *chattaranga*," he once said, referring to the strenuous pose that mimics a long push-up.

In Las Vegas, Murren and Schaeffer existed at equal social levels—each president and chief financial officer of a casino giant. They made an odd pair: Schaeffer, the introvert who loved fine teas and sugary coffees and walked out on his second marriage because, he said, "I don't need to be married"—and Murren, the extroverted family man with juice boxes and schoolwork cluttering his kitchen. Yet the two men discovered shared interests in art and wine. They started investing together—in art and in Schaeffer's New Zealand winery—and were soon describing each other with terms like "soul mate" and "best friend."

They became so close that Schaeffer was once invited along when MGM Mirage's executive crew went on one of those team-building exercises on a nuclear sub. This would be like the president of Pepsi joining Coke's executive team for a bonding ritual.

February, 2004

This is when that deal really started, four months before the hug, at the noon break from one of MGM Mirage's regularly scheduled board meetings. Murren sidled up to two of Kerkorian's friends on the board and casually let it drop that he had been toying with a new development plan.

Kerkorian hadn't built a new casino on his own since the MGM Grand. He had earned a reputation for a weak trigger finger. But he had, at least, not gotten in the way when the MGM Grand proposed building a set of condominiums called The Residences at MGM Grand. Initially, people had been polite about this chuckle-headed condo idea: Who would want to *live* on the Strip? But those condos sold—to speculators, high-rollers, and a variety of jet-setters, many of whom hoped to establish residency in income-tax-free Nevada.

"We sold out five hundred and eighty-three units in seven weeks, which was astonishing to the world," Murren said. "And no one was more surprised than we were."

This fueled an inferno of Las Vegas condo building and got Murren thinking about the urban planning he had studied in college. He wanted to build a city within the city, where people could live and work. When he cornered Terry Christensen, Kerkorian's lawyer, and Kerkorian's old friend George Mason, Murren conveniently had some mock-ups of his idea along. He called his concept "55 West," referring to fifty-five developable acres the company owned on the west side of the Strip.

Christensen and Mason liked it, and so did the rest of the board after Murren's unscheduled presentation. By April, three sets of urban planners were competing to design the project, including the famous Robert Stern, who got the chance "because he's Robert Stern. I had studied him in college," Murren said.

This was not a company with Steve Wynn's self-assured vision. They hired McKinsey & Company to produce a 231-page economic report. It suggested, to Murren's disappointment, that a real city didn't make financial sense: Affordable housing for casino employees and office space for doctors and other professionals wouldn't pay enough.

Four weeks and $4 million later ("We had consultants consulting consultants," Murren said), Kerkorian was looking at a recommendation that the company build three new hotels, 1,640 condo units, and 250,000 square feet of shops and restaurants on the fifty-five acres.

"Gee, I wish we had more land," Murren said to himself.

Mid-May, 2004

"Glenn, what do you really want to do with the rest of your life?" Murren said unexpectedly.

He and Schaeffer were sitting in a small conference room at Bellagio, talking about an art-investing fund and a trip to Art Basel in Switzerland.

"I don't know. I'm having a lot of fun," Schaeffer replied.

Mandalay Resort Group controlled forty-five acres next to MGM Mirage's fifty-five acres. What's more, the company's executives appeared to be indicating that they wanted out. The previous autumn, Mike Ensign (father of U.S. senator John Ensign) and Bill Richardson, Mandalay's chairman and vice-chairman respectively, had inexplicably sold their stakes in the company: Nearly $300 million worth of stock sold over a period of seven months. In Murren's eyes, this was tantamount to hanging out a For-Sale sign.

"Glenn ironically had become the largest inside shareholder at Mandalay. And his interests outside were mushrooming—collecting art, making wine," Murren said. "I wanted to see where his head was at, whether he would go to Mike Ensign and propose this transaction."

So Murren suggested it to Schaeffer. "Well, why don't we put the two companies together? You could go off and do all those other things." Schaeffer cocked his eye. He thought he'd misunderstood.

Murren pressed, "How would that conversation take place?"

"It wouldn't happen here," Schaeffer replied, shocked.

They needed their bosses, Kerkorian and Ensign, to shake hands first. That happened the following Sunday.

Monday, May 31, 2004, 4:00 p.m.

Murren went to Schaeffer's condominium to get started. Schaeffer's 4,000-square-foot condo overlooked the Las Vegas Strip, but was hardly lived in; Schaeffer spent most of his time there reading in the bedroom. The living room was a private gallery—a Richard Serra here, a Donald Judd there.

Murren wasn't sure where to sit. The room was a crowd of minimalist art and furniture, as though Schaeffer embraced the concept of minimalism, but not the practice. Murren lowered his long body onto a low-slung gray couch and stared at large spongy objet d'art at his knees. "Is that a table?" Murren asked. "Can I put my feet on it?" It was a coffee table of foamy black plastic, created by the *Jetsons*-esque designer Karim Rashid.

Schaeffer left the room to choose a New Zealand pinot noir. When he returned, Murren had removed his shoes and was curled into the sofa in his socks, propped up on several colorful pillows.

Schaeffer took a seat on a zebra-striped chair. "This is no Mirage," Schaeffer said, suggesting that Mandalay wasn't in a weak position with respect to the terms of the deal.

They emptied the bottle of wine. Later, Murren called Kerkorian to fill him in on a deal that would make him the unequivocal king of Las Vegas.

"Interesting," Kerkorian said. "Let's keep our options open. Learn more."

Putting MGM Mirage and Mandalay together would give Kerkorian control of the southern half of the Las Vegas Strip just as Wynn was aiming his latest $2.7 billion extravaganza at Bellagio's luxury clientele in the north. With Mandalay, Kerkorian would dominate the baccarat business and the world's biggest gamblers. He would own resorts catering to every level of visitor from lowbrow to highbrow. He would own the biggest casino company in the world.

Of course, they had to have a code name. They had called the deal to buy Mirage Project Platinum. Mandalay was dubbed Project Silver.

Wednesday, June 2, 2004

"We have one bidder," Schaeffer quipped to Mandalay's board of directors. "He's eighty-seven years old. I consider this a time-constrained offer."

Later that day, Schaeffer handed Murren a press release with Mandalay's first-quarter financial results, to be released the following day. The earnings were phenomenal—and Murren realized Mandalay's stock would rise on the news, pressuring Kerkorian to pay more for the company.

MGM Mirage hurried to settle a price for their deal before the earnings became public. Leaving a cluster of more junior executives in the room, Terry Lanni asked Schaeffer and Murren to step outside and offered $66 per share.

"I wouldn't have Kirk call Mike Ensign with an offer like that," Schaeffer retorted. "If you're going to start a bid, you should start at sixty-eight, and you're going to end up with a seven in the front."

Later, Kerkorian offered $67—a handy premium over Mandalay's stock price, which closed that day at $55.48 per share.

Friday, June 4, 2004

The next morning, Mandalay's stock surged so much that Kerkorian, Lanni, and Murren feared that word of their bid had leaked. They sought to put a lid on Mandalay's stock by signaling their price. Kerkorian raised his offer to $68 per share and announced it with a press release.

Over the weekend, bankers at Merrill Lynch, hired by Schaeffer, called trying to get a bidding war going. Schaeffer was hoping Gary Loveman would bid, since Harrah's was one of the few remaining companies big enough to buy Mandalay. But Loveman didn't want to buy a Las Vegas casino company.

That really pissed Schaeffer off. Someone, he felt, should at least pretend to be interested—for no other reason than to weaken Kerkorian by forcing him to pay more for the company. "Don't they teach that in business school?" Schaeffer asked.

Monday, June 7, 2004

Whoosh. Like a rocket, Mandalay was a Wall Street star.

Arbitrageurs assumed that they were seeing Mirage Resorts all over again. And they bid Mandalay's stock up to an all-time high of $72.80 a share.

Ensign and Kerkorian called each other back and forth. Kerkorian raised his bid to $69 a share. Ensign, without expecting so much, asked for $73. "I can't do that," Kerkorian responded, according to someone familiar with the details of the conversation. Suddenly, what had begun as a friendly deal was looking hostile. For three days, Schaeffer studied Kerkorian's purchase of Mirage Resorts, sniffing for clues to the billionaire's behavior. Schaeffer asked Merrill Lynch, " 'Has anyone ever lost a deal over a dollar a share?'

"We were in combat—people's emotions were getting involved," Schaeffer recalls. Schaeffer snapped at Murren during one telephone conversation, then regretted it and called Murren back to invite him to his condo again. But this time Schaeffer didn't invite his friend upstairs. They met in a small conference room by the lobby.

Kerkorian's offer was set to expire, so Mandalay's board was called in to consider the $69 bid on Friday. Bankers, attorneys, and other strategists hurried to catch planes from New York and Los Angeles.

Thursday, June 10, 2004

While MGM Mirage's legal team pulled an all-nighter, Murren drove home to his gated golf-course neighborhood and went to sleep in the huge, carved-wood bed that he and his wife, Heather, had brought back from Spain. When his phone rang at ten thirty that night, Murren reached across Heather's sleeping form to hear the strident voice of Terry Christensen. Kerkorian's lawyer argued to insert a safety clause that would allow Kerkorian to back out if the federal antitrust authorities raised a ruckus about Kerkorian's new control over the Las Vegas casino industry.

Schaeffer had said they wouldn't consider any escape clause.

At least ask for it, Christensen advised. Murren sleepily agreed.

Friday, June 11, 2004

Schaeffer stopped at Starbucks early that morning for a sugary concoction of chocolate and coffee. A short time later, he entered his office—a lavish, sprawling tan and beige suite devoid of family or social photos, but hung with indigenous art from New Zealand, Australia, and the American West.

"Guys, we're gonna have some big decisions today," he told the legal team, who were looking oddly funereal.

"Not actually," responded one of the lawyers.

Mike Ensign walked in. The escape clause that Christensen re-garded as prudent looked outrageous to him. Mandalay would be on tenterhooks with a year-long antitrust review, unable to proceed with any development plans.

At this point, Ensign made a great leap of logic. "Kirk got cold feet. They want out," he told the group. He called the five-bedroom, seven-bath home Kerkorian has maintained since 1992 in the Las Vegas Country Club, a once-tony neighborhood that has lost its ca-chet as suburbs grew to the west and south.

Kerkorian's answering machine picked up and Ensign left a mes-sage. Terry Lanni was also notably absent, attending Ronald Reagan's funeral at the invitation of his friend Nancy Reagan.

Schaeffer and Ensign felt silly for asking the board to fly in for nothing. "We were embarrassed," says Schaeffer. Instead of a sale, Mandalay's board spent two hours figuring out how to shore up the company's stock price once news of the dead deal got out. Arbitra-geurs were going to sell so fast, it'd be like holding a vacuum to Mandalay's ballooned stock.

But Ensign was terribly mistaken. Kerkorian had left for Los An-geles and hadn't received the telephone message. By the time the Las Vegas housekeeper had arrived for work and relayed Ensign's com-munication to her boss in California, Mandalay's board had settled on a new plan: they would turn "The Hotel"—the hipster, boutiquey hotel attached to Mandalay Bay—into an international hotel brand and agreed to announce another casino resort on land just to the south of Mandalay Bay.

Kerkorian did finally call Ensign, but he was out of touch with the details of the negotiation and had no idea about the offending clause. His penchant for leaving the minutiae up to his minions nearly killed the whole deal.

"Kirk, these terms don't seem in keeping with our discussions up to this point," Ensign said. "Are these the terms you mean?"

"Yes," Kerkorian replied, trusting that his team had gotten it right.

Glenn Schaeffer didn't bother to warn MGM Mirage. His gilt tongue worked overtime that afternoon in a series of television and newspaper interviews. "Our offer morphed into an option," Schaeffer sniped. "It is not in the best interest of Mandalay shareholders to agree to a deal that gives MGM control over whether it closes."

Kerkorian seemed resigned. "OK, well, it is what it is," he said calmly. To Murren and Lanni, the public rebuff was a big, humiliating slap in the face—a giant "F-you," Murren said.

Schaeffer left his sprawling office that evening to pick up Chinese take-out and a glass of Riesling—a grape he was studying because his vintner was raising it in New Zealand. Schaeffer figured Murren would never talk to him again. "I thought he'd say, 'Fuck you,'" Schaeffer said.

But when his cell phone rang at the restaurant, he couldn't resist taunting Murren. "Did you see my rocket's red glare over your bow?" Schaeffer teased.

"You're a very funny guy," Murren said. "You're very clever. Ballsy. I love this 'morph' thing. You are the master of the sound bite."

They laughed awkwardly.

"What's going on?" Murren asked. "Is there a way to get this done?"

"Yes."

By evening, MGM's attorneys suddenly became comfortable with the antitrust risk. Kerkorian was willing to buy Mandalay without caveat, if they could settle on a price.

Saturday, June 12, 2004

In a third secretive meeting at Schaeffer's Park Towers condominium building, Murren and Schaeffer searched in the dark for a light switch. They felt with their fingers along the walls for the lights, by the building's wine cellar, and then haggled over price.

"We're still friends," Schaeffer assured Murren.

The next day, Sunday, Schaeffer was invited to Terry Lanni's swank office at Bellagio.

Lanni is studiously svelte, with thinning hair and a cool, formal manner. He has spent so much time cultivating Asian baccarat players that he instinctively holds to their codes of etiquette—not turning the sole of his shoe toward an associate, for example. For years, people have speculated that he would enter politics. He's well behaved. Not flashy. For Christmas one year, he gave Jim Murren an Hermès blanket. It hit just the right note: rich, understated, with just a hint of warmth.

Now Lanni told Schaeffer, "I'm going to give you a price, and I'm telling you, it's not going to be one penny over: Seventy-one dollars."

Schaeffer drove away thrilled. He had been prepared to take $70.

Sometime after five p.m., Schaeffer dialed Jim Murren on his cell phone and delivered a flippant "Hi, boss." With its dual tones of humor and deference, this pleased Murren immensely.

Only months before, Ensign had sold three million Mandalay shares at less than $40 apiece in what must go down in history as one of the worst-timed insider stock sales of all time: Ensign had lost out on nearly $100 million in profits. In the way of these things, Mandalay's board made some of it up to him with a gift of more shares.

With the seal of a handshake, it seemed the only thing left was a grand announcement Monday morning. Murren and Schaeffer were both eager to trumpet their deal. But the Mandalay executives couldn't move as fast as Kerkorian. Only two nonmanagement members had been reached. "We can't have the rest of them read in *The Wall Street Journal* that we have an agreement," said Yvette Landau, the company's general counsel. She wanted to announce that Mandalay "would consider" Kerkorian's offer.

To MGM, this was no trifling detail. Murren hit the ceiling, thinking that Mandalay was backing out. "This is humiliating to us," he stormed, according to a person who witnessed the events. Murren suspected that Schaeffer might screw him again, so Schaeffer headed into enemy territory after dinner, entering through a private executive entrance that bypassed the casino. He did this over the objections of all his advisers. "We told him to get the fuck out," says Joele Frank, a public relations veteran of two decades of big Wall Street deals who was working for Mandalay. "We couldn't believe he went in there."

At Bellagio, lawyers, publicists, and strategists were shouting into telephones or picking at BlackBerrys. "We were like, 'What the fuck

are you doing?' And they were like, 'What the fuck are *you* doing?'"
Murren later said.

People tried to contact Kerkorian. "Luckily, no one reached him,"
said one person involved, who believes Kerkorian would have felt be-
trayed by Ensign. "Kirk is very much a handshake guy."

Strategists on both sides watched in shock as the deal appeared to
unravel again. "It was so frigging weird," says Stephanie Pillarsdorf,
one of MGM Mirage's advisers who was there that night. Joele Frank
calls the whole thing a "total fuck-up." She explained: "Sunday night,
everybody was exhausted. They began to scream at each other over
stupid, stupid stuff. And Jim wasn't exactly calm. Glenn was just sitting there getting yelled at by everybody. Glenn was truly a Ping-
Pong ball."

Around midnight, Schaeffer drew Murren out into the beige-
carpeted corridor. They sat and talked as the deal team watched sur-
reptitiously. Schaeffer leaned into the strung-out Murren and grasped
him in an $8-billion embrace. "Don't worry, we're going to get a
deal," Schaeffer told Murren. "This is all just bullshit—we know
that."

In Schaeffer's arms, Murren muttered, "These damn lawyers . . ."

Monday, June 14, 2004

The deal was announced in sloppy, contradictory press releases.

MGM Mirage claimed to have cinched the deal. Mandalay said its
board would consider the sale. By the afternoon, the distinction was
meaningless.

As Wall Street buzzed, Steve Wynn couldn't help but take a canny
stab at Kerkorian. He waved a red flag for government antitrust regulators by suggesting that Kerkorian would control the whole town.
"Don't worry," Wynn joked by cell phone from New York. "Life'll be
good in Kirkville."

Wynn had just left the Tony Awards, where *Avenue Q* had won
Best Musical. He whispered into his cell phone as he sneaked down a
hallway, heading to a surprise birthday party for the actor Hugh Jackman, who had just won a Tony himself. The world didn't know it yet,

but Wynn had just cinched a blockbuster agreement to bring *Avenue Q* to Wynn Las Vegas.

Days later, Wynn's feat was said to be the dawn of a new era in theater. *Avenue Q* had been lured by the promise of an expensive custom-built theater paid for with casino money. Rather than travel around the country, its cast could live in Las Vegas. This proved so attractive that *Avenue Q*'s producers agreed not to show the production in many regional markets. This was a blow to regional theater owners, for whom a traveling Tony winner is bread and butter.

Broadway insiders griped that *Avenue Q*'s producers had garnered Tony votes by promising to take it on the road—all the while knowing they were about to sign with Steve Wynn. Some theater owners had voted for the R-rated Sesame Street–esque play, hoping to bring it to their theaters and hype its award-winning status.

Broadway fans shuddered that their milieu might be eclipsed by Las Vegas, but Steve Wynn finally had his Broadway show. It wasn't *Miss Spectacular*, but it felt spectacular. Kerkorian had to buy other people's casinos, but Wynn was creating his own. "The only one with growth in their company is me," Wynn gloated over the phone, cackling as he crept toward Hugh Jackman's party. "We're here. Gotta go." *Click.*

Back in Las Vegas, Glenn Schaeffer found the new world strangely silent. He was discovering that he was "yesterday" as far as Wall Street was concerned. "My phone stopped ringing on Monday. Really," he said at the time, surprised. "No bankers. No analysts. Nobody's calling me."

A day or so later . . .

Ken Moelis, a Los Angeles investment banker, stood at the window of his Beverly Hills home. Outside, a group of ladies on a charity tour strolled through his gardens, familiar to some because the Moelis family lived next door to the Osbournes, whose MTV reality show had lately focused on battles between the Moelis family and their heavy-metal neighbors. In a recent episode, some Osbournes had tossed cat feces onto the Moelises' tennis court.

Ken Moelis pondered whether Kerkorian's Mandalay might

generate some business for him. Moelis was head of banking for UBS Warburg, which made him an administrator most days. But he had started out with Drexel in its junk-bond heyday, and he fed off the macho energy of mergers and acquisitions. "Maybe I ought to be a banker again," Moelis thought, according to a person privy to the moment.

Kerkorian's deal-making had left only two other casino giants in Las Vegas: Caesars Entertainment and Harrah's Entertainment. Caesars had a world-famous name and glam properties, but it was loaded with debt and had been undermanaged for years. Stephen Bollenbach, its chairman, was more focused on his day job as chief executive of Hilton Hotels Corp. and with moving about Beverly Hills society. As a result, the company's casinos suffered.

Bollenbach had even broached the subject of selling the casinos to Harrah's a few months earlier. Gary Loveman, who had just won the race for chief executive at Harrah's, had politely demurred. Some CEOs are deal guys; there's nothing they like better than screwing somebody. Their blood heats with the chase. That's not Loveman.

Loveman saw all the work that Caesars required, so he wasn't focused on what a marriage could create: the first truly national casino company—bigger than MGM Mirage and Mandalay together. It would own a powerful arsenal of Las Vegas casinos—including Caesars Palace, Bally's, the Flamingo, and Paris. In the heartland, more casinos could draft gamblers and deploy them like soldiers to resort hubs in Atlantic City, New Orleans, and Las Vegas.

Seize the moment, Moelis advised Bollenbach a day or so later. Take another run at Loveman. "Sell now or wait seven years."

Bollenbach saw what Loveman had missed. In doing so, he cinched the new future of the once highly competitive Las Vegas as an oligopoly controlled by two or three giants. Bankers like to give acquisition deals code names. This one was "Jekyll and Hyde."

chapter twenty-four

CAESARS

Most of our people are still on their first marriages. You won't find us at parties at four a.m.

—GARY LOVEMAN

eading a double life, Loveman was a normal dad in Boston and a casino mogul in Las Vegas.

At home, the Lovemans attended their kids' soccer games and ushered them through homework and friendships, leading a privileged life but not an extreme one. They built a vacation home on the beach in North Carolina, but there were no ski trips with movie stars or Park Avenue apartments. Kathy Welsh did not even want a housekeeper to interrupt her family's privacy. So the Lovemans cleaned their home themselves on Saturdays. Among his various household duties, Gary Loveman cleaned the toilets.

Loveman did have a brief fling with a Ferrari. He sold it. He said it wasn't a practical car.

A distracting consequence of his job as Harrah's chief executive was the frequent requests by parents of his children's friends who sought their own Vegas dreams. A dentist who wanted to work on anything but teeth asked for a job. Schools asked for Vegas getaways to be donated for fund-raisers.

Even as they came with their hands out, Loveman felt the bite of moral judgment. He heard he had been rejected from the Harvard corporate advisory committee when a dean at the university insisted, "No way. Not a gambling company."

"People ask me all the time—old friends, neighbors. They say, 'What's it like to go from being a professor to gambling?' And they're not asking about corporations," Loveman said sadly. "It's a moral question."

In Las Vegas, Loveman lived in a one-bedroom suite overlooking the Rio's swimming pool. He chose this over one of the Rio's Palazzo suites, which had been built for high-rollers in the Rio's baccarat days. "It would send a very bad message for me to be pampered like that," he said. "Very bad."

Hotel staff, concerned about Loveman's increasing girth, kept a cereal bowl of pretzels and a few pieces of fruit on the dining table. He had a computer and an elliptical trainer brought in, and he hung a few suits in the closet, but otherwise lived the life of an ascetic in Las Vegas.

At work, Loveman fielded phone calls from his kids, and he often helped them with their schoolwork. "Your sister's driving you?" Loveman barked into his cell phone once, while lunching at chef Bobby Flay's restaurant at Caesars Palace. "Well, she'd better be taking her homework along to do while she's waiting." He rolled his eyes.

In his early years there, Loveman drove himself around Las Vegas in a used Mercedes. Exiting a casino with Steve Wynn or many other top casino executives can be like accompanying the queen at Buckingham Palace: Doormen snap to attention and a car magically appears at the curb. Leaving the Rio with Loveman was an anonymous act: He walked to the valet stand and waited in line for his turn.

As Loveman ran errands and navigated himself to meetings in Las Vegas, people warned that he and his family could become targets, as Kevyn Wynn had. Once, while buying a toothbrush at a drugstore near the Rio, several men walked up and said, "You're Gary Loveman, aren't you?"

So the company conducted a security study "and they came to the conclusion that I'm an idiot," Loveman said. "They said I'm a moron—they'd never seen anybody in my position who lived as out in the open as I did."

After that, Loveman sold the Mercedes, and Harrah's employed a guard named Tony—a brawny fellow who drove Loveman around in

a big SUV and stuck with him in Las Vegas from early morning until he headed to bed at night. In an attempt to keep his home life as
normal as possible, Loveman did not use Tony in Boston, although
the guard did conduct a security check and notify local police of the
VIP in their midst. It is an example of Loveman's cautious discomfort
with the celebrity of his new role that he asked that neither the
Boston-area town where he resides nor the names of his children be
identified in this book.

♣ ♦ ♥ ♠

Harrah's began to transform itself under Loveman, and the propeller heads' brainy tutelage. Loveman had won the race for CEO without much trouble. Colin Reed read his crystal ball and left Harrah's
after twenty-four years there, taking a job as chief executive of Gay-
lord Entertainment Inc., a Nashville-based convention-hotel operator,
in 2001.

Phil Satre relinquished his role as chief executive in 2003 and as
chairman two years later, after twenty-five years with the company.
"I don't think it makes sense to stay on as chairman when you're not
CEO," Satre said. "You've gotta let the other guy have it." Satre retired with a virtual squeal of joy, settling in on his ranch with his
wife, Jennifer. He fished in Alaska and bought a Montana ski condo.
Trimmer and with a new ruddy health, Satre grinned a lot after his
retirement, his brilliant teeth flashing white. "There's a lot of pressure
in running a public company," he said.

Once, on a visit to Las Vegas, Satre banged Loveman on the
shoulder and said with a healthy smile, "I'm so glad you're doing it
and not me!"

Loveman gained weight and seemed to grow older as the job's
responsibilities sank in. Colleagues worried that he was a stress
eater—and that there was no end in sight to his stress. His bouncy
energy disappeared. Steve Wynn managed to surround himself with
fun and adventure, merging his work with his hobbies. Loveman exhausted himself with work.

Once, in Boston, Loveman was being wired up for an appearance on CNN when his head began to nod. "I realized I was falling asleep," he said.

"I've been chronically fatigued for two years," he said in September 2005, two years after becoming CEO of Harrah's. He was forty-five.

Loveman was transforming Harrah's, though, with his scientific pursuit of gambler satisfaction and his insistence on using new technologies. By 2004, Harrah's hotels were so technologically savvy that when a customer dialed the reservation lines, the computer checked the incoming phone number against its database and placed them into the appropriate service queue—fastest for high-value gamblers—before the operator ever answered the call. Even hotel room prices were calculated in that split second, based on a complex mathematical formula that took into account how long the customer typically stayed, the games they played, and amounts they wagered.

Wynn and MGM Mirage used plush hotel rooms like fishing nets—the idea being to get a customer booked into the hotel so they would be likely to gamble more in the casino. Harrah's took the opposite approach. Harrah's discounted its hotel rooms for the real gamblers and made less profitable customers pay through the nose.

If you weren't a loyal Harrah's gambler, it made no sense to pay the price of staying in the Harrah's hotel. One day in the fall of 2004, a hotel room at the dreary Harrah's Las Vegas was quoted to a non-gambler at a nightly rate of $199—only $14 cheaper than a super-luxury room at Bellagio.

Revenue from gamblers who played at more than one Harrah's casino accounted for half of Harrah's revenues. This meant that gamblers were loyal to Harrah's outside of their home territory. They had, as Loveman had hoped, become less promiscuous, spending about 43 percent of their gambling wallet at Harrah's, up from 36 percent.

Satre and Loveman had bought up regional competitors whenever they could. One coup was the 2003 agreement to buy Horseshoe Gaming—a company started by Jack Binion, the son of legendary casino operator Benny Binion. Loveman even sniffed around Caesars Entertainment a few months later and came close to buying Station Casinos Incorporated prior to the Horseshoe deal. According to someone familiar with the talks, the board rejected the Station deal because the $110 million in golden parachutes—lucrative payments and benefits given to departing executives—for Station's executives was distasteful to Harrah's board.

In his quest to "normalize" the casino business, Loveman sought to connect Harrah's with more mainstream entertainment. He spoke with the owners of media distribution channels such as Liberty Media Corp., Viacom Inc., and News Corp. about melding gambling and interactive television or mobile communication devices. Would it be possible, Loveman posited, to build a gambling game around the outcome of a television show like *Survivor*? He considered buying a game show because marketing research shows that game shows attract viewers who tend to also be avid gamblers.

After repeated rebuffs, Loveman deduced that such an alliance "is the pink elephant at the cocktail party that nobody wants to talk about. So we always bring it up. We have profitable content, and they have distribution and we should find some way to put them together."

Jan Jones tried to hush him, warning that he could end up with a "big red bull's-eye" on his chest as far as several state attorneys general were concerned. She worried that then-New York attorney general Eliot Spitzer would make a gambling-technology battle a part of his upcoming platform in a race for governor.

Some of Loveman's ideas—namely blending games with mobile technologies—were widely viewed as illegal in the United States under federal laws. Undaunted, Loveman wanted to bang the drum with Congress. "Ultimately, you have to hit that head-on. If a family can make the decision to bring in pornography and sports channels," he asked, then why not gambling?

All this while, Harrah's was suffering for its lack of a high-end casino in Las Vegas. After finding little of interest to buy on the Strip—Kerkorian controlled half of it, and much of the rest was either in sorry condition or not for sale—Loveman became enamored with the idea of building a megacasino. He had come a long way from Harvard.

This idea of building so enthused him that when Steve Bollenbach called in the spring of 2004 to propose that he buy the Caesars empire, Loveman said he wasn't interested.

"I wanted to build on the Strip," Loveman says.

To be sure, long ignored by Bollenbach, Caesars was in a corporate shambles, its assets as underused as any in the gambling industry. After Arthur Goldberg's death, Bollenbach had hired Tom Gallagher, Hilton's corporate general counsel, who proved so indecisive that Caesars empire stagnated. Bollenbach finally fired Gallagher and replaced him the easy way—by promoting Wally Barr, the company's chief operating officer.

Barr was a solid choice to finish a sorely needed expansion of Caesars Palace, and he made a fine chief operating officer. But he was a poor public speaker and failed utterly to shine with investors, Wall Street analysts, or other parties whom chief executives are expected to court. What's more, with such poor leadership since Arthur Goldberg's death, Goldberg's management system was still in place, as though on autopilot. Loveman sounded like a professor when he referred, accurately, to the Caesars operations as "*de minimus* corporate overhead and every man, woman, and child for himself."

That summer, it dawned on Loveman that building one casino wouldn't be enough. Kerkorian had changed the equation of competition in Las Vegas by the sheer size of his holdings there. Consider what MGM Mirage properties would consist of once the Mandalay deal closed: Bellagio, MGM Grand, Mandalay Bay, Monte Carlo, Luxor, Mirage, Treasure Island, Excalibur, New York-New York, and Circus Circus.

With the numbers of Harrah's customers clambering to go to Las Vegas, and the need to keep them out of MGM Mirage casinos, Loveman said, "We'd have to build two. And nobody's ever done that." They would cost a couple of billion dollars each, and they wouldn't be expected to open until 2008.

So the banker Ken Moelis's epiphany in his study that day in 2004 was well timed. Moelis egged Bollenbach on, convincing him to take another run at enticing Loveman to buy Caesars Entertainment. This time, Loveman was ready to listen. "One thing that dawned on me—and you might argue I'm slow-witted in my timing—is the advantages of having six properties bunched together. Shame on me, but it took a while for that idea to crystallize," Loveman said.

With Caesars, Harrah's could complete its hub system, feeding gamblers from dozens of local casinos into Las Vegas, Atlantic City, and New Orleans.

Four weeks of discussions ensued between Loveman and Bollenbach. Loveman learned that Caesars Palace was expected that year to make $150 million in earnings before interest, taxes, depreciation, and amortization. The dowdy Harrah's Las Vegas would make $135 million—only $15 million less. "You've just gotta believe we can do better with that than they have," Loveman said.

For two CEOs who appeared to want to marry, the deal was remarkably difficult to cut. It took three weeks to slice the numbers in a way that would allow Harrah's to keep its high ratings with credit agencies. By mid July, Loveman badly wanted the deal. "I got there. They didn't," Loveman said at one point during the talks. "Bollenbach and I have been negotiating this for days."

The emotions of Caesars board members played a role in this drama as well. For Barron Hilton, grandfather of the party girl Paris Hilton, selling Caesars was the end of an era that he had loved. Also, some Caesars board members were loath to relinquish the perks of casino directorship, according to a person familiar with the discussions. These goodies, always enjoyed by the boards of casino companies, included great seats at fights, fancy hotel suites, and sharing the glamour with friends.

"The scariest moment of the Caesars deal was when I looked around the room and thought, 'This board is gonna lose their lifestyle,'" said one person involved in the deal. "When you sell these companies, the board faces a change of lifestyle. They like going to these parties."

As the talks stretched out over the course of a summer month, Bollenbach flew to London and Paris. All of Las Vegas was vacationing. The Wynns took a private train trip through Oregon that summer with former British Prime Minister John Major, George Bush (senior), Las Vegas liquor lord Larry Ruvo, political adviser Sig

Rogich, their wives, and the Bushes' two grown granddaughters. "Every wife and every husband had their own bedrooms," Wynn said.

The Wynns had not joined the ranks of great philanthropists, but they enjoyed discussing the important issues of the day with powerful people. Wynn says John Major encouraged him to consider that he wouldn't always be able to insulate himself from the world's deep poverty. "Steve, there are five billion people in the world," Major said. "Three out of five live on two dollars a day or less. In twenty years, that will be five out of eight living in dire poverty. Now, how big a wall are you going to build around your grandchildren?"

Despite Wynn's pleasure at being included in such conversations, he gave no indication of changing his focus to poverty and hunger from luxury and art in the years that followed.

While everyone else was vacationing, Loveman headed with his family to their North Carolina beach house. His eldest son was leaving for college in a few weeks, and it felt like the end of an era for the family.

So the details were worked out with the Caesars and Harrah's executives scattered about the world. The Caesars vote was, ultimately, unanimous. Bollenbach and Barron Hilton demanded seats on Harrah's board and got them. Bollenbach approved the sale from London, and the Harrah's deal team scrambled to get in touch with Loveman at the beach to tell him he'd be getting a bill for $9.3 billion.

Yet another "biggest deal ever in the gambling industry" was signed, this one from a fax machine at the Dancing Turtle coffee shop in Hatteras, North Carolina. The satellite feeds for network and cable news were conducted from a corner of the homey wooden Cape Cod building with a long wraparound porch and a small parking area out front.

One could almost hear squeals of frustration emanating from MGM Mirage's corporate headquarters. Kerkorian's big deal had been eclipsed before it was consummated. The combined revenue of Harrah's and Caesars would be $8.8 billion, compared with MGM Mirage and Mandalay's $6.4 billion. Harrah's would have 96,000 employees, compared with MGM's 64,000.

It was no vote of confidence in Gary Loveman that Harrah's stock sank 10 percent the following three days. Wall Street, remembering the Rio's fall from grace, feared that Loveman would run Caesars Palace down as well. "The Rio used to be a snazzy place until Harrah's bought it," said Jason Ader, the former Bear Stearns analyst, who had recently launched a hedge fund called Hayground Capital.

Ader saw Loveman's move as a knee-jerk response to Kerkorian that lacked the elder's savvy. "Do they feel pressure to do something because of MGM Mirage? Sure looks that way. . . . The hidden value in Mandalay was the land, and Kirk knows that. But Caesars doesn't have that land benefit. The question is, will the Harrah's marketing machine add value here?"

One of Harrah's most loyal, long-term investors—and a fan of Loveman's—harbored similar concerns. "I think the guys at Harrah's just don't have the mindset for the high-end business. That's just not what they're about," said Mark Greenberg, a portfolio manager with Denver-based AIM Capital Management Inc. "At the Rio, they still don't know how they got hit so hard at high-end blackjack. And I don't know how they can't know that. They should know."

Loveman seemed caught off guard, choosing to stay with his family in North Carolina and doing piped-out television appearances from the Dancing Turtle rather than flying off for the press conferences and hand-shaking photo opportunities that typically accompany big deals.

With Bollenbach in Paris and Barron Hilton staying out of the limelight as always, there was no one on Hilton's side to make an appearance either. Loveman purposely chose not to ask Wally Barr, who hadn't been supportive of the sale, to participate. Loveman, in fact, openly disliked the uncooperative Barr and didn't see the point in a public display of affection. So there was no show of brotherhood between the Caesars and Harrah's executives.

This was a key public-relations misstep and contributed to Wall Street's impression that the deal was poorly hatched. "The market would have liked it if Loveman came out and said, 'I don't know that much about high-roller places, but lemme introduce you to Wally Barr, who's integral,'" says one investment banker who worked on the deal.

Instead, Loveman announced flatly that Caesars Entertainment would be worth more in Harrah's hands, thereby insulting both Bollenbach and the management at Caesars. "What's that mean? It means the management sucks," said one insulted Caesars insider. "I think they're very dismissive of the management."

Weeks later, when a Harrah's executive called to offer Barr, a golf aficionado, lifetime privileges at Caesars golf courses, Barr gruffly turned it down. "I'll never play at any of those places again," he said, according to a person privy to the conversation.

Still, people who know him say that Bollenbach's relief at ridding himself of the casinos—which he had never shown much interest in—was palpable. "I think Steve was like, 'Thank God,'" says one person who worked closely with Bollenbach.

Loveman did little to dispel concerns that he would downgrade Caesars Palace into a low-rolling serf's palace. In fact, he exacerbated them. "We're going to review the profitability of the whale business at Caesars Palace—especially with Steve Wynn about to open his place, which is really going to raise the stakes," Loveman said. "It's just this constant distraction for management. They get obsessed with it."

One thing changed in Loveman's life in a big way, once the Caesars deal came together. Steve Wynn suddenly took great notice of Loveman, signaling that the Harvard professor had finally joined the big leagues. Wynn called Loveman one day, saying he had read something Loveman had written in the *Harvard Business Review* about database management and he wanted to talk some more.

So Loveman had lunch with Steve and Elaine Wynn. They never really got around to talking business, and Loveman says he never really understood the point of the meeting. But it was nice to spend time with the former, and perhaps future king of Vegas.

"Steve *is* Las Vegas," Loveman said. "We wouldn't be here without him."

chapter *twenty-five*

RETURN OF THE KING

We don't want to say anything as crude as that the Bellagio was practice.

—STEVE WYNN, GRINNING

Steve Wynn peered intensely at three ancient Italian olive-oil vessels destined for his Bartolotta restaurant. The baked clay vessels, pockmarked and scraped, varied in size from huge to gigantic—higher than a tall man and bigger around than a bull's belly.

Seven moving specialists were on hand with a "propane-motored crane thingy," Wynn said, to hoist them from inside their necks and lower them into place a floor below. Wynn showed up to see the installation that evening with Andy Pascal, his nephew on his wife's side. As often happens when Wynn gets involved, a tantrum ensued. "They're too big. They won't fit in," Wynn hollered.

"Just let us put them in," Pascal interrupted. "It'll take four hours to move them. If you don't like them, you can take them out."

So Wynn threw his body against the jars to help lift them onto pads that would help them slide along the mosaic floor. Then he sat on a banquette and watched the show until three a.m. When he finally crawled into bed beside Elaine at Shadow Creek, she asked, "What happened? Something bad or something good?"

"Something good," Wynn replied. "I'll tell you about it in the morning." And he went to sleep.

Wynn spent most of the final weeks before his latest casino opening in the grip of this sort of panic. He needed more time, but was afraid to alarm his investors by delaying the opening.

"This is gonna be a squeaker," Wynn said in March 2005, several weeks before the scheduled opening, settled temporarily in the boardroom while his office was being finished. Wynn's dog Bora was gone, replaced by Sela, and the aged Palo lay as usual at his master's feet. Wynn addressed the dogs in their native German: *"Palo! Sitzt dich!"*

Marc Schorr, the resort's president, raced around the facility on a motorized cart, his shoulders hunched habitually forward, a frown etched on his face. "Wall Street will appreciate this because we'll get cash flow six months before," Schorr said, "but we're suffering initially."

♣ ♦ ♥ ♠

It turned out that Le Reve didn't work as a name for a Las Vegas casino. People couldn't pronounce it, and they didn't know what it meant.

Frank Luntz, the Republican pollster who had been doing marketing polls for Wynn for years, ran focus groups on the resort's name. Luntz discovered that Wynn's name alone was worth an extra $80 per night for a hotel room. He recommended naming the casino after its developer. "I call it the Wynn 'extra,'" Luntz says. "People are willing to pay more for him."

Calling it Wynn, of course, sounded like something Donald Trump would do. "I don't like Donald Trump," Luntz said, noting that Wynn and the Donald had called a truce to their long-running feud. "Three years ago, they hated each other. Donald would make blind jokes about Steve, and Steve would make hair jokes about Donald."

Wynn took Luntz's advice and named it Wynn Las Vegas anyway, explaining his decision with a quip: "This is the only place I felt good enough about to put my name on."

At the time, Wynn Las Vegas was probably the most expensive casino resort in the world. It had burled wood paneling, mosaic tile floors, and walls of crinkled fabric. Its $2.7-billion cost irritated some social consciences. This was a billion dollars more than Clark County spent educating 300,000 children. *Vanity Fair* noted the resort cost more than the $2.4 billion that the United States spent on world AIDS research that year.

With 2,716 hotel rooms, the Wynn would be small by the current Las Vegas standards, where most new hotels had more than 4,000 rooms. Each of the Wynn's rooms measured a minimum of 640 square feet—larger than many New York apartments. Luggage was nosed over by bomb-sniffing dogs in the back-of-house area before being delivered to rooms with 320-thread-count linens and at least two flat-screen televisions (one in the bathroom); electronically controlled drapes; and wall-to-wall, floor-to-ceiling windows. Guests were expected to pay, and they soon did pay, on the average, more than $300 a night to stay at the resort. They were the highest room prices in Las Vegas.

The designers who opened shops there included the Wynns' friend Oscar de la Renta, as well as Chanel, Dior, Gaultier, Cartier, Graff jewelers, Louis Vuitton, and Brioni. Manolo Blahnik, the shoe fetishist's designer, agreed to open his first outpost outside of New York there. Treating toe cleavage as an aphrodisiac, Blahnik stocked the shop with delights such as feather-covered stilettos. "After all, Las Vegas is a fantasy town," Blahnik explained in a video recording on Wynn Las Vegas's Web site.

There were three wedding chapels, twenty-two restaurants, and two theaters in addition to the one-of-a-kind Ferrari and Maserati dealership. Once open, the automobile showroom would sell so many Ferraris that Wynn would begin buying up inventory from dealers elsewhere in the country. The lines of people who wanted to catch a glimpse of a Ferrari snaked out of the salesroom, past the gift shop, and down the hall. Wynn, seeing a missed opportunity, began charging admission to walk through the dealership. This did not noticeably shorten the lines.

The resident Ferrari dealership henceforth played a big role in the Wynns' lives. Over dinner at Okada one night in December 2005, the Schorrs and Wynns chatted about their Ferrari habits. Marc Schorr had bought four Ferraris that year, and Steve Wynn had just bought Elaine a new Ferrari Spider. "You're gonna love it," he told his wife. "The engine's got that Ferrari sound, but it's muted inside. It rides like a Town Car."

The Wynn Las Vegas resort even had an 18-hole golf course, designed by Tom Fazio and Steve Wynn. This was remarkable, given how urban the Strip had become in the past twenty years, and how expensive land there had become. The 7,042-yard course had more than 100,000 shrubs, 4,600 linear feet of streams, and a 37-foot waterfall.

In front, the resort had Wynn's mountain: an edifice 140 feet high, with 1,500 freshly transplanted trees—some as high as 50 feet—a 100-foot waterfall, and a 3-acre reflecting pool that had been populated with 4,000 color-changing LED lights and a giant fiberglass head that could be raised and lowered from its depths during nightly sound and light performances.

To enhance the boutique feeling, Wynn turned down the volume on slot machines. He placed blackjack and craps tables near the hotel elevators to draw the attention of Armani-clad guests and heighten the Bond-in-Monaco sense of the place. There were plush salons for high-rollers, who could be ferried into town on one of Wynn Resorts' jets and escorted into the hotel tower through a private entrance. These guests could even slip downstairs to gamble without ever setting foot among the very well-heeled riffraff in the main casino.

Ever the aficionado of clever detail, Wynn placed a few conference rooms overlooking the topless area of the swimming pools—much to the delight and consternation of a group of investment bankers from UBS Warburg in the spring of 2005.

And yet after it opened, many people said they were disappointed in Wynn Las Vegas. The tower's exterior was an architectural departure for the city. The chocolate-and-copper tower, curved in an arc, lorded over the skyline and the Strip. It did not, however, impress architectural critics. Christopher Hawthorne of the *Los Angeles Times* joked, "The theme is mid-rise office tower in Houston, circa 1983."

Wynn was hurt, but unbowed. "You see if they don't start building crescent-shaped buildings around here now," Wynn said with a chuckle one afternoon. (In truth, his wasn't the first: Tony Marnell had built a crescent-shaped tower at the Rio in 1997.)

The fact is that Wynn was a victim of expectations. When they heard him boast that he was building the finest hotel in the world, they expected something bigger and grander-looking than Bellagio, not something more intimate and tasteful. People don't come to Las Vegas for good taste.

Wynn Las Vegas's genius lies in social stratification, the way it guides its human traffic and creates safe zones for the kind of people who stay at the Georges V in Paris or the Pierre in New York. The resort functions something like the Hamptons. A hotel within the hotel, known as the South Tower, serves as Easthampton, with its own exclusive lobby. This region connects to the baccarat salons via the discreet passageway.

This South Tower enclave draws the tanned and siliconed—celebrities and billionaires who withdraw amongst their own. The South Tower's swimming pool and cabanas are elevated above the pools that serve the rest of the resort, which become Westhampton by default—rich, yet lower-crust. The cocktail waitresses there, in discreet-yet-revealing white bathing suits and skirts (designed under the supervision of Elaine Wynn) are sublime in their care and cheerfulness.

There exists an echelon of people with wealth in the world that is willing to spend almost any amount on amusement, as long as it is exclusive enough. The Wynns knew this, from personal experience. "I tried to do here with intimacy what I did with grandeur at Bellagio," Wynn said, echoing his thoughts when he was designing the earlier Atlantic City resort. "Because people with money and discernment don't take pleasure in vast places. They're looking for places to be cozy."

In those final countdown hours before the opening, as morning television crews prepared to record live from the new resort, Wynn roamed and meddled. He might have been in his element while designing resorts, but he was miserable opening them. Five years of design and construction, late nights poring over plans and honing them.

Weeks to pick the perfect color of chocolate for the tower's skin. Two months spent choreographing the show on the lake, in the rain with umbrellas, in the wind. And then putting it out there for the reviews and results: sheer terror.

Farther south on the Las Vegas Strip, Kirk Kerkorian was just about to close on the Mandalay deal and control half the rooms on the Strip. Kerkorian couldn't find his way to the men's room in almost any of them, he'd never been there.

Kerkorian "never breaks a sweat," Wynn said that March with a note of wonder in his voice. "All those deals he's done—and he never sets foot in the building. He never misses a tennis game. He just likes bigger. He measures the cost of construction and the rate of inflation. I like the creative process," Wynn concluded flatly, "so I'm stuck."

Elaine had trouble letting go of Wynn Las Vegas—putting it into the hands of a public that might not appreciate it. The Wynns viewed the resort as an extension of their home and hearth. They had found the chocolate maker in Monte Carlo, discovered the florist via a happenstance meeting at the George V in Paris.

The Wynns' pain at letting go was contagious and spread to executives and flowed out through the rest of the staff. On the day of the opening, Elizabeth Blau, who created his restaurants, winced as the first diners picked up the utensils she'd picked out. Denise Randazzo, head of communications, joked sadly about turning Wynn Las Vegas over to the "unwashed masses."

Wynn was memorizing the resort until he knew it inch by inch. He barreled along the casino's shopping corridor two days before the opening, passing his destination without a glance: the dessert shop called Sugar & Ice. He came to a sudden halt before walking into a tall potted plant. Squinting at the waxy tropical leaves, he pursed his lips and peered upward, with an aspect of minute inspection.

Two days later, his appearance in the hall would draw crowds. People holding out cell-phone cameras would call out: "Steve!" "Mr. Wynn, Mr. Wynn!" "Thank you, Mr. Wynn, for everything you've done for Las Vegas!" But in the resort's preopening privacy, Wynn turned from the plant and swung his head in a wide arc, until his narrowly focused eyes lit upon the ice-cream shop's row of glass doors. He reversed himself and exited into the sunlight, as always, a master of recovery.

♣ ♦ ♥ ♠

After wandering through the Bartolotta restaurant, Wynn decided with only days to go that his designer Roger Thomas's choice of carpeting was gaudy. He insisted on ordering new carpeting at a cost of tens of thousands of dollars. "You better not screw with Roger," Elaine warned him. And Wynn heeded her words, chuckling about his brief mistrust of Thomas.

"The man carries a sketchbook," Wynn said of Thomas. "And he keeps it like Picasso. It's about five by seven. He keeps it in a shoulder purse. You know he's a gay guy," Wynn said, and then his mind leaped to another old friend, Roy Horn, the lion-tamer of Siegfried & Roy. Wynn waved his arm, gesturing around the resort. "This is swashbuckling nerve. Gay or not—Roger and Roy Horn. You can't get sexual preference confused with guts."

To Elaine, Wynn confessed that he feared his anxiety would hamper his employees. "Steve was in that preopening anxiety mode," Elaine said later. "And he gets impatient and he can't wait for things to get finished. He was driving me crazy. I wanted to commit him."

He continued making rounds, involved in every detail. One afternoon, a soprano, blond and thirtyish, auditioned for a lounge singer's job at the casino's Parasol Up bar. She wore a clingy string-strapped evening dress of maroon satin. Accompanying her were a bearded pianist and the last-minute drilling and hammering of construction crews.

Wynn arrived in a natty pink polka-dot tie, straight from his lunch and a manicure. He leaned across the piano, so close that she must have felt his breath. Without taking her eyes off of him, the singer leaned in to Wynn and shimmied her torso.

She finished her song, languid and throaty, and began another. Her index finger tickled the piano's lid. "I like that," Wynn said. When he turned and headed across the casino to inspect the baccarat pit, the back of his head revealed a bald spot, artfully concealed by blackened hair.

Outside, three Clark County cranes tied up traffic working overtime to build three pedestrian overpasses to the Wynn. An emergency call was routed through to Les Henley, a county public works director. The emergency was Steve Wynn, who had gotten caught in a traffic snarl on the way to work that morning.

Wynn's side of the conversation was typically bombastic:

> *"Les? Steve Wynn."*
> *(. . .)*
> *"A little hassled by my trip this morning. It took me forty minutes to go the length of Treasure Island."*
> *(. . .)*
> *"We've got a two-point-seven-billion-dollar hotel opening with ninety-seven hundred employees. The county can't pretend they didn't know it was coming. My employees can't get to work."*
> *(. . .)*
> *"Your guys have gotta work on a graveyard shift. Unless you're gonna cut us loose here."*

♣ ♦ ♥ ♠

Shadow Creek had long since ceased to feel like a permanent home. Wynn's anger lurked just beneath the surface. Staff at Shadow Creek told Wynn a year or so after MGM took over that they had been ordered to shoot his exotic birds—pheasants and others—that Wynn had loved like pets. "They did it because the feed was sixty thousand dollars a year," Wynn growled, his eyes angry.

People at MGM Mirage profess to know nothing about any birds being shot.

Eventually, Bobby Baldwin called Steve Wynn to tell him he'd sold the two hundred acres around Shadow Creek, where Wynn had once planned to build a luxury community.

"The sixty-four-thousand-dollar question is who'd you sell it to?" Wynn asked.

"Centex Homes," Baldwin replied, according to Wynn.

Wynn called his wife. "Elaine, the neighborhood is about to change," he told her.

They sold the Shadow Creek home to MGM Mirage that summer in accordance with their contract. They settled into one of Wynn Las Vegas's high-roller villas. Thereafter, Steve Wynn could be found haunting the resort at all hours, scratching his chin and reworking his decisions like Banquo's ghost. Wynn Las Vegas became the Wynns' own Versailles—the palace where they entertained the world and their friends.

At Okada one evening, the Wynns signed for the check for the table of five, leaving a crisp $100 bill for a tip. Elaine Wynn dismissed one of her guests' attempt to pay with a firm wave of her hand. "If I cooked for you, you wouldn't pay," she said, motherly.

Her office was a study in feminine chic—all creamy, sheer curtains and walls covered in squares of rice paper, surrounding a living area where she liked to nap on the couch in the afternoons in front of the television. Elaine Wynn kept a framed photo of herself and Steve in their youth. It was taken at a costume party, and they are dressed country-western. Her head is thrown back, laughing, while the young mogul-to-be nuzzles her neck, a white cowboy hat on his head.

"I have never been as stressed as I was in the endgame here," she said one morning three months after the resort opened, her legs curled on that couch. "Will they like it as much as what we've done before?

"The expectation that was created out of Bellagio for this place was overwhelming to us. We'd go out to the movies, to dinners— Steve and I are regular Joes really—and people would come up to us and say, 'I can't wait to see how you exceed that place.' Of course, it was a double-edged sword."

Her role had grown at each of Wynn's resorts until she was her husband's most trusted adviser. She had warned him at Bellagio not to place the spa far from the hotel tower elevators: He had ignored her, leaving spa guests to march through the entire casino, their faces flaming from the latest chemical peel or facial. "I had a good I-told-you-so," she says. "You'll notice that in this property, the spa is by the hotel tower. I think he trusts my instincts more and more as things have progressed.

"Steve's process is his unique process, and it drives me crazy," she said of her husband's way of going about designing. "He draws it out, and he'll call me in and I'll critique it and the next morning I'll go in and he'll have thrown it away. He wants me to sit there on the stool with him while he measures, *da-da-da-dupp*"—she took her hand and mimicked drawing in the air.

♣ ◆ ♥ ♠

That spring of 2005, Wall Street experienced a wave of enthusiasm for Wynn Resorts Ltd. Ground had broken for Wynn Macao, off the coast of China, and drawings were underway for the second phase of Wynn's Disney-esque plans in Las Vegas, christened Encore by Elaine Wynn.

Steve Wynn spoke of an empire with more resorts in Singapore, perhaps even Thailand. "We're going to be an Asian company," he said once, his eyebrows raised in surprise. Wynn knew how to do business in Asia. To help this along a few years later, he would buy a rare Ming vase at auction for $10.1 million and donate it to a museum in Macao—currying great favor in China while overlooking his hungry hometown art museum, the Nevada Museum of Art in Las Vegas.

With no properties open and no revenues, Wynn Resorts stock was trading on pure speculation. It shot up like one of the dot-coms of yore. From its initial offering price of $13 in October 2002, it had risen to $76.45 a share on March 16, 2005. Wynn was a billionaire.

Wynn noted cheerily in a moment of uncanny prescience that winter that the reality of his casinos could hardly live up to the expectations. "I've made more money in four years with this company than in fifteen years at my old one. I open that property, and I screw the stock," he said, chortling.

He had finally figured out the stock market.

♣ ♦ ♥ ♠

And in fact, the casino hadn't yet opened on the April Saturday when David Anders put on a pair of Levi's and a T-shirt in his Upper West Side brownstone and decided to pull the plug.

Anders covered the casino business as a stock analyst with Merrill Lynch. It was his job to advise the firm's clients on when to buy and sell stocks. At thirty-nine, he was one of the older analysts in the field, and he felt he was seeing something he'd seen before—a bubble of irrational investor enthusiasm in China.

This bubble was creating all sorts of new billionaires. The eccentric Sheldon Adelson had recently taken public his Las Vegas Sands Corp., parent of the Venetian, which was built on the property Adelson had bought from Kerkorian years before. Going public catapulted Adelson from obscurity to number 19 on the *Forbes* List of World's Richest People with a net worth of $15.6 billion. This happened to Adelson because he, like Wynn, had obtained permission to build a casino in Macao that would cater to millions of Asians on their own continent. And Adelson's Macao casino was going to open long before Wynn's.

Adelson's astounding jackpot unseated Las Vegas's reigning billionaire, Kirk Kerkorian, who racked up a mere fortune of $8.9 billion that year.

As Anders headed out into the damp Manhattan springtime for a coffee and newspaper, he concluded—wrongly, as time would prove—that China couldn't possibly deliver on the high expectations. Wynn's stock was an obvious "sell," he thought. There was no news that could drive the price up further. He said later, "It just popped into my head."

On Tuesday afternoon, while Wynn was fretting over Bartolotta's carpet, Anders presented Merrill's research committee with his thesis. "We knew it was going to be a controversial call," he says. "This was a very high-flying company."

Anders called Wynn's balance sheet "exhausted," and he argued that investors were assuming a best-case scenario for the opening of

Wynn Las Vegas. Had Wynn any idea of the icy blast that was about to hit his company, he would no doubt have felt the chill of déjà vu.

Anders spent the evening prior to his report's release on his couch, nursing his nerves. His report was released around 7:15 a.m. He sent calls from Las Vegas's 702 area code into voice mail to "let them cool down for a few hours." Unfortunately for Anders, Ron Kramer, president of Wynn Resorts, was working out of his New York office that day. Anders picked up the phone and received the full blast of Kramer's freshly minted wrath.

When the markets closed for the weekend, Wynn's personal net worth had been shorn by $153 million.

Franco Dragone is an old friend of the Wynns. A cofounder of Cirque du Soleil, he created *Mystère* at Treasure Island and *O* at Bellagio. Dragone split from Cirque while Wynn was building his comeback casino.

With the trust of years of friendship, Dragone was given carte blanche to design Wynn Las Vegas's main entertainment attraction. Wynn had initially ordered up an outdoor show on a lake, with Jet-Skiers and other water performers—much like he had once planned for Bellagio. But by the time he added a roof and climate control to keep away the desert heat, the lake became an elaborate indoor theater-in-the-round.

Wynn built his Belgian friend Dragone a theater unlike any in the world—2,080 seats encircling a million-gallon pool of water in which lifts could rise and fall, creating sets for performers, some of whom worked in scuba gear. A domed roof rained on the pool, housed pigeons, and served as another point of entry to this circus of the surreal.

Originally, Wynn wanted to call the show *Genesis—the Comedy*. But when pollster Frank Luntz tested the name in focus groups, baby boomers were confused. They were unsure whether this was a reference to the Bible or to the Phil Collins rock group of their youth. What's more, the show wasn't funny. "Thank God Elaine talked him out of that," said Luntz. The show inherited the name *Le Reve*.

Unfortunately, *Le Reve* was just plain bad. Conceptually, it followed a character named Wayne as he dreamed from nightmare to redemption. But few early viewers even realized there was a character named Wayne. Populated by aerialists, acrobats, and swimmers, the show was dark, depressing, and confusing. For no apparent reason, pole-dancing women were beaten by men in a sadistic dream sequence. Wynn executives warned that women's groups would be picketing outside the resort. In another scene, pregnant women dressed in white were dropped, over and over, from high in the theater's domed ceiling. Even some of the show's collaborators winced.

Wynn watched the rehearsals and became frantic. Daily, he asked Elaine Wynn to attend the rehearsals. "Please," he begged her. Each day, Elaine refused. "My plate is full," she told him. "I can't go—I'll be sick if I don't like it."

The following August, four months after the opening, at which time she still hadn't managed to see the whole show, she said, "I love Franco. That's another reason I didn't want to go see the show. I didn't want to see my opinion of Franco diminished."

So the unnerved Wynn turned to Frank Luntz, who was on business in Britain. When Wynn insisted it was an emergency, Luntz bought a $6,000 plane ticket and flew in for the job.

"If Steve says 'shit,'" quipped Luntz, "I say, 'How much?'"

Luntz's test audience complained. "The only thing they liked is the theater," Luntz said.

Dragone, a chubby doe-eyed man with unruly dark hair, acknowledged that Wynn was "freaked out" and scared. But he clung to his show with palpable desperation, resisting Wynn's push for a clear narrative. "I don't want to have a story line that pulls us by the nose and we don't see what's going on around," he said in French-accented English.

"With his eyes, he can't see everything that's going on," said Dragone, his voice rising in frustration. "My shows are the opposite of Steve. He can't see all that's going on onstage."

A day or so later, a group of Wynn's artists gathered over a slow dinner and several bottles of wine at the resort's SW Steakhouse, which had served them for a test run.

The group included the puppeteer Michael Curry and the lighting designer Patrick Woodroffe, who wanted to work out kinks in the timing of *Fiesta Fatale,* one of several short shows that would play on a reflecting pool at the foot of Wynn's mountain. Wynn called the pond the Lake of Dreams. In it, a tall stone wall served alternately as the spillway for a dramatically lit waterfall and as a film-projection screen.

Curry is best known for his creations for Disney on Broadway's *The Lion King.* He is small of stature with boyish, round features and a self-contained Oregonian manner that contrasts with the angular features and heart-on-sleeve manner of Woodroffe.

Drawn to Las Vegas for work, they had each become unexpectedly affectionate about Las Vegas. Woodroffe, a Brit more accustomed to working concert tours with the Rolling Stones or Bob Dylan—although he once lighted Buckingham Palace—had been working in Mexico City when Wynn called to say he wanted to turn his lake red. "He hired me before we even talked about money," Woodroffe said, and he thereafter spent so much time working on the Wynn project that he purchased, in addition to the London home he shared with his wife and kids, a vintage ranch house in Las Vegas that had formerly been built for Bill Boyd, one of the town's early gambling entrepreneurs. Wynn sent Woodroffe four double beds as a housewarming present.

After dark, the Lake of Dreams became a theater for nine brief shows that melded video, music, light, and, in the case of a three-minute bit called "Jungle Bill," large, elaborate puppets. At times, a 27-foot fiberglass head rose from the depths, water sheeting from its face. The features of a woman could be projected onto it, wriggling her eyebrows and making smooching expressions with her lips.

Under the lake's water were 4,400 LED lights whose colors could be programmed with the aid of a computer. They turned the lake into a crude pixel screen. At times, air bubbles were released underwater. When the light was diffused through the tiny bubbles, the lake became a broiling psychedelic cauldron.

Curry joined Woodroffe around 11:15 one night shortly before the opening wearing a white, gauzy peasant shirt. They sat on a cushioned bench at the Parasol Down bar.

"I'm having a hard time letting go," Woodroffe confessed gloomily.

"Do you always have this postpartum depression?" asked Curry. Earlier in the evening, he had told an installment of an ongoing bedtime story to his small children at home in Oregon.

Woodroffe gestured toward a terrace that overlooked the Lake of Dreams. "That was my terrace for months," Woodroffe said.

Curry nodded. "I always have this," he said. "And the bigger the hit, the bigger the depression."

Outside, people were already lining up on the Strip to gawk at the mountain. Television news stations had been running nightly updates. Newspapers griped that they hadn't been granted open access. Security guards chased people who sneaked in for a forbidden peek.

Inside, employees, dressed shyly in their Sunday best, brought their families to dine, sleep, gamble "on the house," and put the place to the test. At eleven o'clock the following morning, Marc Schorr's daily staff meeting became a litany of things gone awry. Missing ashtrays, ice buckets, lightbulbs, remote-control batteries, construction dust clinging to furnishings—things expected in any new resort.

Employees caused bigger problems by taking advantage of their chance to romp. Resort operators handled six hundred calls from employees trying to change their assigned restaurant reservations. Front-desk managers upgraded friends to suites the hotel wasn't prepared to fill. The SW Steakhouse ran out of steak when people ordered two and even three entrées.

"Our employees are pigs," Schorr griped. "The general public will not be eating and drinking like that."

A dozen oversized banquet waiters were still waiting for their Armani uniforms to be re-cut, because Armani, being Armani, didn't make sizes large enough for them.

Wynn was still meddling. He wouldn't allow his restaurant prices to fall below Bellagio's. So at Bartolotta, the price of a 28-ounce prime rib-eye steak was hastily raised from $38 to $48.

A customer due to arrive the next day was causing a ruckus about his suite. "[He] likes to stay in number seven but he won't stay in a red suite," reported a hotel operations manager. She suggested that the villas be renumbered. "I don't want to change it for one gentleman. Just leave it. He'll get over it," said Schorr.

The casino was full of rumors that Dragone's show was in trouble. Marc Schorr filled the staff in on the latest news on *Le Reve*. "They took the pole act out," he said. "That made such a difference—the slapping of the women around.

"They're still dropping the pregnant ladies," Schorr added.

chapter twenty-six

BLIND MAN'S BLUFF

MGM thought they'd gotten rid of Wynn—they never thought he'd get the money. If you're gonna hurt 'em, be sure to kill 'em: They didn't kill Wynn.

—Anonymous inhabitant of the Las Vegas Strip

pril 2005. Steve Wynn likened Wynn Las Vegas to a beautiful model on the cover of *Vogue*. He tended to think in more explicit terms, but he told a G-rated audience of his new employees, "This hotel is about having that woman *hug* you. Let the huggin' begin."

On a rainy spring Sunday three days before the opening, Wynn had stood in a hallway outside the doors that led into the resort's Lafite ballroom. The floor beneath his big feet was a brilliant swirl of red and gold and green—inspired by a Cézanne painting that had caught his fancy. He shrugged his shoulders, a showman preparing for his debut.

In his sixth decade, he was taut, artfully sculpted, polished. His face was burnished from forty-seven days of skiing that winter at Sun Valley. As always, he wore his hair Vegas style: blown dry with sideburns, brushed back at the sides and a tad long in back so that it swept into the merest hint of a ducktail behind his lantern jaw.

In a spirit of renewal that befitted his return as a Las Vegas casino mogul, Wynn had embarked six months earlier upon a low-carbohydrate diet. He liked to say it was no diet, but a way of life. Wynn said he had shed thirty pounds by eliminating pizza and pasta from his diet and dining instead on Atkins cereal with Silk soymilk for breakfast, and poached salmon for lunch.

In the past year, Wynn's sixty-three-year-old waistline had dwindled to a svelte 32½ inches. He did not shy from boasting about this after trying on pants at the Mojitos Resort Wear shop that week. He did not mention liposuction, though one executive in Las Vegas who is closely familiar with the Wynns says, "They don't lose weight like you and I do."

Wynn wore a dark suit over a silky black Chinese-collared shirt. Between the shirt and his hairy chest lay a silver pendant with the initials "CM" placed vertically, the C facing backwards. For as long as Wynn could remember, this necklace had been worn by his father's former bookie, Charlie Meyerson. After Wynn's father had died, Meyerson had befriended Wynn and later went to work for him as a casino host, catering to gamblers. He had died of cancer the previous November, shortly before turning eighty-nine. A few weeks later, a package arrived. The note said with understatement, "Thanks" and there was the pendant. "So I put it on and I haven't taken it off since," said Wynn.

Wynn Las Vegas was set to open the following Thursday at the stroke of midnight. On the other side of the ballroom doors, about a third of the resort's 9,700 employees waited as though expecting a rock star. They were card dealers, cocktail waitresses, housekeepers, sous chefs, security guards, dog handlers, gardeners, lighting techs, and a few special guests. Wynn's daughter Kevyn sat in the front row, her first baby gurgling on her lap. Soon she would have two more babies—twins—with her new husband, a Las Vegas cantor and former stage actor.

Many in the cultish audience had quit better jobs elsewhere, wagering that higher tips and upward mobility at the Wynn would pay off in the long run. One, Michael Martin, thirty years old, said he had left a bigger guest-services job and ten years of seniority at the Paris and the Flamingo casinos (not to mention four weeks of annual vacation) to park cars at Wynn Las Vegas.

Music from *The Wiz*—the '70s soul musical based loosely on *The*

Wizard of Oz—filled the ballroom. With a vaudevillian's sense of timing, Wynn entered the room at its crescendo and walked unescorted through the wild applause. His gaze was fixed on a short set of stairs that led to the stage. He climbed these steps carefully, wobbling once. Reaching the dais, Wynn grinned sassily, doffed his jacket, and shimmied.

The crowd was screaming now.

It is worth contemplating what Wynn saw from this vantage point. The light in the Lafite ballroom was low, and would have seemed even darker to Wynn—people like shadows, disappearing in the dark. Yet he walked to the platform's edge and opened his mouth and laughed big.

"Upstairs on the roof is a sign that says 'Wynn period.' And it's the name of the hotel and it's my last name," he told them. "And I, on behalf of myself and Elaine, I'd like to get something straight. As of this minute, you will be doing me a big favor, each of you who are in this room, if you refer to me as Steve and her as Elaine. There's enough Wynn plastered around this building."

They cheered.

"I was self-conscious about calling it Wynn. Elaine didn't want to do it. I didn't want to do it. It had come up before in the past, but it turns out that names do make a difference before the fact; before it opens, it's helpful to create expectations. The research and the focus groups and the advertising people that did these polls said that it was important, before the place was opened, to remind everybody that this was a hotel by the guy who did—or the team that did—Mirage, Bellagio, Golden Nugget, Treasure Island."

As he spoke, Wynn approached the stage's edge and moved away, always looking out into the rapt audience.

"The cast is assembled. The show's about to begin in what is undoubtedly the fanciest theater that ever was. OK, it's the fanciest theater that ever was. When it comes to the physical plant, you don't have to be a rocket scientist. We don't have to use hyperbole.

"It's game. Set. Match. We won the beauty contest. And we knew we were gonna win the beauty contest." He grinned.

"This is the most complicated, high-tech, cutting edge, technological environment ever created on earth—including the Space Station. This is a tricky building. It does stuff. It opens, it closes, it squirts, it yells, it sings, it saves people's lives. How Tony Marnell managed to finish the place is a miracle to me. We did it in thirty months, and that was too short a schedule. It should have been thirty-two. Bellagio took thirty-six. This is the same size and it's ten times more complicated.

"All right. It's new. It's fancy. It's done. And now you guys gotta take over the place."

Wynn became serious, the father urging his children to make the most of themselves, in a speech that sounded a lot like the ones he gave to employees before Bellagio opened. "You are the fanciest group of people ever assembled in terms of your backgrounds and knowledge. It is a privilege to work with you. . . . The name on the sign is nothing but a bunch of bulbs. This place on Wednesday belongs to you.

"Any chance that you have of experiencing a better life, of finding more self-esteem, of looking in the mirror and saying, 'Yeah,' is gonna come from someone other than me. And you can meet that person by going to the closest ladies' or men's room and looking in the mirror. As much as possible, I'll be right there with you. Especially if it's not the ladies' room."

Chuckle. Wave of appreciative laughter.

"Everybody and their uncle of every description from every country is gonna beat a path to this door. And they won't be disappointed. They're going to walk in and go, 'Wow.' And after they get through looking at the flowers and the trees and the vistas that are open to them in this place, they're gonna get real serious and they're gonna turn around and look at *you.*

"The future is in this room. And the only way that you can make their dreams come true is, you have to decide that it's OK to play with these people. They're coming here to play. That's what Las Vegas is all about. It's a playpen. And this is the fanciest playpen of them all. Anywhere.

"This hotel wasn't built to be the best hotel in Las Vegas. We had done that a couple times already. This hotel was designed to be the best thing that was done *on earth*.

"It was created to give people an experience that they couldn't get anywhere else on the planet. And that's not developer-speak. That's actually what we set out to do. Which is why it cost so much money. This was a very serious effort to create an experience that could not be duplicated on earth.

"I'm very serious today. This is not a pep talk. . . . I'm short-tempered sometimes and don't make the best impression. But today I'm trying real hard to make an impression, a sincere impression, mano a mano, [that] all the dreams you've got can only come true because of you.

"My biggest fear is isolation. That somehow I'll get disconnected from you guys and I won't know what's really going on or how it's working. . . . This market's not going to stay the same. Indian tribes are building casinos. Companies are merging, getting bigger, trying to figure out how to . . . spell their name. Like it's not tough enough to run one joint, you wanna run twenty-four of them or fifty-six of them or ninety-three. That's not us. We will never be the biggest at any-thing, 'cause I don't wanna be the biggest. I just want to be the best.

"So it's time for us to perform. The show's about to begin. It's time for us to give this place its real vitality. . . . Being successful in busi-ness ain't being right or wrong, it's about being nice, gettin' them to love us."

Then Wynn roared.

"They came to play. *PLAY* with them!"

♣ ♦ ♥ ♠

To film the resort's television ad, Wynn waited for a cloudless day. Exit-ing through a door near the top of the building, he climbed a ladder to a higher rooftop. From there, he walked along a parapet to stand atop the fifty-story tower, where he was invisibly harnessed to the building. A cinematographer—who had been recommended by Wynn's friend Steven Spielberg—filmed from a hovering helicopter. Wynn delivered his lines and ad-libbed at the end, "Can I get down now?"

As the first guests were checking into their hotel rooms, crews were still planting flowers and brushing black paint on wrought-iron fencing. Forgotten in the hubbub were the protective plastic sheets that covered the newly installed skylights of the luxury villas. For days after the resort opened, the sheets flapped in the desert spring breeze like white flags waving from the roof.

The Wynns had decided to open with a four-day party for their friends much the same way they'd opened Bellagio. The party started with a benefit for the Foundation Fighting Blindness and two local education charities. Invited guests paid as much as $7,500 per couple.

Dan Lee, Wynn's former chief financial officer from Mirage, was there. Gary Loveman bought tickets for Harrah's entire board of directors.

The pollster Frank Luntz arrived on Wednesday afternoon. His reaction suggested that Wynn might manage to impress people who aren't typical Vegas types. The Washington political junkie was so enthused at wandering about the place that he failed to check his e-mail for two whole hours. "I love this place!" Luntz announced, sweating, his sandy hair mussed and his shirt coming untucked from his wrinkled khakis.

That evening, *Le Reve* was the centerpiece of the evening's entertainment. At around ten p.m., near the show's midpoint, Loveman rose from his seat in the theater and left with Robert Miller, chairman and chief executive of RiteAid Inc. Their reactions foretold the host of troubles facing the show.

"I didn't get it," Loveman said, as others filed out as well. "The guy sitting next to me said, 'Is the target audience for this gay Asian males? Because that's pretty much all you get in the first half.'"

"I'm tired," Miller added, looking it.

At midnight, the doors opened and the hordes poured in. A blubbery couple in shorts raced in, pumping their arms—first in! They ran for slot machines. A man in a wheelchair whizzed by in white tube socks but no shoes.

Elaine Wynn went home to bed, saying she was unable to watch and too worried about the following evening's gala. Steve Wynn, with a walkie talkie in his hands, wandered the casino floor flanked by his friend Allan Zeman, a Hong Kong entertainment developer. Wynn posed for pictures that the crowd, wielding cell-phone cameras, was shooting in violation of every casino rule. "Mr. Wynn! Mr. Wynn! Thank you for everything you've done for Vegas," they called, jostling for his attention.

Within moments, visitors began to e-mail their photos, which landed on the Internet, scooping a heavily protected photo-exclusive that had been offered to *Vanity Fair*.

Then Wynn went to bed. "Look," he explained, "once the casino's open, you know what it looks like, right?"

On Thursday, the Wynns' out-of-town guests began to arrive. People joked that private jets were stuck in airborne traffic jams trying to land in Las Vegas. (By September, the number of people flying into Las Vegas by private jet had risen 50 percent from the year earlier, according to Douglas Gollan, editor in chief of *Elite Traveler* magazine, which is distributed on private jetcraft and in other places the super-rich hang out.)

The *Today* show's Katie Couric got right to the point when she began an interview with Wynn. She asked him about being blind, catching Wynn off guard. He was furious and later screamed at his publicity executive, Denise Randazzo, "Didn't you prep them?"

The following evening, Hugh Jackman performed a bit from his Broadway show, *The Boy from Oz,* to celebrate Elaine Wynn's birthday. The elastic actor sang "Happy Birthday" and pulled Elaine onstage, where she did a demure bump and grind in her ruffled red Oscar de la Renta gown. The evening's guest list included Elizabeth Taylor, who arrived in a wheelchair; Jackman briefly sat in her lap. Siegfried and Roy were there. Former President George Bush had as his dinner partner the actress Teri Hatcher. In the kitchen cooking were Wolfgang Puck and Alain Ducasse.

At around five thirty p.m., the hotel's exclusive South Tower lobby was doing its job to separate the classes. While the masses filled slot machines beyond, the singer Harry Connick Jr. chatted near the exit to the swimming pool. The music mogul David Geffen looked bored in a queue waiting to check in. The actor George Hamilton preened in a corner, his trademark tan glowing a strange orange. Richard Branson strode past, a gray-blond billionaire adventurer with a wicked grin.

Sirio Maccioni, restaurateur of the famous New York Le Cirque, was there despite his anger that Wynn had hired away twenty-two of his people, including the chef. "For his opening, I wasn't going to go, because you don't do that, said the old-world restaurateur. "But they explained to me that's what happens when they open a new restaurant. [So] I told him, 'When you took away twenty-two people, you did me a favor. Because the young people who stayed, they're fresh and ready. The older people were getting tired. The chef was getting presumptuous.'"

The night was billed as the "international premiere" of poor *Le Reve.* An hour into the show, Barry Sternlicht, who had sold Wynn the Desert Inn, peered down into the greenish glow of a wireless e-mail device. It illuminated his seat for much of the rest of the show. His wife appeared to sleep on his shoulder. Sternlicht looked up once as a topless female performer did a brief, melancholy dance.

A few seats down, newlyweds Donald and Melania Trump chatted and gazed around the audience in a sea of empty seats. The Wynns had quietly warned their friends to avoid seeing *Le Reve.* "Go have a nice dinner. It isn't ready," Elaine Wynn told them.

Several months later, she exclaimed, her azure eyes wide, "Thank God it wasn't the centerpiece of the entertainment for the gala. We had Hugh Jackman."

Wynn Resorts' president, Ron Kramer, ate breakfast the next morning at Tableau in the South Tower. This had been Kramer's first casino opening, and he had been so excited the night before that he took photos of the crowds taking photos of Wynn.

Kramer estimated that 40 percent of his net worth was invested with Wynn. He had not moved from New York when he took the job, but he'd wanted to be "part of creating something" after the terror attacks of 9/11. Kramer had been in a downtown conference room staring out the window at the World Trade Center when the first plane crashed into it. "I saw the planes hit," Kramer said, his eyes reddening. He continued in a staccato voice, "My anger. From that. Has not. Dissipated."

He changed tracks. "Wynn Resorts is considered one of the premier companies in the resort industry. We got our first dollar of revenue less than twenty-four hours ago," Kramer said proudly.

As he spoke, the fat fellow from the previous night scooted by in his wheelchair, his tube socks now gray with filth. Headed toward the baccarat salons, he held a Budweiser between his thighs.

♣ ♦ ♥ ♠

At the other end of the Strip, Jim Murren and Glenn Schaeffer were finally closing the MGM Mandalay deal that would briefly make Kerkorian the biggest casino owner in the world.

A "war room" for lawyers, bankers, and support staff was set up in one of Bellagio's big spa suites. Jim Murren's eldest son, Jack, who was nine years old, was off from school that day, so Murren brought him along. Jack wore a jacket and tie.

Schaeffer and Murren's friendship had continued to propel their careers over the ten months since their dramatic agreement. Instead of riding off to his homes in Taos, Los Angeles, and New Zealand, Schaeffer had landed his shot at being a CEO. He had joined Fontainebleau Resorts, a start-up venture that would have two flagships: the Fontainebleau Hotel in Miami—a Morris Lapidus–designed mid-century resort—and a new extravaganza on the Strip to the north of Wynn Las Vegas that Schaeffer would be responsible for developing. "My building—it won't have my name on it—is going to be great architecture," Schaeffer said. "It will be sexy. It will be different. It will be quiet. It will show people something they haven't seen before."

As the party geared up at the Wynn, the Mandalay deal officially closed. Schaeffer was feeling melancholy. He stopped off at Piero's Trattoria for a drink. "It was a humbling day," Schaeffer said. "I had no idea it would be so emotional."

Schaeffer's eyes were slightly bloodshot. He wore a black zip-front sweater and gray pants—his minimalist uniform. As he rested his elbows on the bar, he swallowed.

That afternoon at the closing of the deal, Ensign had walked into the room. "Come here," he said, and kissed Schaeffer on his right ear.

"I love you," Mike Ensign said.

"I love you, too," Glenn Schaeffer replied.

"You're my son," Ensign said.

Hours later Schaeffer was still overcome. "I've been a wreck ever since," he said, leaning on the bar. "He's the best executive I've ever worked for. I'm going to tell him that. He came through for me, and I'm going to do the same for him."

Shaeffer's fingers stroked his wineglass, his face enveloped in emotion.

"He told me he loved me."

chapter twenty-seven

META-VEGAS

Ladies and gentlemen, Elvis has left the building.
—AL DVORIN, ELVIS PRESLEY ANNOUNCER

The Las Vegas barons were forever spying on one another. It wasn't just an extraordinary coincidence that Kirk Kerkorian and Steve Wynn announced their next megacasino resorts within days of each other in the spring of 2004.

Kerkorian's concept had been studiously assembled by architects and city planners over months of secret effort. Wynn's was largely in his head.

Hedge funds, banks, and other investors were flush from an extended economic boom. These Wall Street decision makers were rich and readily influenced by the new Vegas cool. Moreover, they needed to park huge tranches of cash. Casinos offered a sweet deal: big construction projects that promised ripe cash returns.

Thus, well-connected casino operators were raising billions of dollars of capital to build casinos that dwarfed Wynn Las Vegas's cost of $2.7 billion. As the prices of steel and concrete soared in the United States—a global outcome of China's economic boom—Las Vegas saw the starting price of a new casino more than double to $2 billion in just a few years.

It's hard to imagine that a tycoon wouldn't be satisfied with controlling half of the Las Vegas Strip. But Kerkorian's architects were already drawing up plans for all the new land he had acquired. It was to be the biggest privately financed development in the world, which they called CityCenter.

Themed resorts were history, but this new one was to have a futuristic urban milieu. The construction cost: $7.4 billion (excluding the land value) for a mass of high-rises that Loveman wryly dubbed Kerkorian City.

Kerkorian hadn't built a resort of significance in fifteen years, and this one wasn't his idea. But CityCenter grew from his seed and he *loved* it like an expectant father whose chest swells proudly as his wife's belly grows. "He knows it's transforming the city," said Jim Murren, MGM Mirage's president.

The concept was Murren's inspiration—the same idea that had caused him to approach Glenn Schaeffer about buying Mandalay Resorts: a city within the city of Las Vegas. Its sixty-six acres amounted to an area larger than New York's Times Square, SoHo, and Rockefeller Center combined, and it would be packed nearly as densely. It was set to open in late 2009, with four hotels and residential towers and 6,800 rooms, suites, and condos. The primary sixty-story City-Center Hotel would have 4,000 rooms and suites. A Mandarin Oriental luxury hotel and three other projects called the Vdara, the Harmon, and Veer Towers would contain another 2,800 hotel rooms, suites, and even condominiums.

Billed as "a place to live—and live it up as never before," CityCenter suggested that the Las Vegas Strip would evolve into a place where people might want to live full-time.

Condo buyers were pitched on living like high-rollers. They were promised all manner of VIP invitations to concerts and boxing matches and automatic entry past velvet ropes. When a Middle Eastern casino customer agreed to buy forty-two condo units for himself and his entourage in December 2006, Terry Lanni, MGM Mirage's chief executive, rewarded his $60-million purchase with permanent privileges to golf at Shadow Creek. It was the first exception Lanni had made to the Shadow Creek "guests only" rule.

Kerkorian didn't try to screw with Wynn's winning formula.

People might have wondered if there was room for yet another surrealistic Cirque du Soleil show in Las Vegas, but Kerkorian signed up. The French-Canadian group agreed to create a show that would appeal to the aging baby boomers who are expected to be Las Vegas's primary spenders for the next twenty years.

None other than the King of Rock 'n' Roll was expected to return in November 2009 with a posthumous "Elvis Experience," involving live musicians, singers, dancers, and the best that multimedia technology could accomplish to reincarnate a long-dead star. The show was announced during "Elvis Week"—a time set aside by fans to commemorate the singer's untimely August 16, 1977, passing.

Murren's original concept for an open-air shopping district—so SoHo-like that MGM executives took to calling it SoBella, for "South of Bellagio"—was killed in favor of climate control. Planners feared that visitors would be unwilling to walk through the desert heat as they shopped at Chanel and Louis Vuitton. "We're creating our own urban environment," Murren said—albeit an air-conditioned one.

Murren was CityCenter's financial architect, but Kerkorian lacked an artistic creator, so he hired the best and most expensive. For the first time, renowned architects were vying to work in Las Vegas.

They included Daniel Libeskind, whose wacky rectangular eyeglasses had entered the American mainstream a few years earlier when he submitted plans to rebuild the World Trade Center site. Cesar Pelli, whose work includes the world's tallest buildings—the Petronas Towers in Kuala Lumpur—was the lead architect on the main casino and 4,000-room hotel. New York–based Ehrenkrantz, Eckstut & Kuhn Architects, the architects responsible for the Battery Park City esplanade in New York and the Baltimore Inner Harbor East, initiated the master planning—the linking of the hotels, residences, shopping, and other elements. Adam Tihany would design the luxury hotel; Sir Norman Foster, a Pritzker Architecture Prize–winner, was to design the exterior of one of the boutique hotels. David Rockwell was brought in for the retail areas.

The futuristic result seemed fit for Dubai or Tokyo. The shopping district was a collection of tentlike planes juxtaposed against angular high-rise towers. Executives at MGM Mirage felt CityCenter was moving Las Vegas into the realm of major cities.

Steve Wynn snorted at their aspirations—Las Vegas did not embarrass him—as well as the heavy-hitter architects. He boasted that he did his own in-house design without paying fees to people with egos as big as his own. In fact, Wynn proved correct in his prediction that others would start building crescent-shaped towers like the Wynn's. One of the first was CityCenter's 1,500-room Vdara Hotel.

Wynn called CityCenter "the most revolutionary idea I've seen—to create Times Square." It wasn't a compliment.

"I don't believe in it," Wynn continued one afternoon, clad sleekly in a black Wynn-logo golf shirt and white pants. "The most expensive real estate in New York is not Times Square. They sell CD's there. People don't get on a plane to go to Times Square. I'll take Central Park South any day. The human scale of Madison Avenue."

Cantankerous, Wynn wiggled his eyebrows and slyly hedged his bets. "But I want to understand, because I can do it too!"

Blindness be damned, Wynn went skiing that winter and popped a ligament in his knee—just standing on his skis and turning the wrong way. During three weeks on crutches, he told colleagues it was the most painful surgery of his life.

He was struggling to get Wynn Las Vegas right. The La Bete nightclub had been a stinker—failing to draw attractive young women who could lure male customers. Wynn fired the manager and brought in a new nightclub operator who created the more successful Tryst.

As Gary Loveman's reaction on opening night suggested, *Le Reve* turned out to be an even stickier mess. The show played to a sea of empty seats night after night. Wynn was forced to break his contract with his friend Franco Dragone and remake the show. The improvement might have played well in many cities, but in Las Vegas, it just didn't stand out against Cirque du Soleil's productions elsewhere. Wynn and Cirque had already done the water theme, after all, with *O* at Bellagio.

Rather than leading Las Vegas entertainment, Wynn found himself the bargain-priced entertainment option. Tickets to *O, KÀ,* and

Love ranged as high as $165 in early 2007. Wynn could garner only $119 for a ticket to *Le Reve*—about 40 percent less than Kerkorian was getting at Bellagio, MGM Grand, and the Mirage.

Similarly, the Broadway show *Avenue Q* had been a hit in its small New York theater, but it played to half-full houses in its big 1,200-seat Las Vegas venue. Wynn had been so tickled with the racy Muppet-esque takeoff—he even kept a Steve Wynn puppet in his office. But he finally threw in the towel and closed the show. He announced a deal to bring in Monty Python's more populist *Spamalot* in 2007.

"Yeah, we blew it," said one senior Wynn executive. "Can you imagine how great things would be if we'd got the entertainment right?"

Still, much ended up just as Wynn had planned. Fashionistas and the moneyed flocked to the Wynn, helping it maintain the most expensive rooms in Las Vegas. Bellagio, less fashionable but bigger, cost a hundred bucks a night less.

Yet Wynn needed a bigger place to compete. He had assembled around the resort more developable land than Kerkorian had. With 250 acres, Wynn was planning a resort spread among gardens and a lake from the same well of inspiration he had dipped into before. Just a few days before Kerkorian's CityCenter was announced in the fall of 2004, Wynn said, "If I talk about it, it'll sound a lot like Walt Disney talking about Epcot."

It turned out that the $22 million he spent on the Tom Fazio golf course was just a temporary placeholder, reserving the spot for a number of waterfront resorts. "Not high-rise. Medium-rise," Wynn said. He would "create a pedestrian village where you walk, where there's stores and shopping in a beautiful environment with no cars." He would build right up to the edge of the Las Vegas Convention Center at the back of his property and haul in conventioneers in shuttle buses, offering them his goodies before they managed to set foot onto the Las Vegas Strip.

In the center of it all would be Wynn's boyhood lake, only better— with water-skiing and a boardwalk leading to the hotels. "I'm going to fix it up so you can look from the convention center into the lake," he said.

The precursor to all this was Encore, a second $2.1 billion high-rise tower on the Strip with 2,034 huge hotel rooms—1,030 square feet with a 230-square-foot bathroom. His aim was to draw "suite" people. "Remember, when I fill rooms with suite customers, I get a higher-spending customer," Wynn said.

The name Encore was Elaine Wynn's idea. "It was a working title, and it sort of stuck," Wynn said. "This is for my grandchildren," he said with great cheer. When Ron Kramer sewed up all the financing for Encore a few weeks later, Wynn was so tickled he could hardly sit still. "One of the best days of my business life," Wynn shared in somewhat of an off-color way. "I feel like a kid who has to go to the bathroom."

He crowed, "We went out for a billion dollars. We were triple over-subscribed. We did one-point-three billion, six and five-eighths percent, ten-year, non-recourse to the parent." What's more, he'd put in more of his own equity and got the bonds upgraded from the humiliating junk status. "We are in fan-ceee shape!

"I never had a day like this in twenty-seven years at Mirage Resorts. I'm done. If I get hit by a truck tomorrow, we are a fucking institution!" Wynn said, once more the king. He planned to celebrate in Sun Valley. "This is going to be the best vacation ever! I'm going skiing!"

Before hanging up the telephone, Wynn couldn't resist taking a swipe at his rival at the Venetian. Sheldon Adelson had recently taken the Las Vegas Sands, the Venetian's parent company, public.

The seventy-two-year-old Adelson, who was a diabetic and disabled, blamed Wynn for troubles he'd had financing the Venetian in the late 1990s. Several years later, as Adelson sold his public offering, potential investors became inexplicably and suddenly concerned that he might die before completing the Sands development plans. Adelson was infuriated by the awkward rumors and insisted that his health was fine even if he needed help walking.

Unlike Wynn's difficult offering, though, Adelson's was perfectly timed to take advantage of the booming interest in stocks and Macao, where his second resort would be built. The public offering vaulted him to the fourteenth richest person in the world, according to *Forbes* in 2006, at a worth of $16 billion.

Yet Wynn took a moment to pity Adelson that afternoon. "It's too bad he's not in better health and able to enjoy it more," Wynn said cunningly. "He's in a wheelchair."

♣ ◆ ♥ ♠

As Kerkorian's stake in Las Vegas grew, his circle of friends shrank. Fred Benninger, the man who had developed all three of Kerkorian's first hotels, died in February 2004 at the age of eighty-six. George Mason, sick with cancer, worked right up to his death in October 2005 at the age of seventy-four. Walter Sharp, who had variously served Kerkorian on the boards of MGM Mirage and the MGM movie studios since the 1970s, died two months after Mason at the age of eighty-nine. Kerkorian's old friend and corporate caretaker James Algian died of cancer in April 2007, having worked up until the day of his death.

Mort Viner, an old friend of Kerkorian's who was once Dean Martin's and Jimmy Stewart's Hollywood agent, dropped dead on a fine June Sunday in the midst of his notoriously competitive tennis game with Kerkorian. "You've got to say there's something extraordinary about someone who will play tennis to the death," said Dan Lee, Wynn's former chief financial officer, when he heard about it.

Kerkorian, at eighty-seven, was becoming more stooped and was losing his sight to macular degeneration. He was deaf in one ear. Yet no one wanted to suggest publicly that he wouldn't live forever. Not even Steve Wynn. "He'll live to a hundred and forty, and he'll still look the same," Wynn said.

Privately, people in Las Vegas wondered what would become of Tracinda and Mirage Resorts when Kerkorian died. Outsiders gossiped about Kerkorian's estate planning. "Kirk's not going to live forever. And nobody knows if there is enough money to pay the taxes," said one Las Vegas casino developer.

The thing was, even the people on MGM Mirage's board were in the dark on this. They simply assumed Kerkorian would take care of things and that his daughters would somehow inherit. Kerkorian kept the various parts of his organizations so in the dark that it came as a surprise to executives at MGM Mirage when he made a sweeping move in May 2005 for General Motors Corp. in Detroit—another city that had drawn Kerkorian's attention time and again.

Kerkorian started by quietly buying shares in General Motors. The day he announced a tender to buy more, Kerkorian had a trusted lieutenant named Jerry York call to warn GM's vice chairman, Robert Lutz. These moves were textbook Kerkorian.

Wall Street suddenly suspected that Kerkorian had espied a hidden gem and started buying up the stock, sending the price above Kerkorian's $31-a-share tender offer. Kerkorian later sold twelve million shares at a substantial loss, purportedly for tax purposes, but the move made a point to GM's recalcitrant management that Kerkorian held sway with the company's stock price: GM's stock sank to its lowest price in twenty-three years.

"Contrary to what most people say, Kirk is not an easy guy," says Henry Gluck.

As the GM news played out in daily headlines, Kerkorian's rising age contributed to an unspoken sense of urgency among those jockeying to succeed Terry Lanni as chief executive at MGM Mirage. Because of Kerkorian's hands-off management style, the role was a substantial one—nearly on par with Wynn's.

Lanni had long promised to retire when his contract came due in 2006, setting up a poisonous atmosphere of rivalry in the top ranks at MGM Mirage. Bobby Baldwin, who ran the former Mirage Resorts, and a casino veteran named John Redmond ran the MGM Grand and Mandalay casinos. This left Jim Murren to find another way—for example creating CityCenter and pushing expansions into hotels in China and Dubai—to prove he could add the most value to the company.

The power triangle pleased Lanni. "I like having a little competition between them. I think that's healthy if one of them wants to do better than the other," Lanni said.

Murren said that Kerkorian had indicated that he was next in line for Lanni's job. This, in 2006, was keeping Jim and Heather in Las Vegas despite the yen to cash in and move to Europe. Others in Las Vegas were also noticing Murren's talents. Loveman once said he would have tried to recruit Murren except that it would take a "truckload of gold bars" to lure him away from his contract with MGM Mirage. Even Wynn had his eye on Murren. "That guy is added-value over there," Wynn said without affection. "He is smart."

It was a nasty surprise, then, when Terry Lanni extended his employment contract until 2010, the year CityCenter would be open. "I'm forty-four years old," Murren said one day, frowning, noting that he'd be approaching fifty by the time the job came open.

When Lanni handed responsibility for building CityCenter over to Bobby Baldwin, Murren gulped gracefully and acknowledged Baldwin's years of experience building things for Steve Wynn. "I'm good friends with Frank Visconti, who's head of retail, so at least I'll have some input there," Murren said sadly.

Bound together by their rich employment contracts, the top five executives at MGM Mirage were the highest-paid chain gang in the gambling business. Collectively, thanks to their pre–Wynn-Las Vegas employment contracts, they earned $51.2 million in compensation in 2006—far more than the top five executives at Harrah's ($29.5 million) and Wynn ($31.5 million).

Murren, who earned $6.3 million in 2005, resented Baldwin's $6.5 million that year. Murren's frustration that Baldwin and Redmond earned more than him simmered beneath his wide-eyed, boyish exterior. "I know I've added a lot more value to this company than they have," he fussed, frowning over a lunch of chilled salads in the kitchen of his sprawling, gated home in a gated subdivision in the suburb of Summerlin.

Loveman, chairman, chief executive, and president of the world's biggest casino company, distanced himself from the group as usual. "I don't care who's bigger," Loveman said. "Jim, I'm sure, gets paid more than I do. I like the fact that I don't live in Las Vegas and I don't have a need to be the big guy there."

♣ ♦ ♥ ♠

So he said.

Harrah's investors questioned whether Loveman had any business getting involved in high-end Las Vegas properties. But once he'd had a chance to see what was going on at Caesars, Loveman finally grasped that high-rollers did more than gamble at Caesars Palace. The glamour of their surroundings drew other big spenders. They might not gamble, but they'd check into a $300 room in the Palace's new tower, get a $180 basic facial at the Qua Baths and Spa, and eat a $300 dinner for two at Bradley Ogden's restaurant before plopping into $225 seats at the Celine Dion show.

These travelers were creating a New Las Vegas gold rush. Loveman and the propeller heads had been so focused on Harrah's low-rollers that they hadn't bothered to study their Las Vegas rivals. They were more familiar with the operations of RiteAid drugstores than MGM Mirage.

It took nine months to dawn on Loveman that he'd bought entrée to a whole new world. It hit him in Tokyo in May 2005 at a board meeting for the handbag maker Coach, where he is a director. As the board discussed the hardships of building new luxury brands in Japan, Loveman realized that the legwork had been done at Caesars. "The Caesars brand has tremendously powerful impact internationally. I didn't fully appreciate that when we bought it," he said a few weeks later. "I feel better than I did a year ago. We made the decision [to buy Caesars] on less interesting grounds than we might have."

Loveman began to direct his analytic brain to Las Vegas entertainment—looking for productions that would attract the masses of shoppers, diners, and tourists.

In the spring of 2006, Loveman and the Hollywood director James Cameron emerged from a white Caesars stretch limo and walked together into an interview for a CNBC broadcast in Singapore.

"Just don't use the C-word. Don't say 'casino,'" Loveman coached the director of *Titanic, Terminator,* and *Aliens.*

"It's a theme-park environment," Cameron rehearsed, looking earnest. His casual blue suit was slightly disheveled, and he wore a denim shirt with no tie.

On camera, Loveman and Cameron discussed plans for a huge casino resort in Singapore. If they won the bid, Loveman would build a twenty-first-century theme park with an art center by the architect of Paris's Centre Pompidou; entertainment programming by News Corporation's STAR, Asia's biggest broadcaster; and an immersive entertainment zone called iPort produced with Cameron.

At iPort, people would eat in a replica of the *Titanic*'s first-class dining room, re-created "right down to the flatware." Visitors could experience the moment the *Titanic* hit the iceberg, every ten minutes, in a replica of the ship's boiler room. "The 'I' in iPort stands for immersion. A totally immersive environment," Cameron said that afternoon. He seemed nerdily unlike the pompous-sounding director who shouted, "I'm king of the world!" when *Titanic* won eleven Oscars in 1998.

"I'm pretty pumped to be part of the [Harrah's] team," Cameron said. "They actually had me about halfway through the first meeting. I'm kind of a gearhead, and I love to explore the engineering. iPort for me is basically Christmas morning."

Loveman lost the Singapore bid to Sheldon Adelson. This blow left Loveman, like Kerkorian, struggling to catch up with Wynn and Adelson in the promised land of Asia, where people believe in luck. Superstition and wagering are part of Chinese and other Asian cultures that goes back centuries.

Kerkorian finally got a foothold in Macao when MGM Mirage agreed to join Pansy Ho, daughter of Macao gambling magnate Stanley Ho, to jointly own a $975-million casino called the MGM Grand Macao that was set to open in 2007.

Loveman needed in on Asia, so he was glad to hear Wynn's voice on his cell phone one afternoon while Loveman was shopping with his family. Wynn offered to sell Harrah's a piece of his action in Macao. He wanted $800 million for the legal right to build a casino there.

Loveman feared he'd look like a "chump" if he paid that high price for nothing more than a right to build. This soon appeared to be a gross misstep. Wall Street was rewarding anyone with a toe in Macao with high valuations. One investment banker estimated that the Macao concession would have added more than $20 a share to Harrah's stock value. Wynn turned around and sold the concession for even more money—$900 million—to James Packer, the son of Australian magnate Kerry Packer.

With his continued focus on smaller markets, Loveman successfully pressed to secure casino licenses in Ciudad Real, Spain, 118 miles south of Madrid; and Nova Gorica, Slovenia, on the border with Italy. There was even an opportunity in Holland, and several in England. Loveman wanted to explore a business involving *pachinko* machines in Japan—slot-machine–like gambling devices that are all the rage there.

Loveman had planned to change the parent company's name to Caesars shortly after the deal closed. But then he was in Washington, dropping off his son at college, when Hurricane Katrina was bearing down on New Orleans and Biloxi, where Harrah's had casinos. He stayed up all night in a Washington hotel room figuring out what to do. "We know how to batten down—we practice that twice a year," he said on Tuesday as Katrina blew. "But what about after the storm?"

Loveman was profoundly affected by the storm's tragic human aftermath. He promised to pay the 6,000 Harrah's and Caesars workers at the destroyed casinos for ninety days—forcing resentful rivals to try to match the offer. "Our people come first, Harrah's comes second," Loveman told his management in a conference call.

"This is the end of the riverboat era," the politically facile Jan Jones predicted. "They'll all get rebuilt, but it'll be on land." And she was right.

When Loveman finally broached the name change at an April 2006 management meeting, his top executives were adamant. "I had to get business cards once that said Caesars, because nobody would talk to me if I said 'Harrah's,'" said Tom Jenkin, president of Harrah's western division. "I might as well have said Procter & Gamble—it just didn't mean anything to them."

Rich Mirman, one of the first propeller heads, believed that the Harrah's name was slowing the company's international expansion. "People associate us with Wal-Mart," Mirman said, as though that was now a bad thing.

♣ ♦ ♥ ♠

Disneyland is eighty-five acres. The Magic Kingdom in Orlando is a hundred and seven acres. Epcot Center is three hundred acres. Harrah's had collected three hundred fifty acres along the Strip in Las Vegas. Loveman was planning a giant resort that he claimed would change the "gestalt" in Las Vegas. Its working name was Epicentre.

Loveman conceded he had been slow to accept his new role as a casino developer. "I have on certain occasions underestimated the importance of buildings and have thought we could manage our way out of any problem," Loveman said. "We let the competition get too far ahead."

Loveman hired dozens of consultants from theme parks and casinos. Among them was Tony Marnell, former owner of the Rio and the construction contractor for the Mirage, Bellagio, and Wynn Las Vegas.

For the first dozen meetings or so with the propeller heads, Marnell discussed the value of customers who don't gamble. Food, drinks, shows, shops . . . More than 60 percent of revenues in Las Vegas casinos come from not gambling—a gap that grows wider every year. Harrah's hadn't bothered to collect this data because the propeller heads had been so focused on gambling.

Another epiphany followed. "We had never really looked at how people behaved by age patterns," says John Boushy, the Harrah's executive who was leading the Las Vegas effort at the time, "because we were focused on how to get more revenue out of existing customers." And Harrah's customers were mostly . . . retired. It turned out that Generation Y customers in their twenties were willing to spend huge amounts of money in casinos. Soon they would discover other lucrative subgroups. Harrah's would begin promoting Paris Las Vegas's "gay-friendly staff" and placing photos of gay and lesbian couples on its Web site.

Marnell and Boushy pinned scores of photographs and drawings cut from magazines representing the spectrum of people of legal age to gamble. To one side was Generation Y, driven by style. There was

Generation X, driven by status. There were the Boomers, aged forty to sixty, and the older-than-sixty Silent Generation—Harrah's "avid experienced players."

"Gen-Ys don't give a rat's patootie about Total Rewards," Boushy said. "They're just interested in having a good time."

One afternoon in March, two dozen of Harrah's consultants—almost exclusively white males—gathered in a Las Vegas conference room to brainstorm. They tossed around ideas to build an arena and a sports stadium, sketched out mass transportation systems, and fantasized about "omnimovers"—moving dinettes where people would drink, party, eat, and maybe even loll about in beds while being transported around Harrah's three hundred fifty acres. "Can you gamble in these vehicles?" asked Craig Hanna, principal of Thinkwell Design and Production, a Los Angeles creator of theme-park attractions.

Sheldon Gordon, the developer of the Forum Shops at Caesars Palace, was there. Gordon's Bluetooth earpiece wasn't picking up sound properly, so he fetched the amplifier from his suit pocket and moved it to the center of the conference table. "If this all comes to pass," Gordon said, "the Strip is going to be yesterday's newspapers."

Loveman stayed up late on April 24 to edit his son's eight-page college paper on John Locke. The next morning, he led Harrah's board meeting, listening to a complaint from director Frank Biondi, former CEO of Viacom, about plans for Jason Alexander to appear in a ninety-minute version of *The Producers* show at the Paris casino. "Not Jason Alexander! He's terrible!" said Biondi. ("He's been on the board for two years now, and this is the most heated he ever got on any subject," Loveman later told his management team with a grin.)

Loveman also presented his directors with a development plan that would cost at least $13 billion and take as long as ten years to complete. The plan called for ten new hotel towers, including new casinos designed to cater to Gen-Xers and Gen-Yers.

At the development's center, Loveman decided to build an avenue leading from the Strip into the deep interior of Harrah's property. This had the effect of moving the street action away from the gridlocked boulevard and entirely inside Harrah's domain. In effect, it would create a new Main Street, where Harrah's would control every shop, restaurant, hotel, condominium building, and theater in the whole destination, much like what Kerkorian was doing at CityCenter.

"This is a tale of two cities," said one of Harrah's consultants. "CityCenter and Epicentre."

With his rise, Loveman found that like all new CEOs, he was often lonely. "It's an isolating job," Loveman said. "It's hard to have relationships with people absent any business motivation." Rich Mirman, one of the original propeller heads, left his job at Harrah's, saying he didn't expect to work at another casino company, but Harrah's just wasn't the same familial place that had drawn him. Old friends didn't always fit into Loveman's new life. He took friends of fifteen years to Las Vegas. "It was a mind-blowing experience for them to see me here after the way they know me all these years," he said.

Friends told him that a nasty rumor was making its way around Wellesley that spring. People were saying, "Gary is involved with the Mob."

Loveman had planned to ask his board to approve his big development plans at the July 2006 board meeting, and then to announce them with a splash in September. Word was leaking that Harrah's had some big development planned—and the stock was tumbling as a result. "Absolutely nothing had changed. It was just what the public markets had done to us," Loveman said, sounding a lot like Steve Wynn in his last days at Mirage Resorts.

Instead of discussing his plans with directors, Loveman found himself explaining the vagaries of the stock market's evaluation of casinos. "This is the time for private equity in our industry," he said.

As it turned out, the private-equity guys were sniffing over Harrah's Entertainment. Representatives of two heavyweight fund groups, Apollo Management L.P. and Texas Pacific Group, came knocking at Loveman's door that fall with an offer to buy the company. Loveman was so eager that he entered into discussions with them before he notified his board. Still, after several months of high-profile dickering, Apollo and TPG agreed to buy Harrah's for $17.1 billion in cash.

So Loveman once again beat Kerkorian at doing the biggest deal in Vegas. This time, his feat was more extraordinary. Loveman managed to break the trend of publicly traded ownership of gambling: Casinos had become so profitable—and the billionaires so rich—that investment funds wanted to gobble them up for themselves.

Loveman had also managed to sell the company and keep his job at the same time.

Loveman was a fast learner. He got something else that Wynn had wanted: Bette Midler. Word got out that Steve Wynn was talking to Midler about doing a show at Wynn Las Vegas. In the midst of those talks, Wynn was peppy with optimism, chatting about his plans over dinner at Okada.

It was an odd twist that Loveman managed to beat out Steve Wynn for a star like Midler. It proved Harrah's was now in a whole new league. Midler signed a long-term deal to replace Celine Dion at Caesars Palace. A year later, in 2007, Loveman announced plans to build a $470 million sports arena behind Bally's or the Flamingo. It was the precursor to nabbing Las Vegas's first professional sports team—which at the time looked likely to be with the National Hockey League.

Loveman, though, sometimes seemed surprised to find himself in league with Wynn. He would ask about the king of Vegas from time to time, sounding amused, at times, by Wynn's behavior. He became incensed once when he heard a rumor that Wynn had suggested he might be tutoring Loveman.

In the midst of Harrah's negotiations with Apollo and TPG, Wynn called Loveman on his cell phone and proposed talking again about opportunities in Macao. Wynn's focus was on two fronts at the time: He had one foot in Las Vegas and the other in Asia as he pursued the strategy that Kerkorian had either forced or allowed him to follow—to be the best, but not the biggest.

Loveman was eager—both for a shot at Macao and for another close-up of Wynn. A week later, Loveman arrived at the appointed time at Wynn Las Vegas. Steve Wynn, though, wasn't there. He was "at the ball game," a car valet said.

Wynn's nephew, Andrew Pascal, rushed up and said, "Steve wants you to come to the game." Pascal then drove Loveman directly into the University of Nevada Las Vegas basketball arena. Loveman was ushered to center-court seats on the floor and was seated smack dab between Steve and Elaine Wynn. "I'm like, 'Oh, God, it's going to be in the paper that Steve and I were meeting,'" Loveman recalled later.

Nothing came of the meeting. In fact, Loveman was still wondering about its purpose months later. With Wynn, you never know; he might have had a purpose in being seen publicly with Loveman at that moment. Or maybe he just felt like going to the game.

"We got about eight substantive sentences in between hot dogs," Loveman said. "It was just another visit to the theater of the bizarre."

chapter twenty-eight

NO END

Are those people suckers? Honey, I have to answer that like this:
You're talking to a sucker. Gambling is a vice. Drugs are a vice. Pros-
titution is a vice. You can't sell the poison unless you're willing to take
it yourself.

—BOB STUPAK, GAMBLER AND CREATOR OF VEGAS WORLD,
NOW THE STRATOSPHERE CASINO, IN 1997

It's hard to love a place that tries so hard, yet can't respect itself—
like the class slut.

Kirk Kerkorian owns a home in Las Vegas, but lives in Beverly
Hills, California. Terry Lanni's real home—the one where his wife and
kids live—is in Pasadena, California. Gary Loveman commutes from
Boston. Richard Mirman bought a summer home in Chicago. Ron
Kramer, Wynn Resorts' president, lives in New York City.

Dan Lee, who has a pilot's license, flew his young family out of
Las Vegas almost every weekend when he worked for Steve Wynn.
Phil Satre commuted from his ranch in Reno. Glenn Schaeffer bought
homes in New Zealand, Taos, Los Angeles, Miami, Barcelona, and
Orange County, California. Jim Murren aches to move to Europe.

It is gambling that brought Elaine Wynn to Las Vegas, and it's
gambling that keeps her there. "I consider Sun Valley my real home,"
she once said.

The fortunes of Las Vegas's gambling leaders may be tied to the
kingdom of Las Vegas, but they flee the place with alacrity.

Many Las Vegas executives yearn to push their companies beyond the confines of casinos, dreaming of partnerships with Disney, film studios, media giants, and big hotel chains. Those deals have been few so far.

All that will change. They will manage, because they'll never give up and because the more we all go to Las Vegas to do something other than gamble, the more normal the place can claim to be.

In coming years, gambling profits will continue to dwindle as a percentage of the casino resorts' total take. Las Vegas visitors today are overwhelmingly married and well-educated—nearly two-thirds have attended college. Thirty-two percent have household incomes greater than $80,000 per year—making them far wealthier than the average American—and a lucrative bunch of consumers. Big media companies will soon relax about hobnobbing with casinos as young Harvard, MIT, and Cornell graduates take jobs in Vegas. The town will get better private schools, arts programs, top-notch hospitals—and surely even a major-league sports franchise.

As the rest of the country seeps into Las Vegas, Las Vegas is seeping into the rest of the country. Consider Times Square, which resembles the neon and billboard flash of the southern end of the Las Vegas Strip, and the Time Warner Center in New York City—an oversized mix of shopping, dining, and other heavily marketed pleasures. Consider Palm Springs, Tampa, and even parts of Connecticut. Gambling has come to Pennsylvania now—surrounding New York City with casinos in every direction except the Atlantic Ocean.

When the anticelebrity chef Anthony Bourdain visited Las Vegas for his travel show a few years back, he wandered through Kerkorian's New York-New York casino, with its imitation Greenwich Village streets, and he wondered aloud where the pigeons were. But he found the place all too weirdly familiar and he concluded his film diary with a philosophical thought.

"My fear," Bourdain said, sounding melancholy, "is that my beloved New York, with each passing year, is beginning to look more like Las Vegas."

So where does it all end?

It doesn't. There is no end of Las Vegas.

AUTHOR'S NOTE

inner Takes All comes of the eight years I spent covering the business of gambling for *The Wall Street Journal*, from 1997 until 2005, and the additional two years that I spent researching and writing the book. Unless otherwise stated as taken from newspaper or magazine articles, the conversations quoted in this book took place during my interviews, in my presence, or, if noted as such, were relayed to me by the participants.

In addition to numerous books and newspaper and magazine accounts that I used to acquaint myself with times and places I hadn't witnessed, my research benefited from many years of knowing and writing about the people who are described in these pages. Although they might not like what I've written over all these years—in fact, they often have not liked it at all—they became at the least accustomed to me. In many instances, they offered unusual access to meetings and strategic documents as well as their thoughts. For that, I am grateful.

So many people helped with this book by providing documents, sharing memories, and confirming facts that it is impossible for me to acknowledge them all. They include casino executives, employees, customers, investors, and vendors; gamblers and entertainers; government officials; Wall Street analysts and bankers; print and broadcast media; college faculty, staff, and students; a fair number of old chums, relatives, and neighbors of the people in this book; a couple of dolphin trainers; and at least one taxi driver. I hope these people, whether named in the book or not, will understand that I appreciate their generosity.

BIBLIOGRAPHY

Bellagio Gallery of Fine Art, edited by Libby Lumpkin,
   Mirage Resorts Inc., 1999.

Bringing Down The House, Ben Mezrich, The Free Press, 2002.

Casino, Nicholas Pileggi and Martin Scorsese, Faber & Faber Ltd.,
   1986.

Empire: The Life, Legend, and Madness of Howard Hughes, Donald L.
   Barlett and James B. Steele, W.W. Norton & Co., 1979.

Fly on the Wall, Dick Odessky, Huntington Press, 1999.

Fountains of Bellagio, Mary Stayton and Tammy Edmonds,
   Wet Design, 2004.

The Green Felt Jungle, Ed Reid and Ovid Demaris,
   Buccaneer Books, 1963.

Hughes, Richard Hack, New Millennium Press, 2001.

In Nevada, David Thomson, Alfred A. Knopf, 1999.

Jackpot!, Robert L. Shook, John Wiley & Sons Inc., 2003.

Kerkorian: An American Success Story, Dial Torgerson,
   The Dial Press, 1974.

The Man Who Invented Las Vegas, W. R. Wilkerson, III,
   Ciro's Books, 2000.

Neon Metropolis, Hal Rothman, Routledge, 2002.

Nevada's Golden Age of Gambling, Albert Woods Moe,
   Puget Sound Books, 2001.

The Players: The Men Who Made Las Vegas, edited by Jack E.
   Sheehan, University of Nevada Press, 1997.

Resort City in the Sunbelt, Eugene P. Moehring, University of Nevada
   Press, 1989.

Roadside History of Nevada, Richard Moreno, Mountain Press
   Publishing Co., 2000.

Service Breakthroughs, James L. Heskett, W. Earl Sasser, Jr.,
   and Christopher W. L. Hart, The Free Press, 1990.

The Service Profit Chain, James L. Heskett, W. Earl Sasser, Jr.,
   and Leonard A. Schlesinger, The Free Press, 1997.

Sharks in the Desert, John L. Smith, Barricade Books Inc., 2005.

A Short History of Las Vegas, Barbara Land and Myrick Land,
   University of Nevada Press, 1999.

Sirio, Sirio Maccioni and Peter Elliot, John Wiley & Sons Inc., 2004.

Starting Over in Eastern Europe, Simon Johnson and Gary Loveman,
   Harvard Business School Press, 1995.

Super Casino, Pete Earley, Bantam Books, 2000.

Tales from the Art Crypt, Richard Feigen, Alfred A. Knopf, 2000.

Tales Out of Tulsa, Bobby ("The Owl") Baldwin, Gambling Times Inc., 1984.

The Value Profit Chain, James L. Heskett, W. Earl Sasser, Jr., and Leonard A. Schlesinger, The Free Press, 2003.

Welcome to the Pleasuredome, David Spanier, University of Nevada Press, 1992.

Yakuza: Japan's Criminal Underworld, David E. Kaplan and Alec Dubro, University of California Press, 2003.

"Ambient Frontiers: The El Rancho Vegas and Hotel Last Frontier: Strip Pioneers," David G. Schwarz, *eGambling: The Electronic Journal of Gambling Issues,* www.camh.net/egambling.

RESOURCES

Federal Budget of the United States, FY 2007, Summary Tables
Las Vegas Convention and Visitors Authority
New York Convention & Visitors Bureau
Internet Movie Database—www.imdb.com
www.armeniapedia.org
Hyde Flippo—www.german-way.com
www.yachtspotter.com

INDEX

Kerkorian, Tracy, 8, 12, 167
kidnapping, of Wynn daughter, 57–58
King, Larry, 5, 6, 7
Kramer, Ron, 210–11, 251, 263–64, 271, 283

Lake Charles, Louisiana, 54
Lake Tahoe, 19, 20, 48, 70, 72, 93, 98, 195
Lanni, J. Terrence "Terry": Bellagio offices of, 225–26; and buying Mirage stock, 126; at Caesars, 11; contract/salary for, 215, 274; dogs of, 158; home of, 283; and Kerkorian estate planning, 273, 274; Kerkorian's hiring of, 11, 129; and Macao licenses, 210; and Mandalay-MGM Mirage deal, 222, 224, 225–26; and MGM Grand growth strategy, 116; and MGM Grand-Mirage deal, 147, 148, 150, 152, 153, 155, 156, 157–58, 159, 160, 161; as MGM Mirage chairman and CEO, 11, 155; personal and professional background of, 129; personality of, 129; and propeller heads, 170; resignation as MGM Grand chairman of, 129–30; retirement of, 273; and Shadow Creek, 267; and Wynn, 11; Yemenidjian's rivalry with, 130
Las Vegas: ambience of, 1–3; beginning of goofy modern era of, 29; change in, 283–84; Disneyland compared with, 23; economy of, 1–3; education of media about, 83; elite charity events in, 5–7; entertainment in, 133–39; as family place, 37; history of, 21, 22; image of, 21, 83, 87–88, 169, 201, 207, 208–9; implosion of casinos in, 34–35;

inconveniences of, 2; investment capital in, 22; Kerkorian's first visits to, 15; New York's similarity to, 284; non-gambling revenues in, 278; organized crime in, 22, 23, 24, 203; popularity of, 1, 2–3; on reality television, 209; rebirths of, 1–2, 283–84; shopping in, 2; slogan of, 209; tourists in, 22, 29, 207, 284; Wynn's comments about, 31, 39–40, 99, 256, 259; Wynn's first trip to, 47–48; and Wynn's legacy, 100
Las Vegas Convention and Visitors Authority, 2, 3, 270
Las Vegas Sands Corp., 250, 271
Las Vegas Strip. *See* The Strip
Last Frontier, 15
Le Cirque Restaurant (New York), 75, 78, 79, 213, 263
Le Jardin (Atlantic City), 121–22
Le Reve (casino). *See* Wynn Las Vegas
Le Reve (show), 251–53, 255, 261, 263, 269, 270
Le Reve (*The Dream*) (Picasso), 199–200
Lee, Daniel R.: accomplishments of, 125; and art purchases, 89; and Bellagio costs, 91; and Bellagio opening, 105; departure of, 124–26, 134, 142; and Gallin, 134; and "giving guidance" to Wall Street, 123; and Haverty-Wynn meeting, 75; and investors, 91; and Las Vegas, 283; and Marnell audit, 82–83; and MGM Grand-Mirage deal, 154, 158; and Mirage employees as family, 55; and Mirage financial reports, 111; and Mirage's last annual meeting, 154; offices of, 218; personal and professional